In wellis Latexis Plodamus

This book belongeth to
Lord Dicky Tottering,
of Tottering
and Daffy, his wife.

Annie Tempest

Lady Tottering's Journal

by

Annie Tempest

ANALYSIS

ELEMENT: Daffy

SYMBOL: TBg

ATOMIC MASS: 11 stone, but known to fluctuate between 10.5 and 13.5 stone

OCCURRENCE: Indigenous to North Pimmshire with trace elements in outlying regions

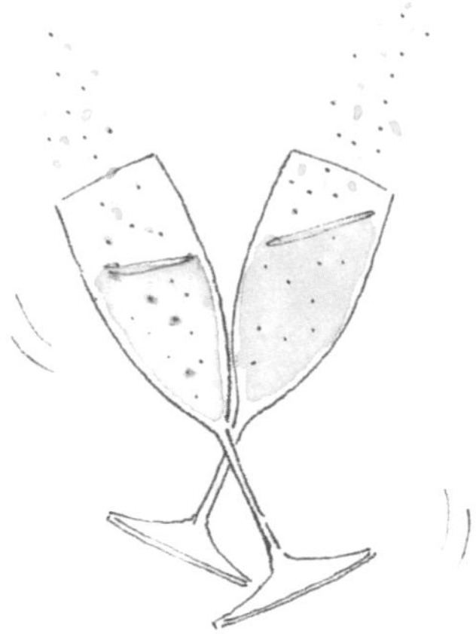

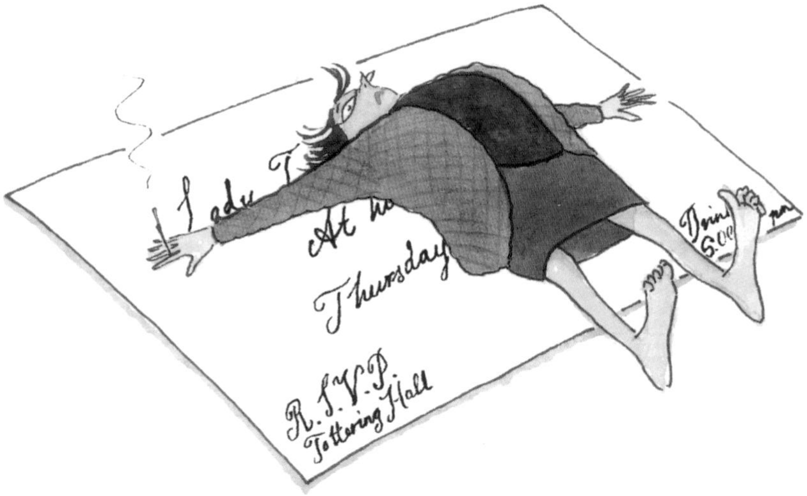
R.S.V.P.
Tottering Hall

LADY TOTTERING
DATA SHEET

PHYSICAL PROPERTIES:

1. Surface covered in creamy substances, often appearing to have a light film of powder.
2. Alternately boils and freezes for no known reason.
3. Melts if given special treatment.
4. Combusts if carelessly handled.
5. Yields to pressure if expertly applied.
6. Grading fluctuates between absolute rock and pure gold.

CHEMICAL PROPERTIES:

1. Affinity with gold, silver, platinum and most precious stones.
2. Absorbs large quantities of expensive substances.
3. Volatile when saturated in alcohol.
4. Powerful money-reducing agent.
5. Cyclically unstable.

COMMON USES:

1. Source of nutrients.
2. Effective cleaning agent.
3. Can be excellent aid to relaxation.
4. Occasionally ornamental.

TESTS:

1. Turns red when complimented.
2. Turns green when placed alongside leaner specimen.
3. Extremities turn blue when heating is withdrawn.
4. Turns purple when crossed.

HAZARDS:

1. Unpredictability.
2. Known to be addictive.

January

1

2

3

4

5 Peggys Birthday

6

7

8

9

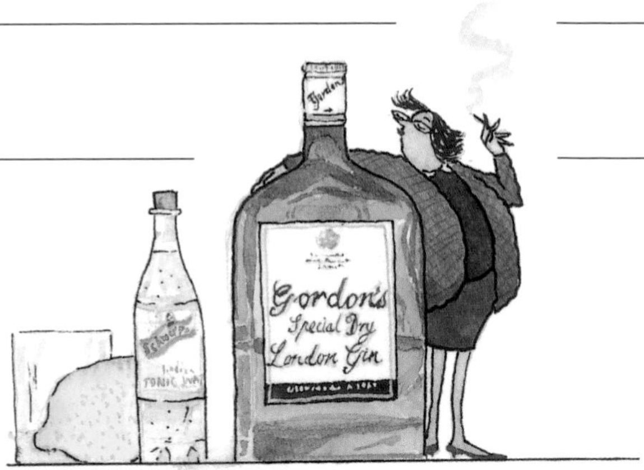

Gordon's
Special Dry
London Gin

Methinks my scales deceive me...

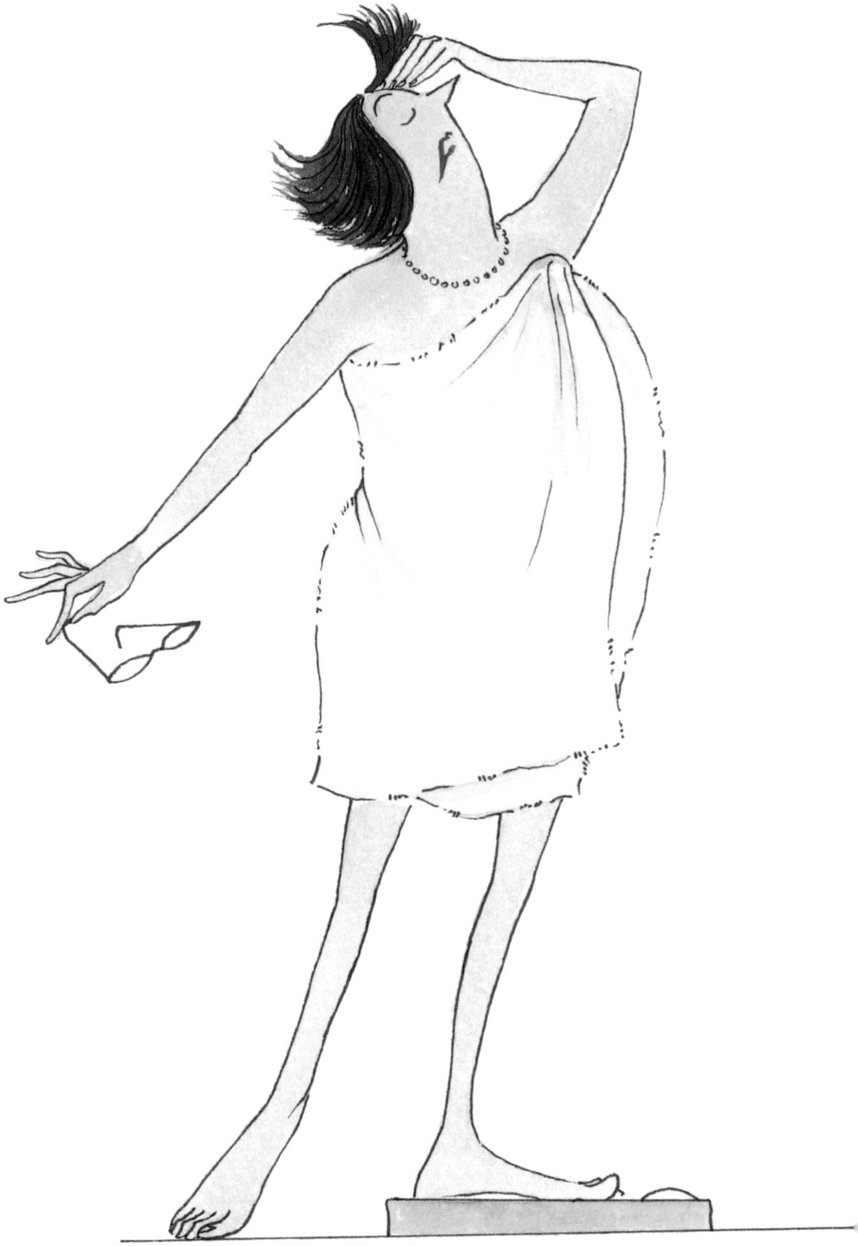

A Sonnet*

Oh that this too too solid flesh would melt,
Thaw, and resolve itself into a dew
Shall I betake myself this night to Forest Mere?
Methinks my scales deceive me. Fourteen two.
How weary, stale, flat and unprofitable
Seem to me all the creases in my chin.
Fie ont! O fie! Pass me a double gin
Frailty thy name is woman, tis an uneaten grapefruit
That goes to seed. I vow to go a jogging
And then once more into the breach,
dear friends. Eye of newt and tongue of dog
Adders fork and blind worm's sting
Gall of goat and lizard's belly
Cooked by Pierre White or Novelli.

*by Alistair Sampson.

THE MALE AND FEMALE CHARACTERS

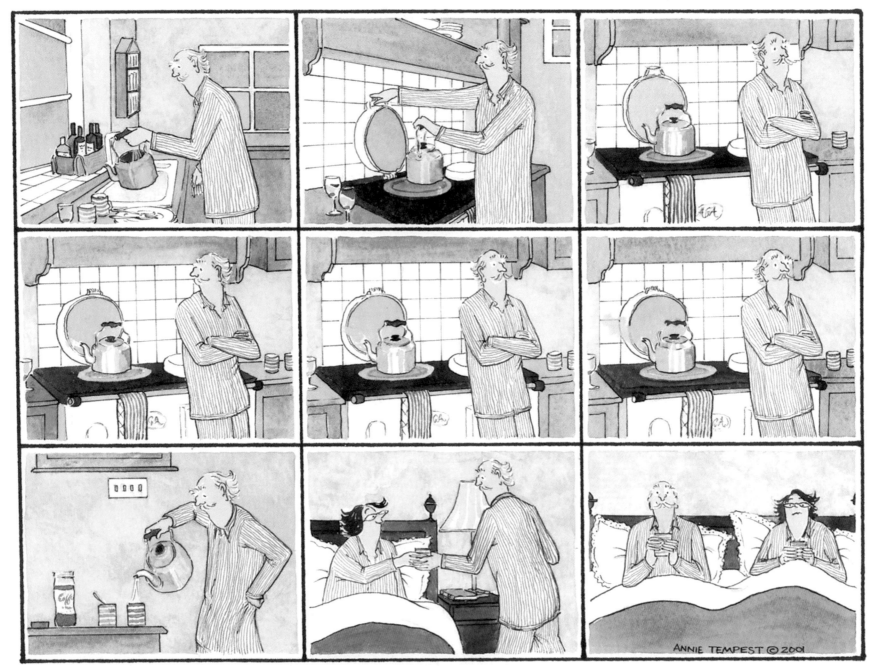

He makes coffee...

ANNIE TEMPEST © 2001

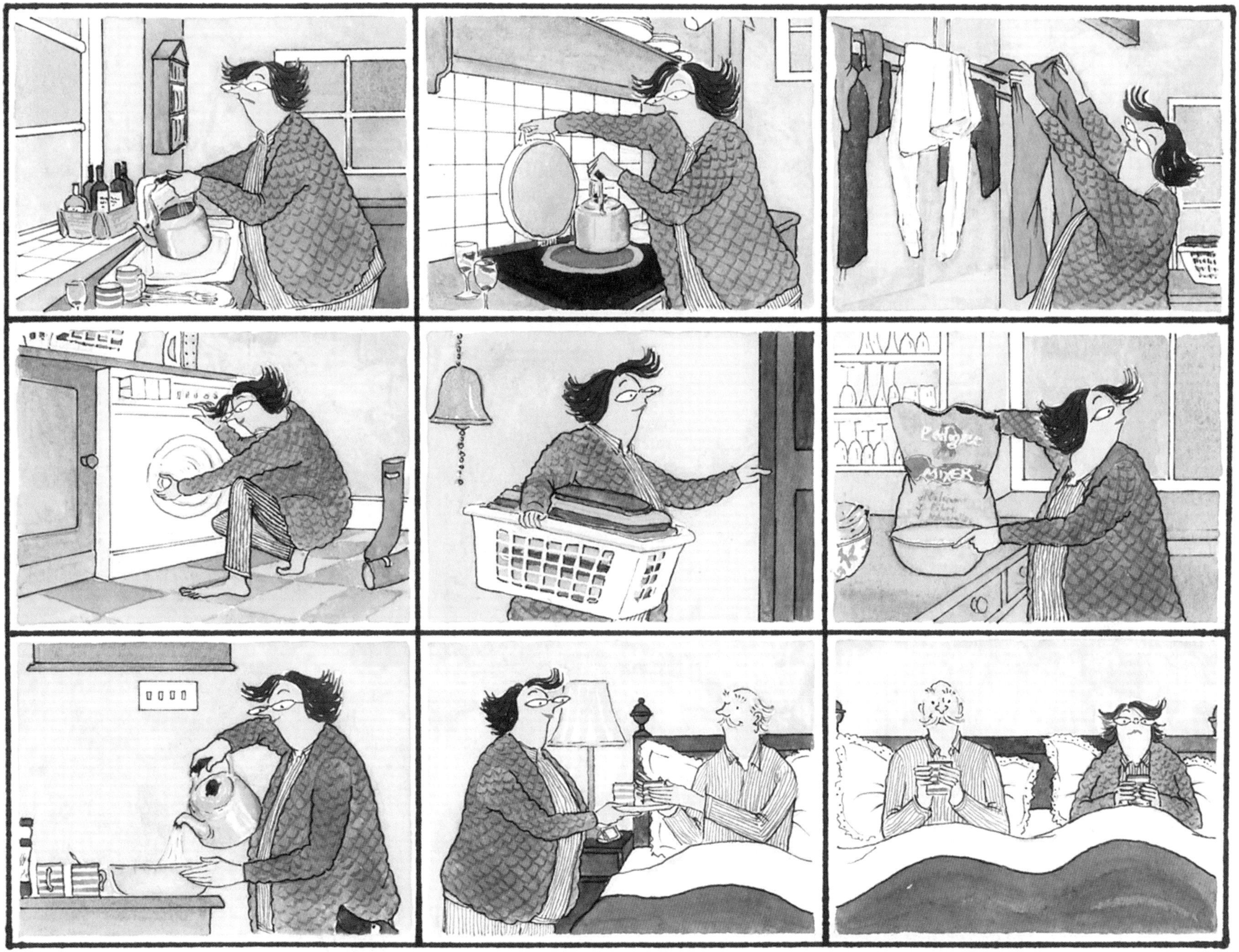
MIXER

She makes coffee...

January

DON'T GIVE UP ON NEW YEARS RESOLUTIONS!

Pay the milk bill.

Iris 01742 662

10 _____

11 _Snowdrops & Aconites are up_ _____

12 _____

13 _____

14 **DAVID WEBSTERS BIRTHDAY** _____

15 _____

16 _____

I dunno... maybe Pilates is easier... Mrs Shagpile says there's a new class in Rattling-by-Furiously on a Wednesday morning...

And anyway...

... doing yoga at home on your own can be dangerous for your self-esteem.

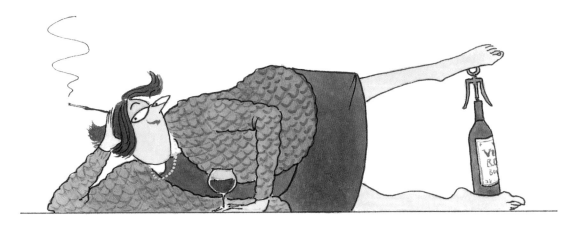

Oh! What the hell! Red wine's good for your heart too, isn't it?...

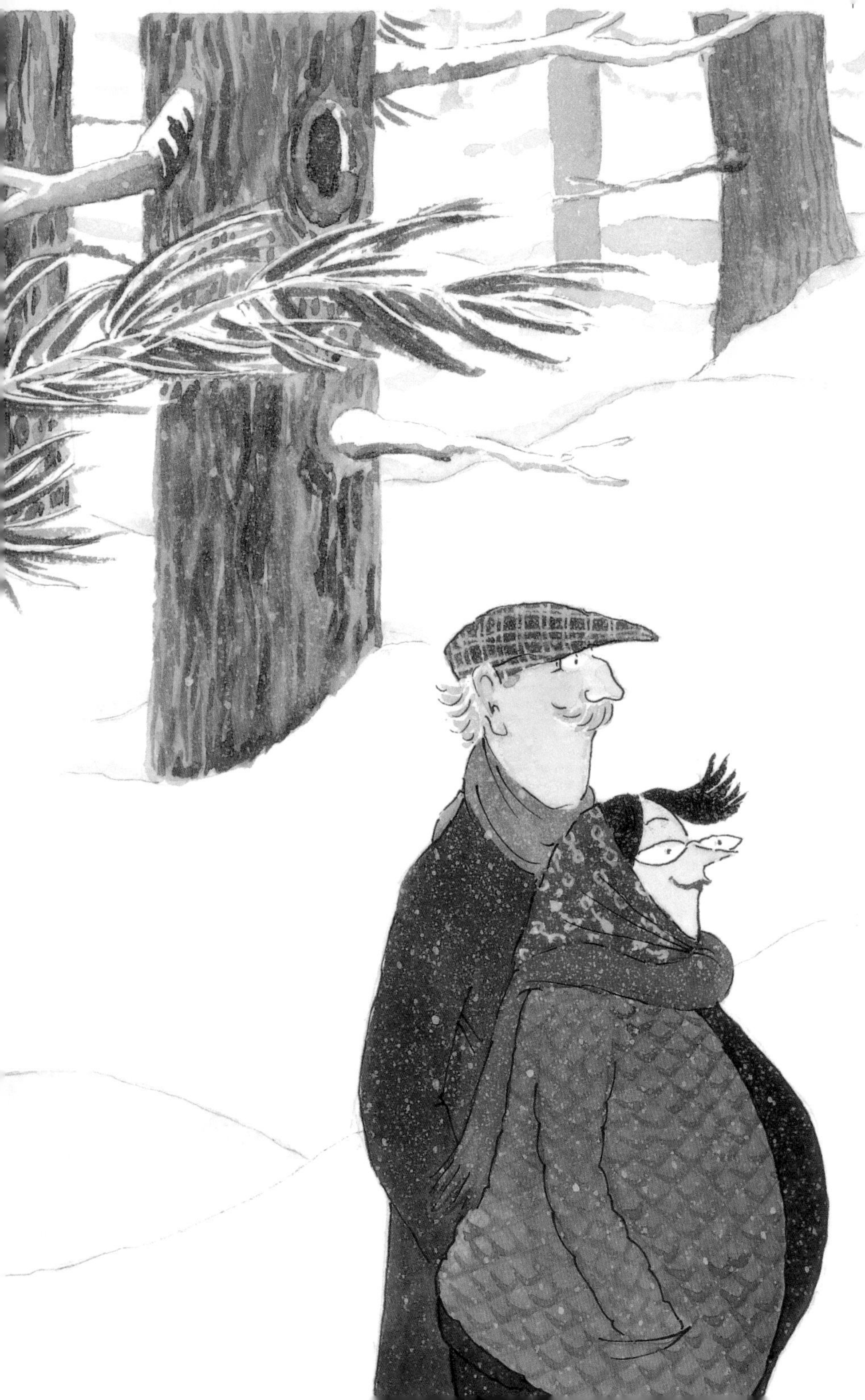

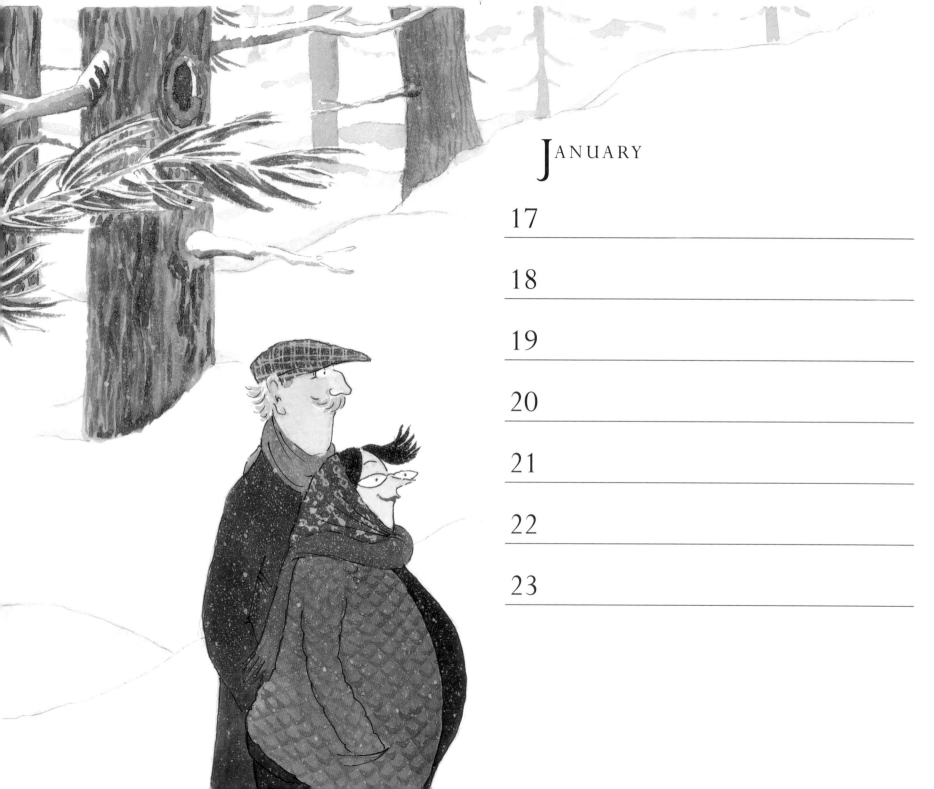

JANUARY

17

18

19

20

21

22

23

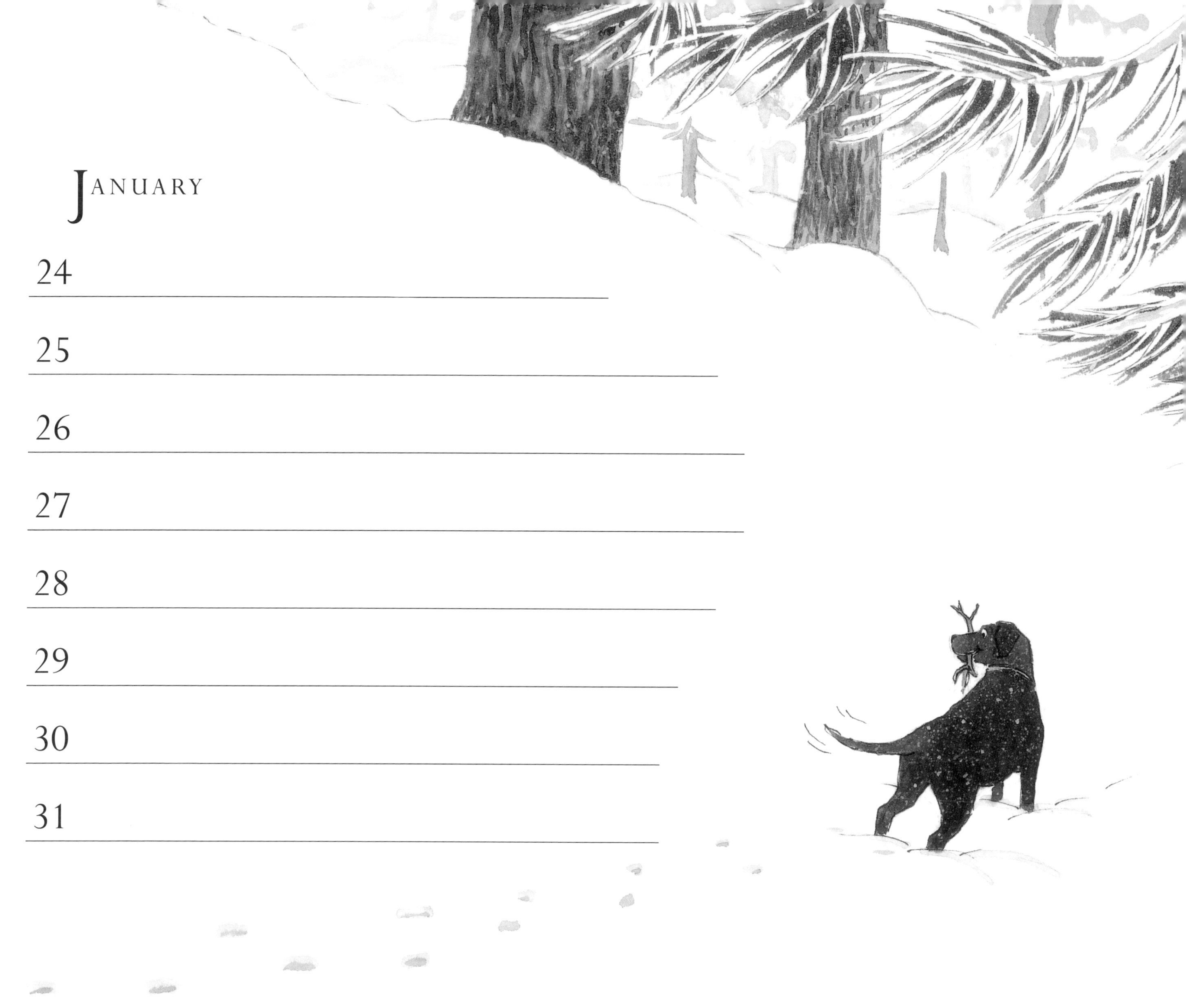

January

24

25

26

27

28

29

30

31

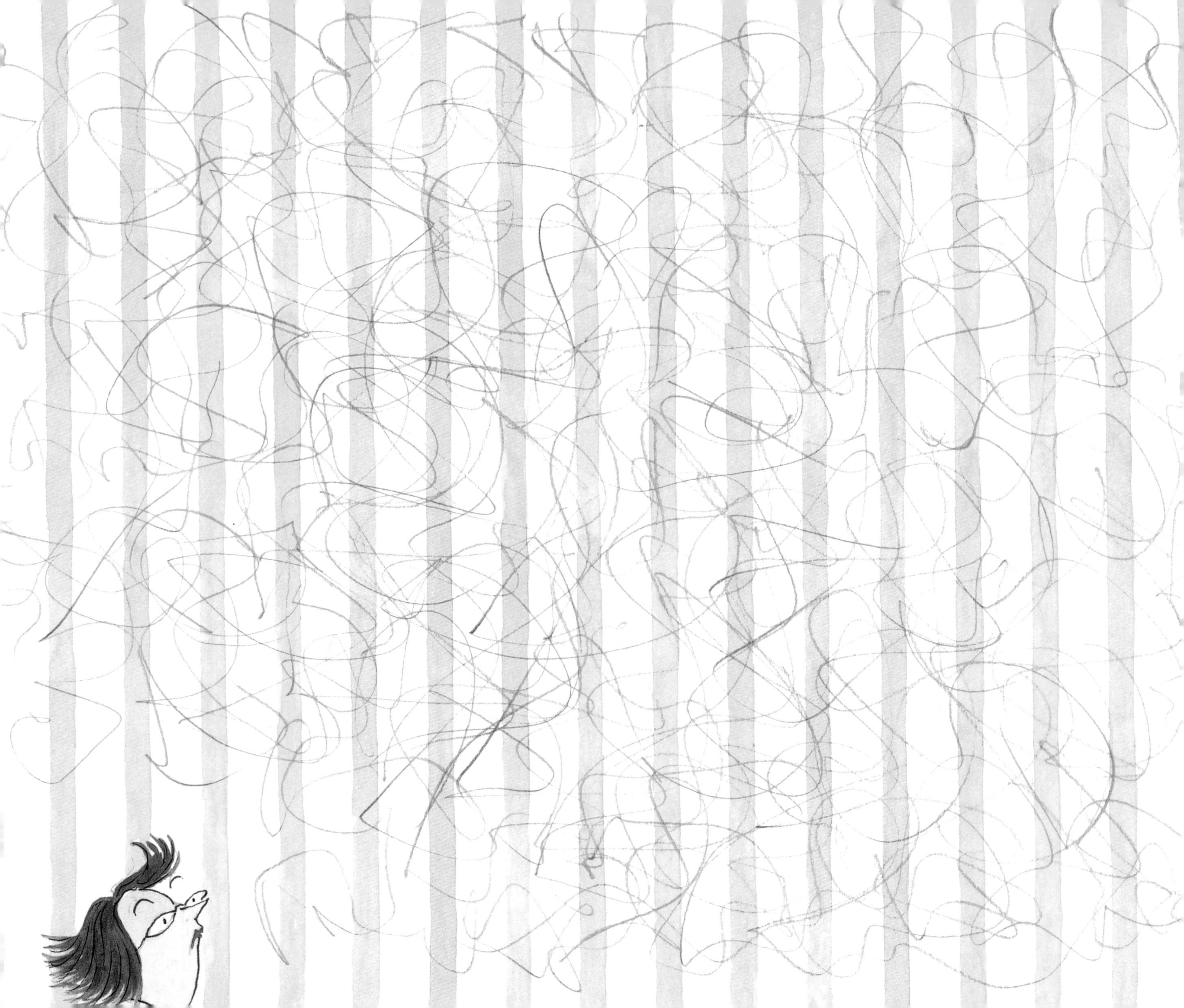

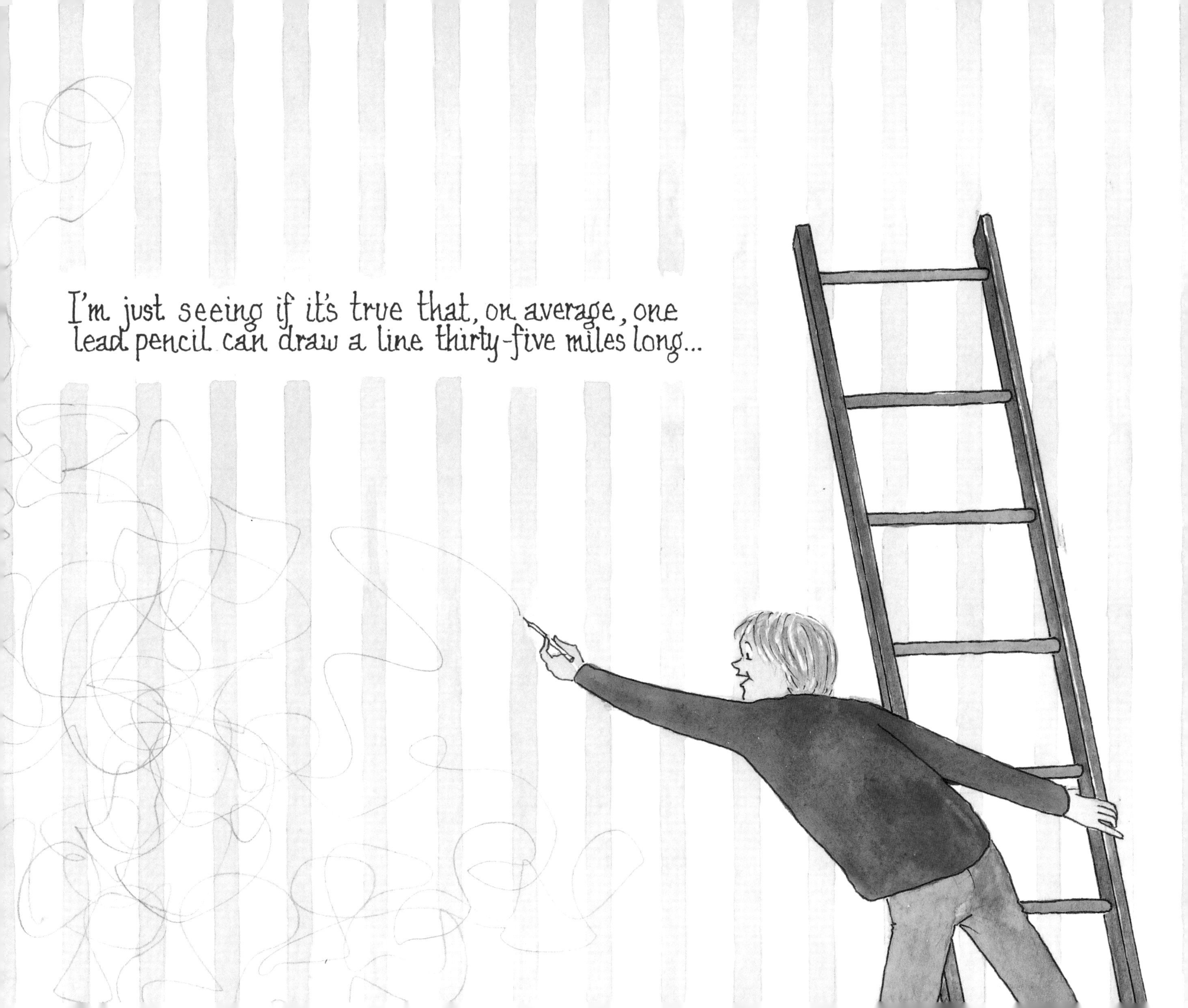
I'm just seeing if it's true that, on average, one lead pencil can draw a line thirty-five miles long...

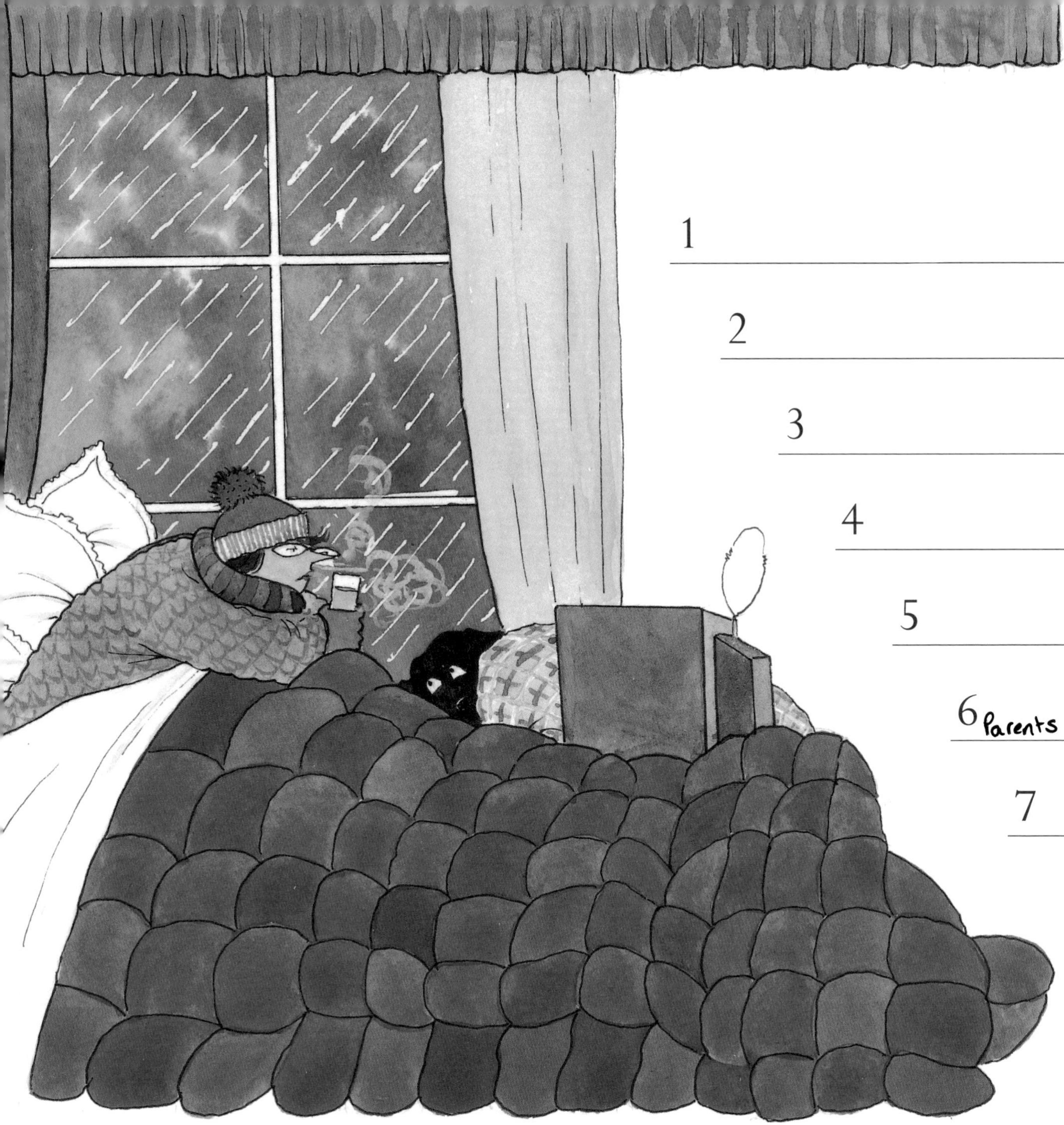

Symptoms of Februaryitis...

FEBRUARY

1

2

3

4

5

6 Parents wedding anniversary

7

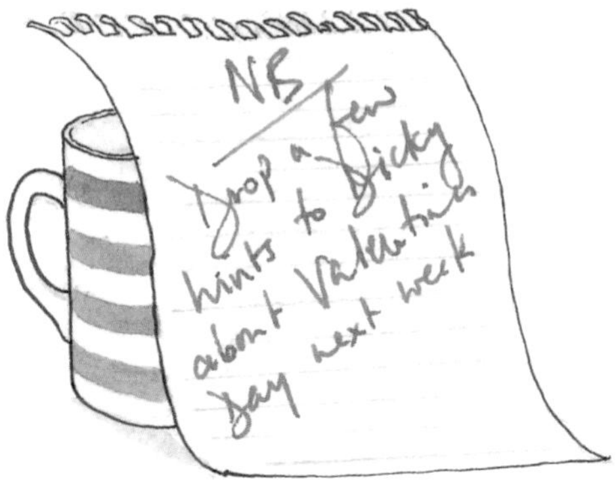
NB
Drop a few hints to Dicky about Valentines Day next week

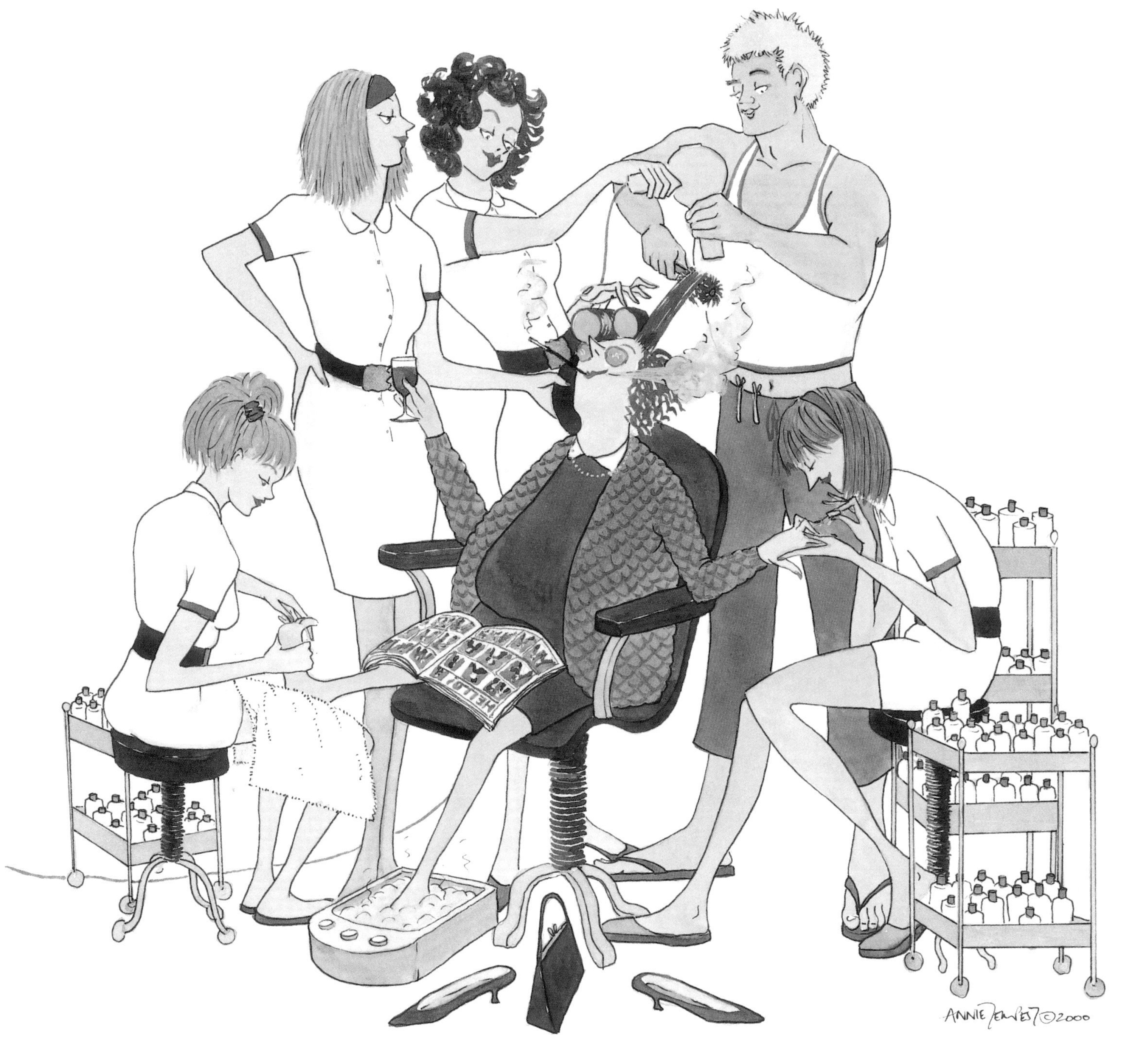
ANNIE TEMPEST ©2000

An effective treatment for Februaryitis...

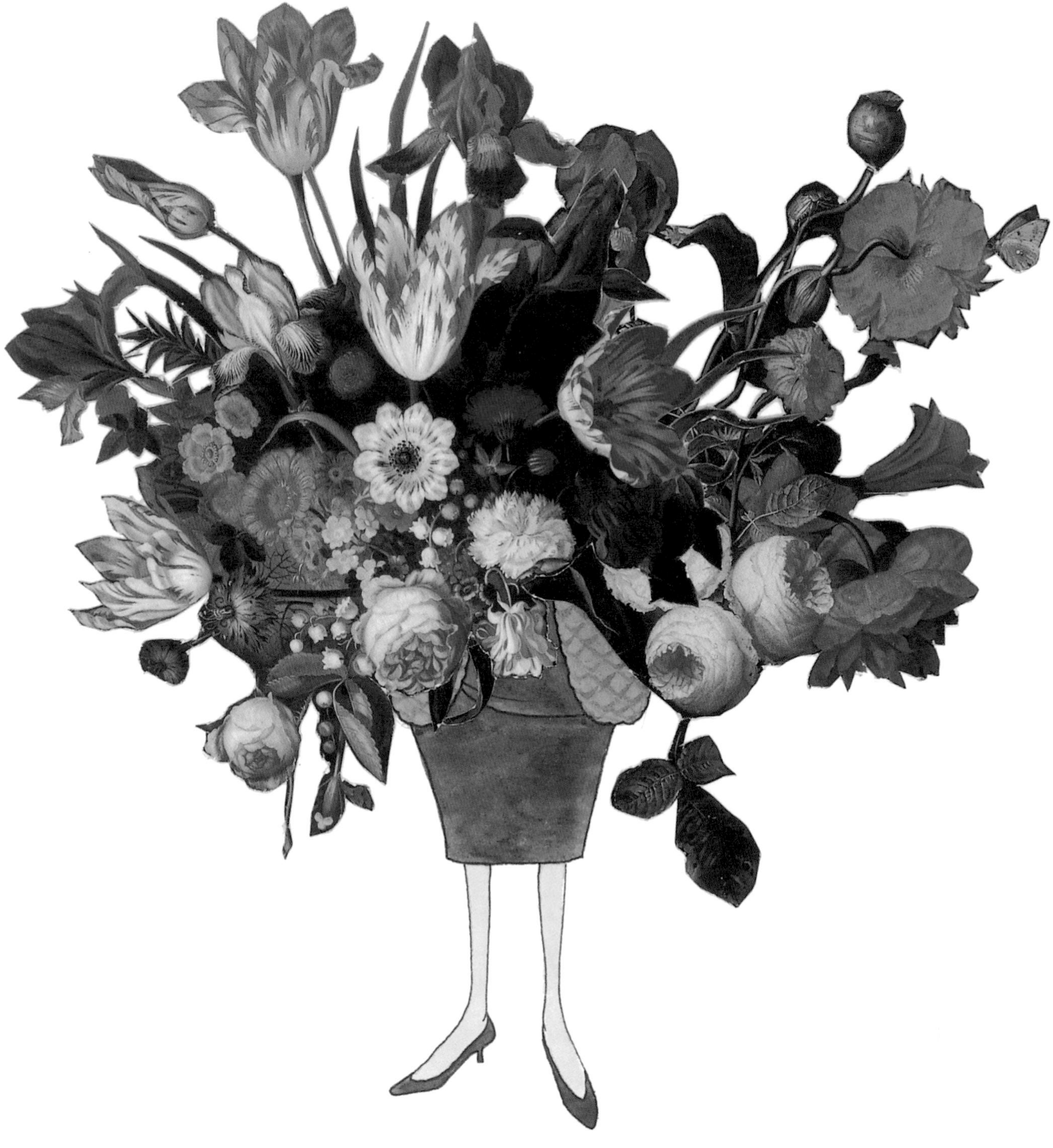

FEBRUARY

8

9

10

11

12

13

14 Send the old trout flowers!

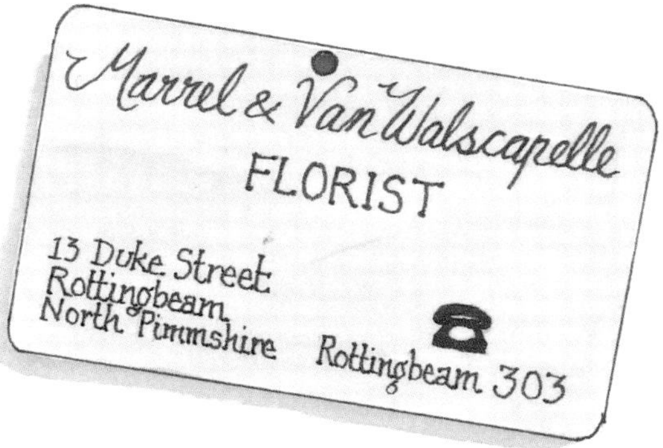
Marrel & Van Walscapelle
FLORIST
13 Duke Street
Rottingbeam
North Pimmshire
Rottingbeam 303

Jolly good - you got them, then.
Can I have my coffee now?

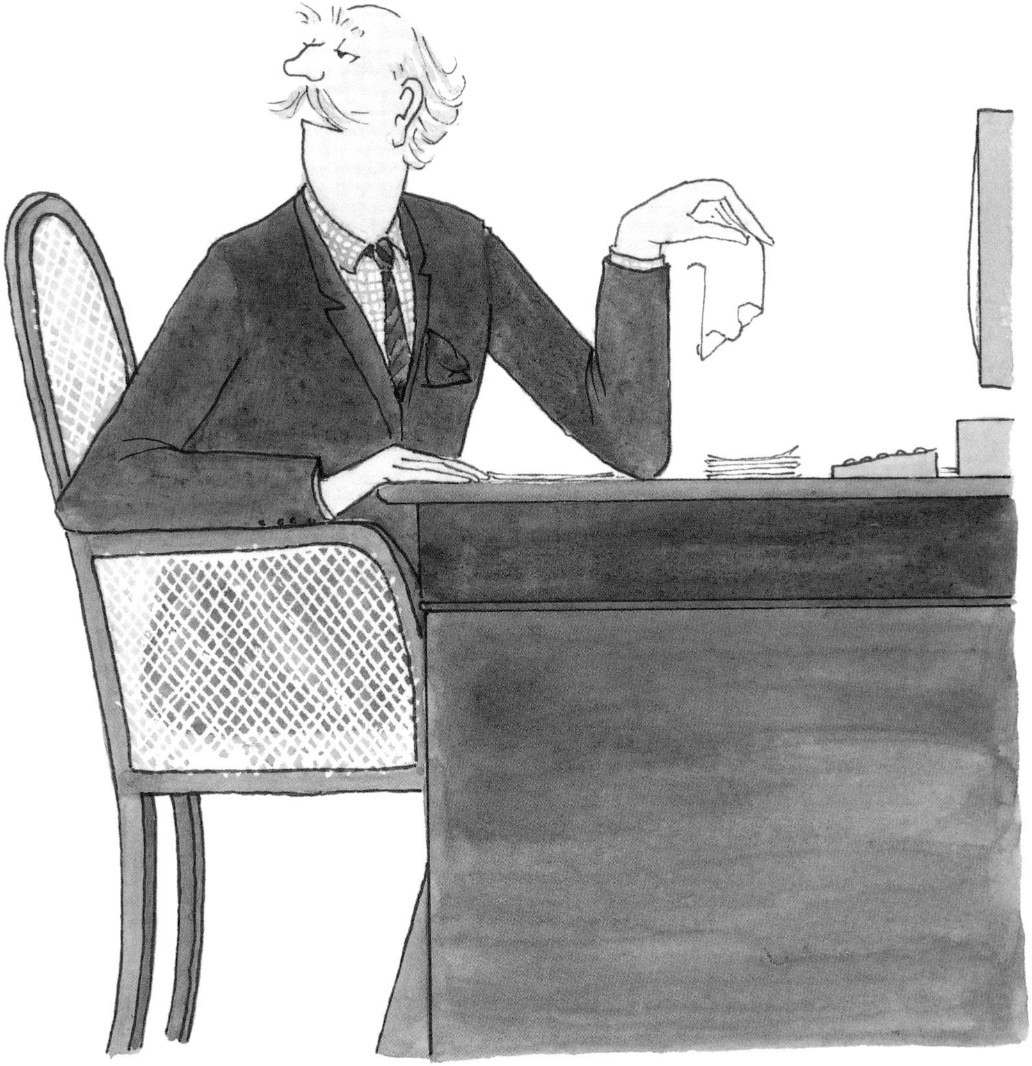

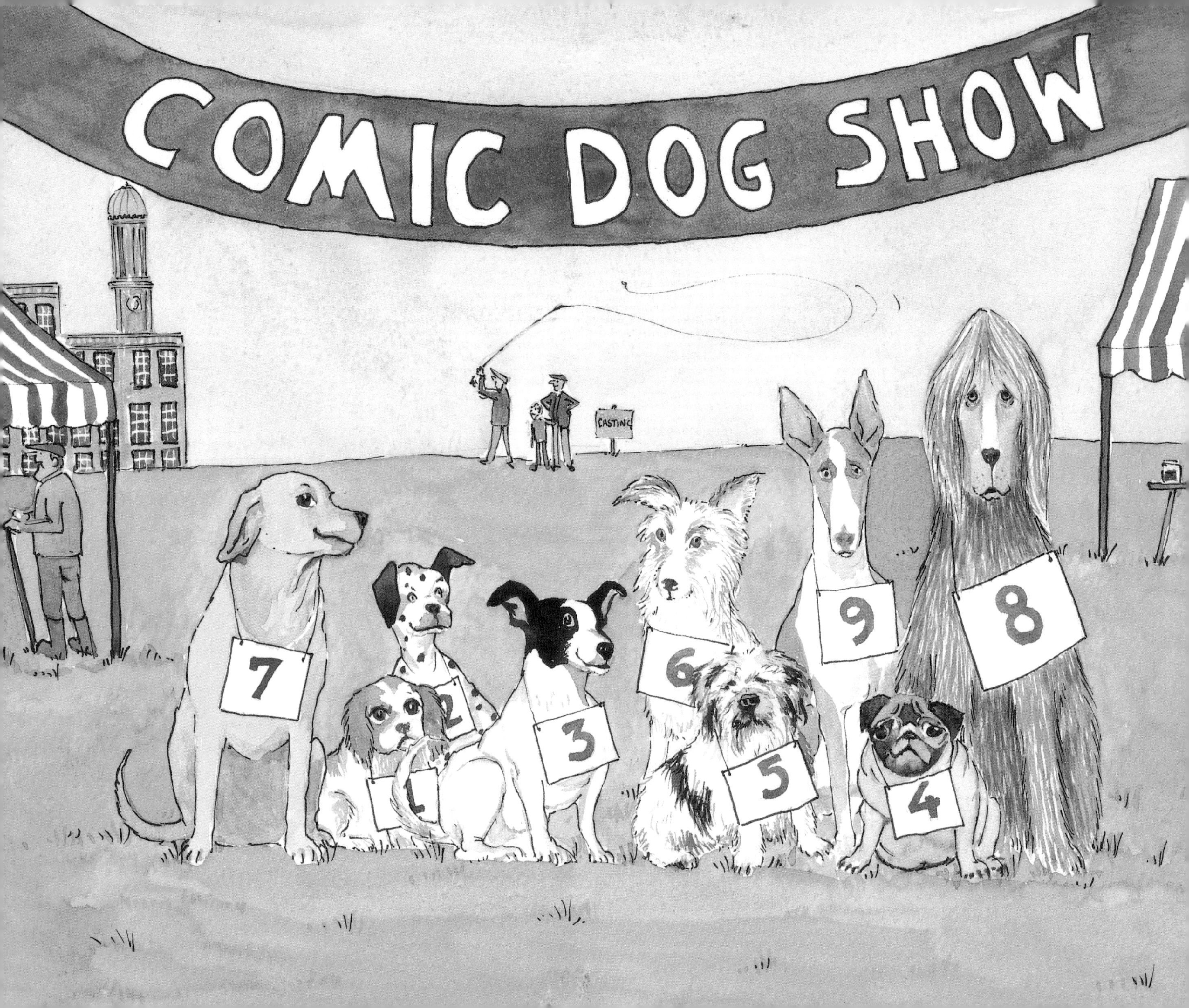

COMIC DOG SHOW
CASTING
7
2
1
3
6
5
9
8
4

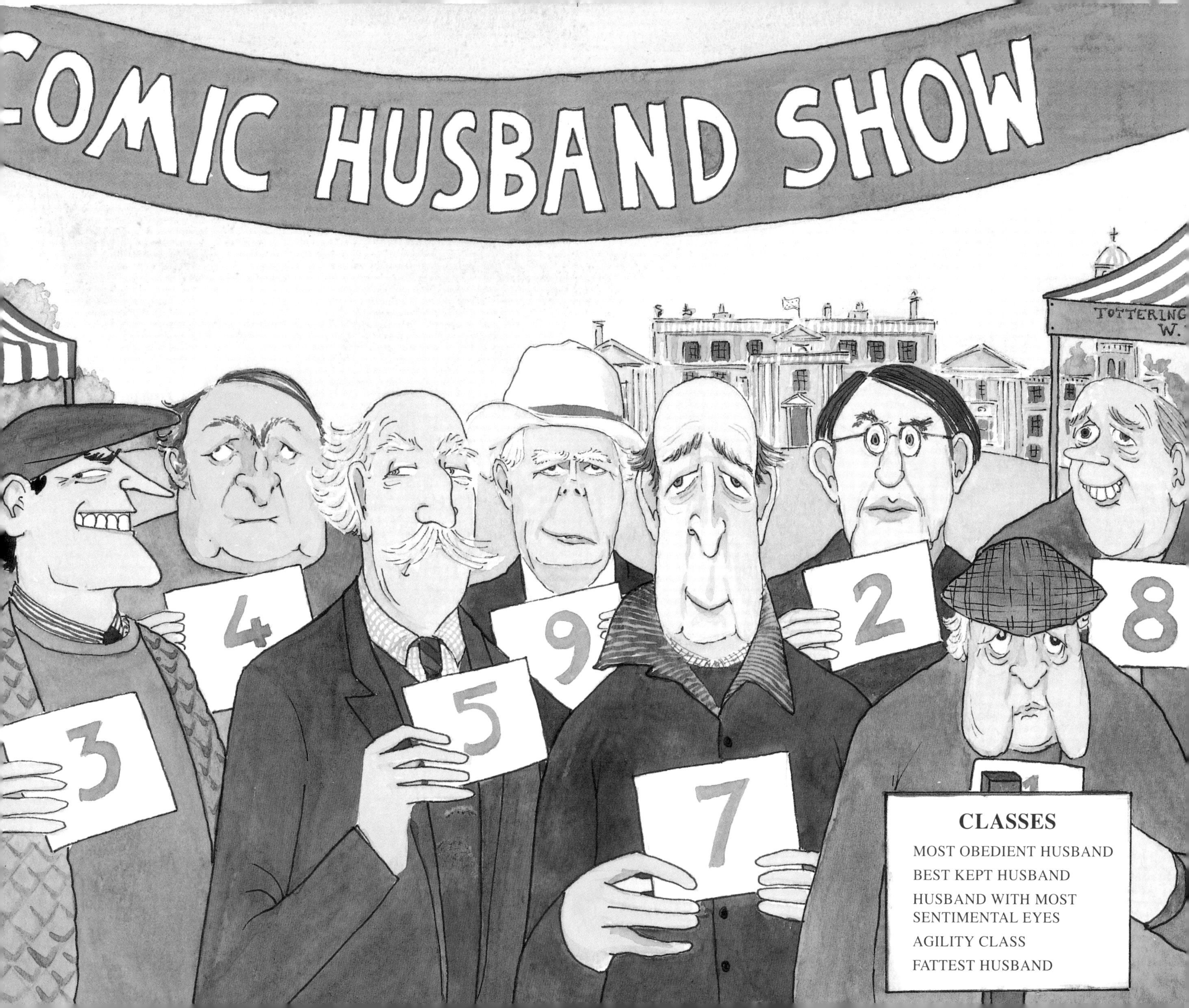
COMIC HUSBAND SHOW
TOTTERING
W.
3
4
5
9
7
2
8
CLASSES
MOST OBEDIENT HUSBAND
BEST KEPT HUSBAND
HUSBAND WITH MOST SENTIMENTAL EYES
AGILITY CLASS
FATTEST HUSBAND

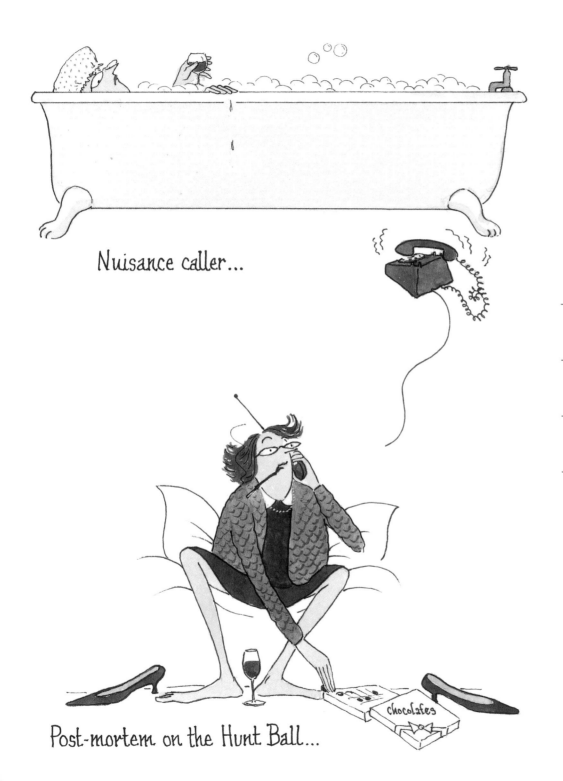

Nuisance caller...

Post-mortem on the Hunt Ball...

FEBRUARY

15

_____

16

_____

17

_____

18

_____

19

_____

20 Jakie Hughes

_____

21

_____

Oh! My God! Must go - The Archers has started

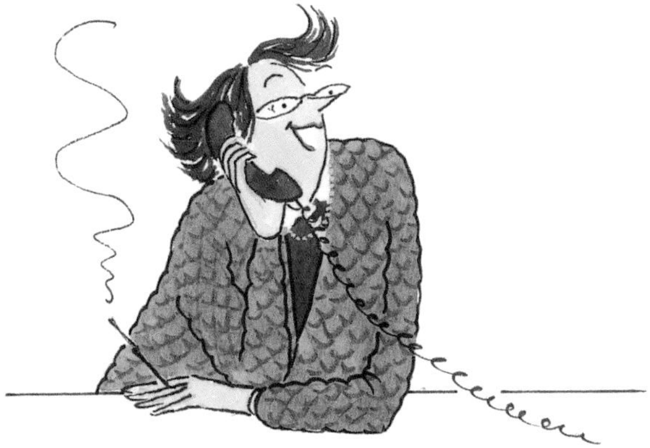

How ghastly! Really?...

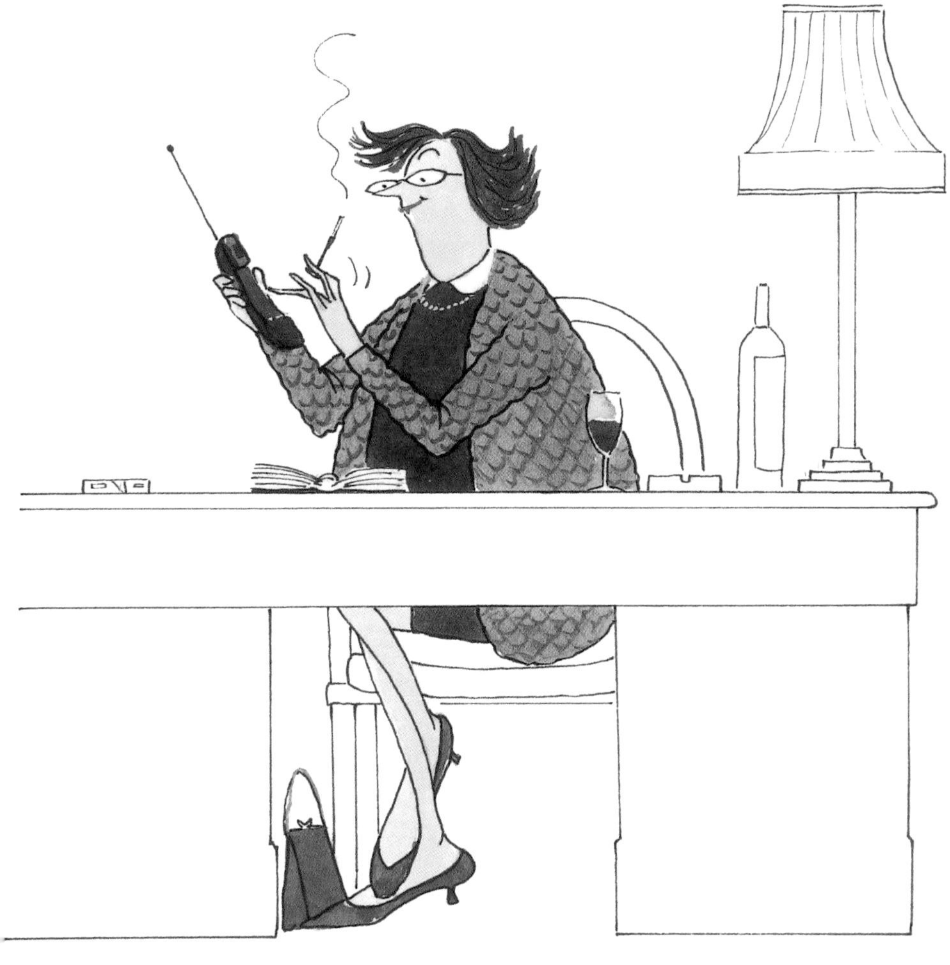

About to spread some juicy gossip...

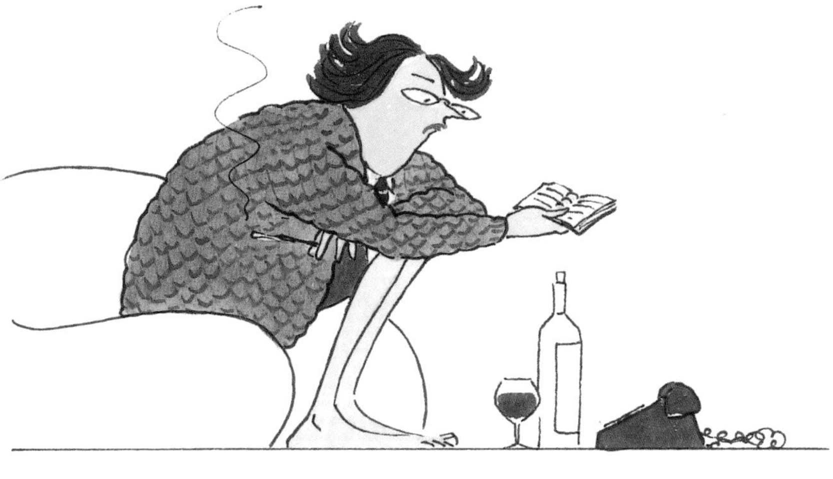

Who else can I ring at this time of night?..

PANCAKES
Makes 8
125g. plain flour
pinch of salt
1 egg - ½ pint milk
veg. oil for frying
sugar + lemon juice
METHOD
Sift flour + salt in to a bowl -
make well in centre - break egg into
well and beat in with wooden spoon.
Gradually beat in milk - drawing
flour from the sides to make a
smooth batter.
Heat oil in frying pan - add just
enough batter to coat thinly + cook
for 1-2 mins. TOSS + cook other
side. Sprinkle with sugar + lemon.

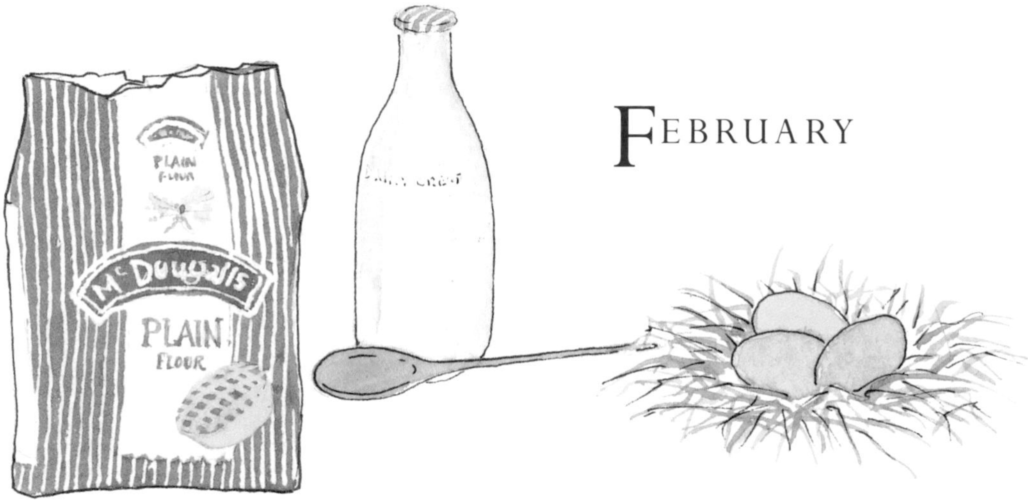
McDougalls
PLAIN
FLOUR

FEBRUARY

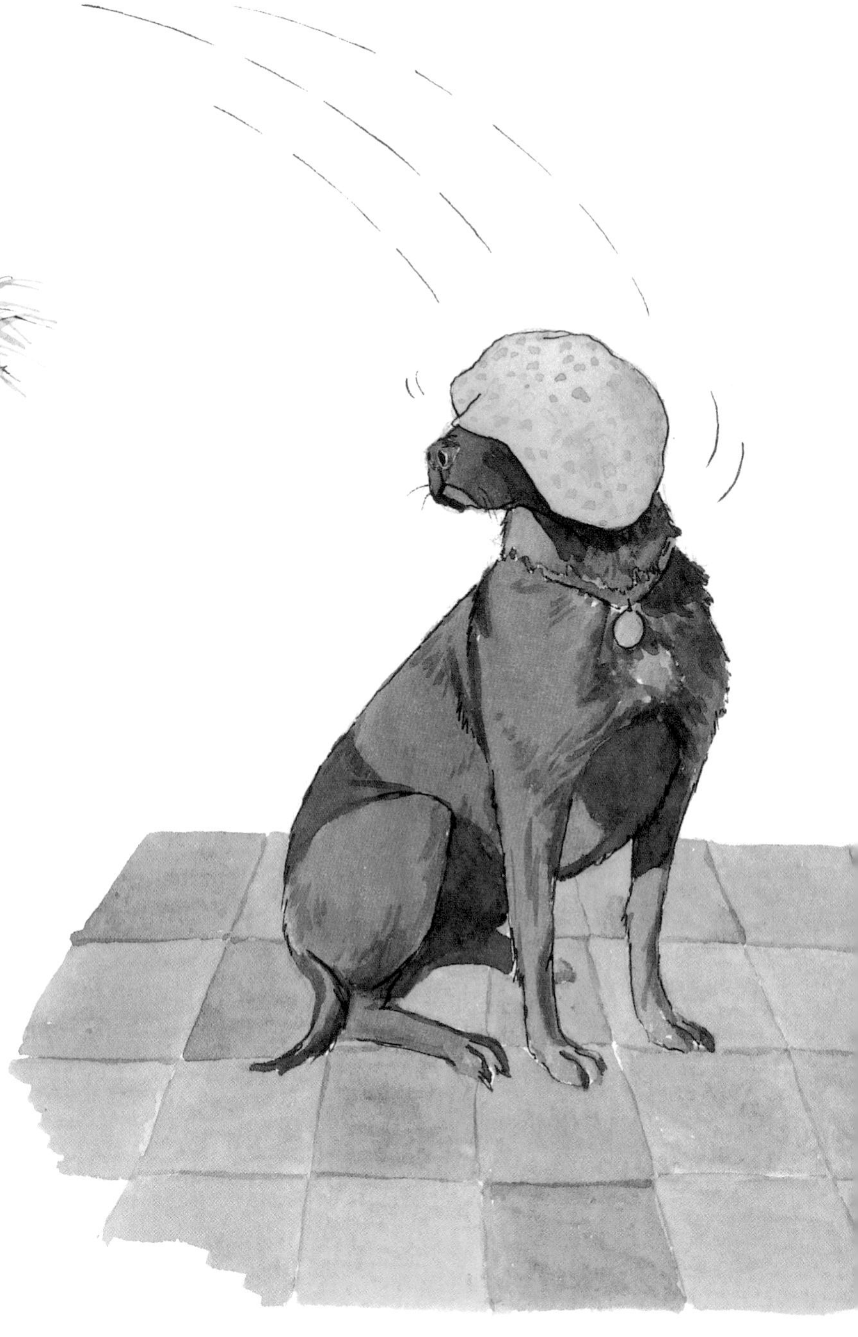

22

23

24

25 Issy Birthday

26

27

28

29

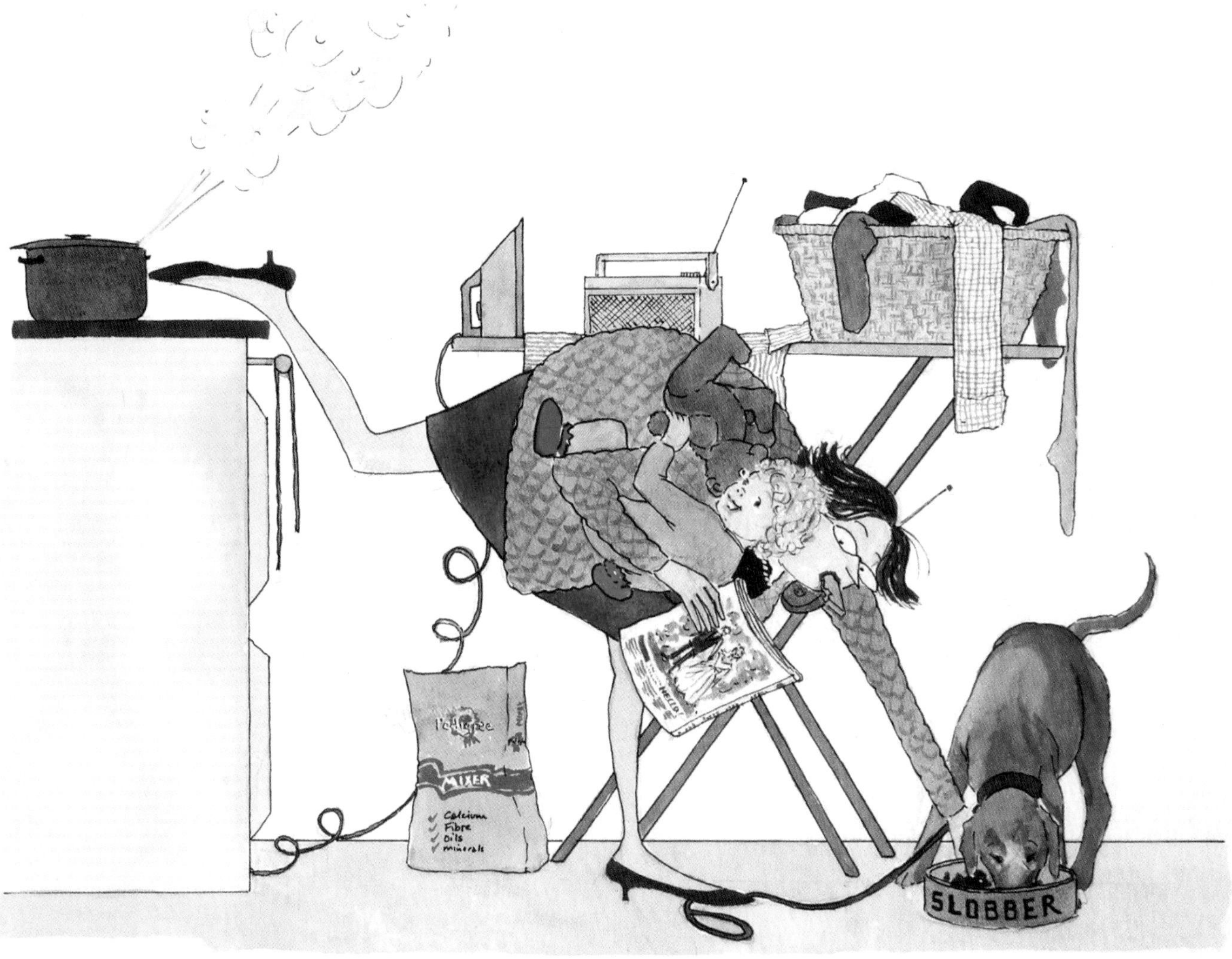
MIXER
Calcium
Fibre
Oils
minerals
SLOBBER

THE FEMALE CHARACTER: A predilection for doing six things at once...

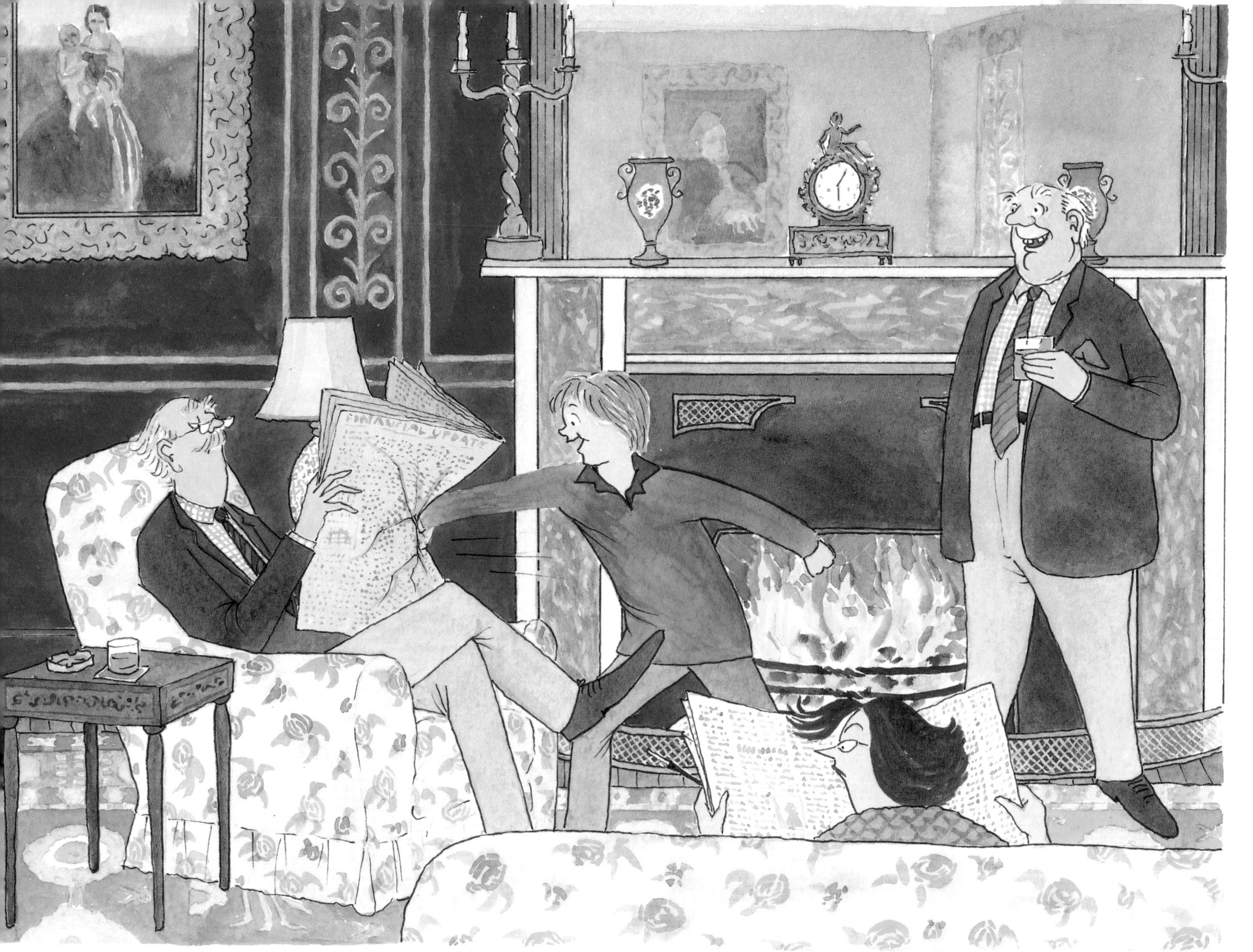
FINANCIAL UPDATE

"It amazes me how you two manage to juggle retirement with having grandchildren..."

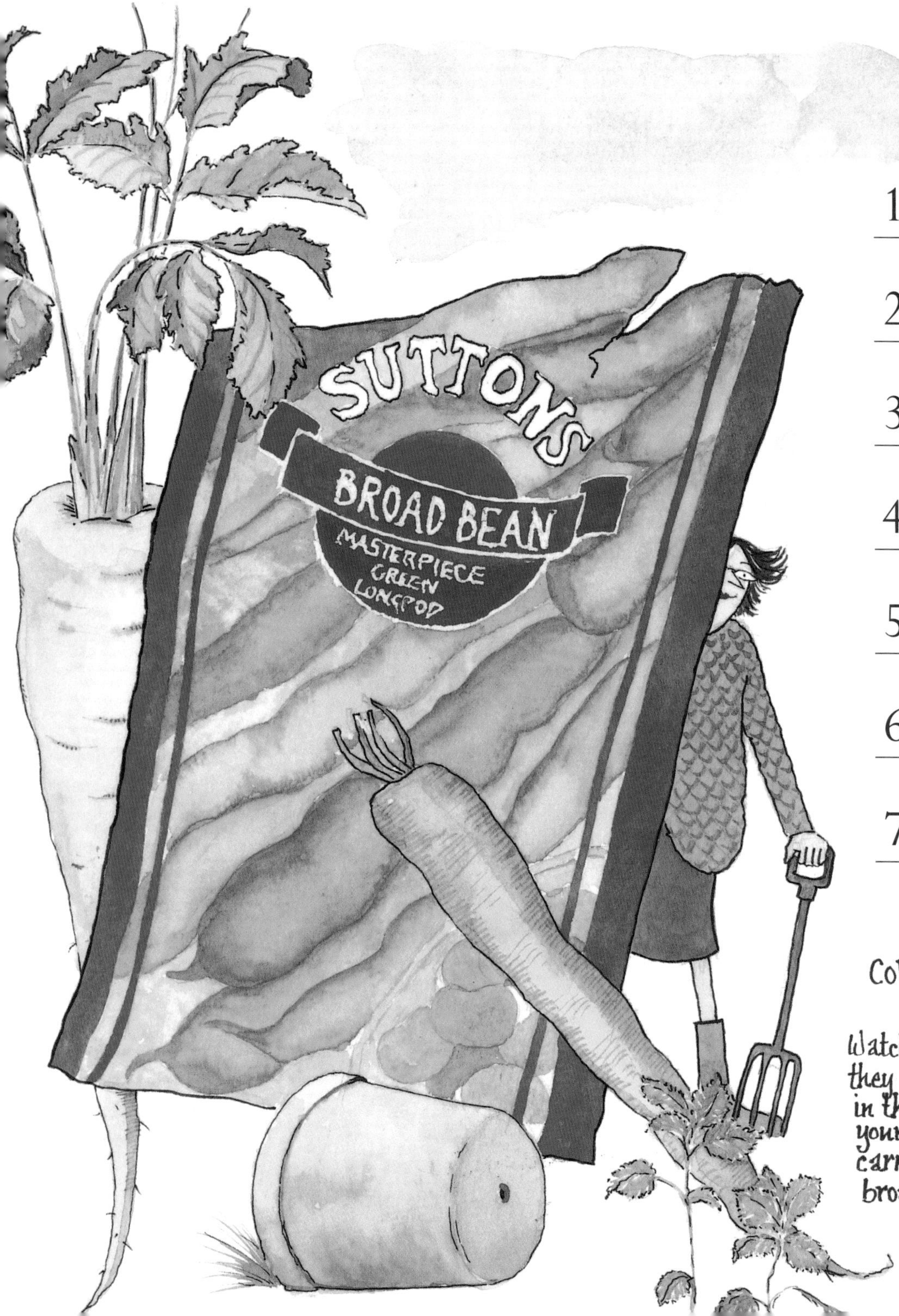
SUTTONS
BROAD BEAN
MASTERPIECE
GREEN
LONGPOD

MARCH

1 St. David's day

2

3 Pops Birthday

4

5

6

7

CORKY MEADOWGRASS SAYS...

Watch for nettles on the banks – once they start to shoot there's warmth in the soil so you can start sewing your veggies – start with early carrots, parsnips and broad beans...

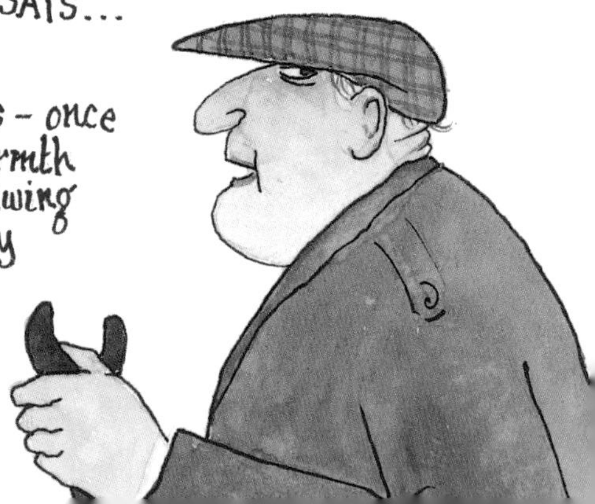

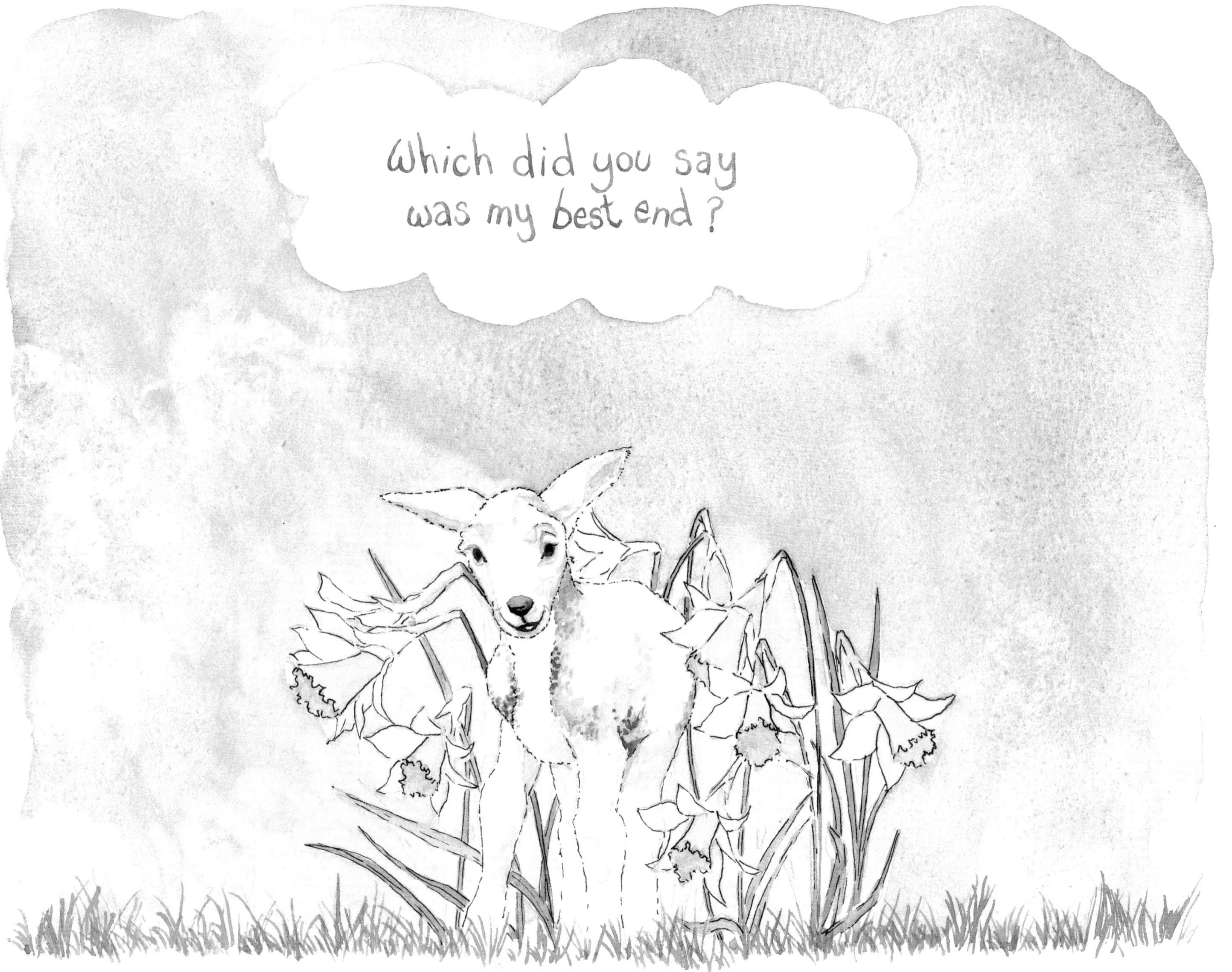
Which did you say
was my best end?

New ways to exercise at home...

Pop your Georgian mahogany bootjack onto an old skateboard and whiz up and down the bedroom corridors...

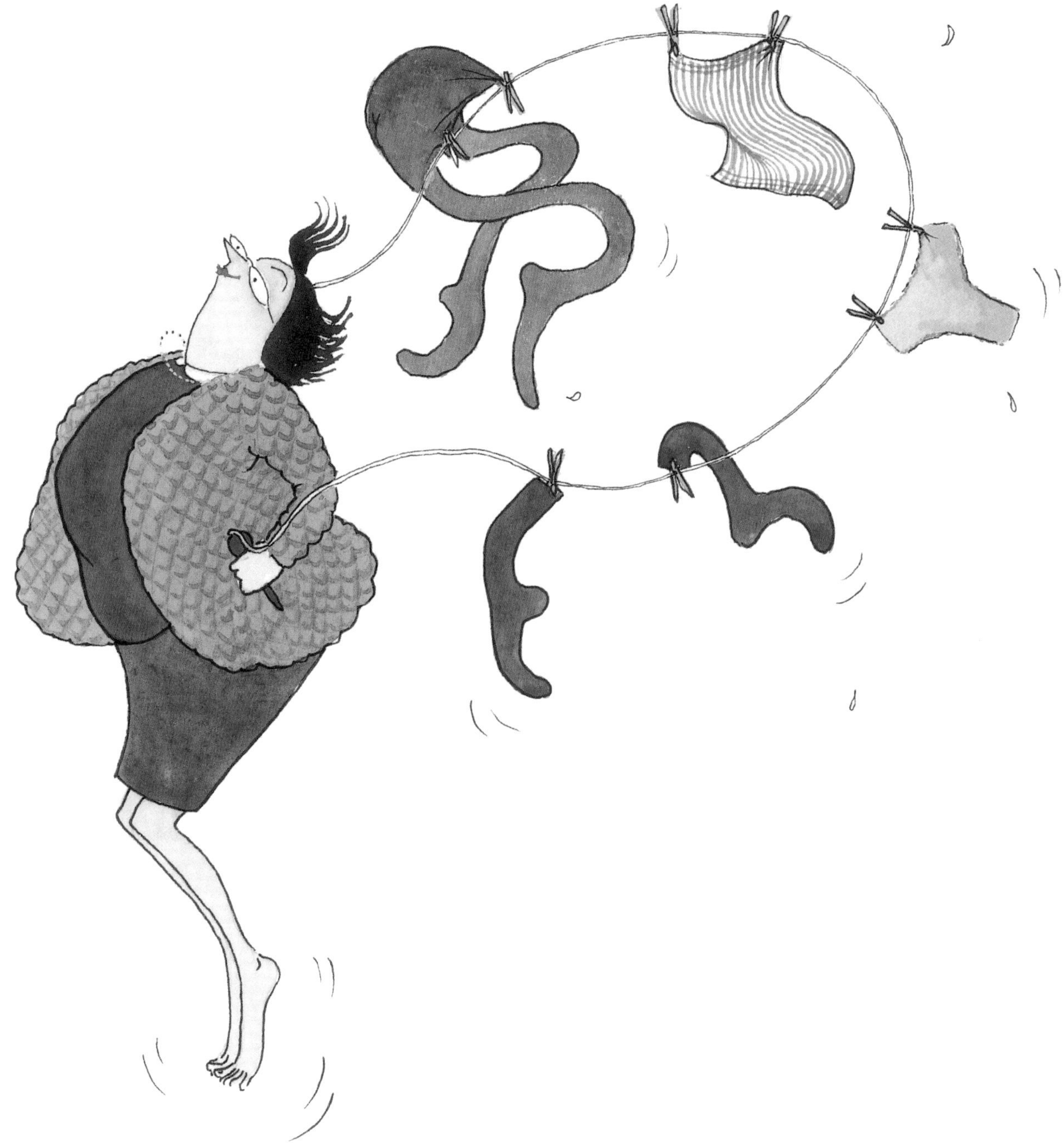

Peg your wet laundry to your grandchildren's skipping-rope and start skipping.
Not only will you burn calories, but your clothes will dry quicker too...

Avoid the embarrassment of streaming eyes when chopping onions by wearing a snorkel and swimming goggles...

MARCH

8

9

10

11

12

13 ELAINES BIRTHDAY (DANNY BROWN)

14

15 MY BIRTHDAY
SUSANS BIRTHDAY

CORKY MEADOWGRASS SAYS

Get your Arran Pilots, Ailsa Craigs and Walton Mammoths in...

"If I haven't made a million by the time I'm eighteen,
then I'll just have to go into something my parents approve of..."

Dicky — Whilst rootling through the library with the N.A.D.F.A.S. ladies, I found this extract in a Home Economics text book printed in the early 60s...

Have dinner ready. Plan ahead, even the night before, to have a delicious meal ready on time for ~~his~~ *her* return home from ~~work~~ *shopping.* This is a way of letting ~~him~~ *her* know that you have been thinking about ~~him~~ *her* and are concerned about ~~his~~ *her* needs. Most ~~men~~ *wo* are hungry when they come home and the prospect of a good meal (especially ~~his~~ *her* favourite dish) is part of the warm welcome needed. Prepare yourself. Take 15 minutes to rest so you will be refreshed when ~~he~~ *she* arrives. Touch up your make-up, put a ribbon in your hair and be fresh looking. ~~He~~ *She* has just been with a lot of work weary people. Be a little gay and a little more interesting for ~~him~~ *her*. ~~His~~ *Her* boring day may need a lift and one of your duties is to provide it.

Clear away the clutter. Make one last trip through the main part of the house just before your ~~husband~~ *wife* arrives. Gather up school books, toys, papers, etc. and then run a dust cloth over the tables. Over the cooler months of the year you should prepare and light a fire for ~~him~~ *her* to unwind by.

Your ~~husband~~ *wife* will feel ~~he~~ *she* has reached a haven of rest and order and it will give you a lift too. After all, catering for ~~his~~ *her* comfort will provide you with immense personal satisfaction.

Minimise all noise. At the time of ~~his~~ *her* arrival, eliminate all noise of the washer, dryer or vacuum. Try to encourage the children to be quiet. Be happy to see ~~him~~ *her*. Greet ~~him~~ *her* with a warm smile and show sincerity in your desire to please ~~him~~ *her*. Listen to ~~him~~ *her*. You may have a dozen important things to tell ~~him~~ *her*, but the moment of ~~his~~ *her* arrival is not the time. Let ~~him~~ *her* talk first. Remember, <u>~~his~~ *her* topics of conversation are more important than yours.</u> Make the evening ~~his~~ *hers*. Never complain if ~~he~~ *she* comes home late or goes out to dinner or other places of entertainment without you. Instead, try to understand ~~his~~ *her* world of strain and pressure and ~~his~~ *her* very real need to be at home and relax.

YOUR GOAL: Try to make sure your home is a place of peace, order and tranquillity where your ~~husband~~ wife can renew ~~him~~herself in body and spirit. Don't greet ~~him~~ her with complaints and problems. Don't complain if she's late home for dinner, or even stays out all night. Count this as minor compared to what She might have gone through that day.

Make ~~him~~ her comfortable. Have ~~him~~ her lean back in a comfortable chair or have ~~him~~ her lie down in the bedroom. Have a cool or warm drink ready for ~~him~~ her. Arrange the pillow and offer to take off ~~his~~ her shoes. Speak in a low, soothing and pleasant voice. Don't ask ~~him~~ her questions about ~~his~~ her actions or question ~~his~~ her judgement or integrity.

Remember, she is the master of the house and as such will always exercise ~~his~~ her will with fairness and truthfulness…

Couldn't resist a bit of editing…
Love Daffy x

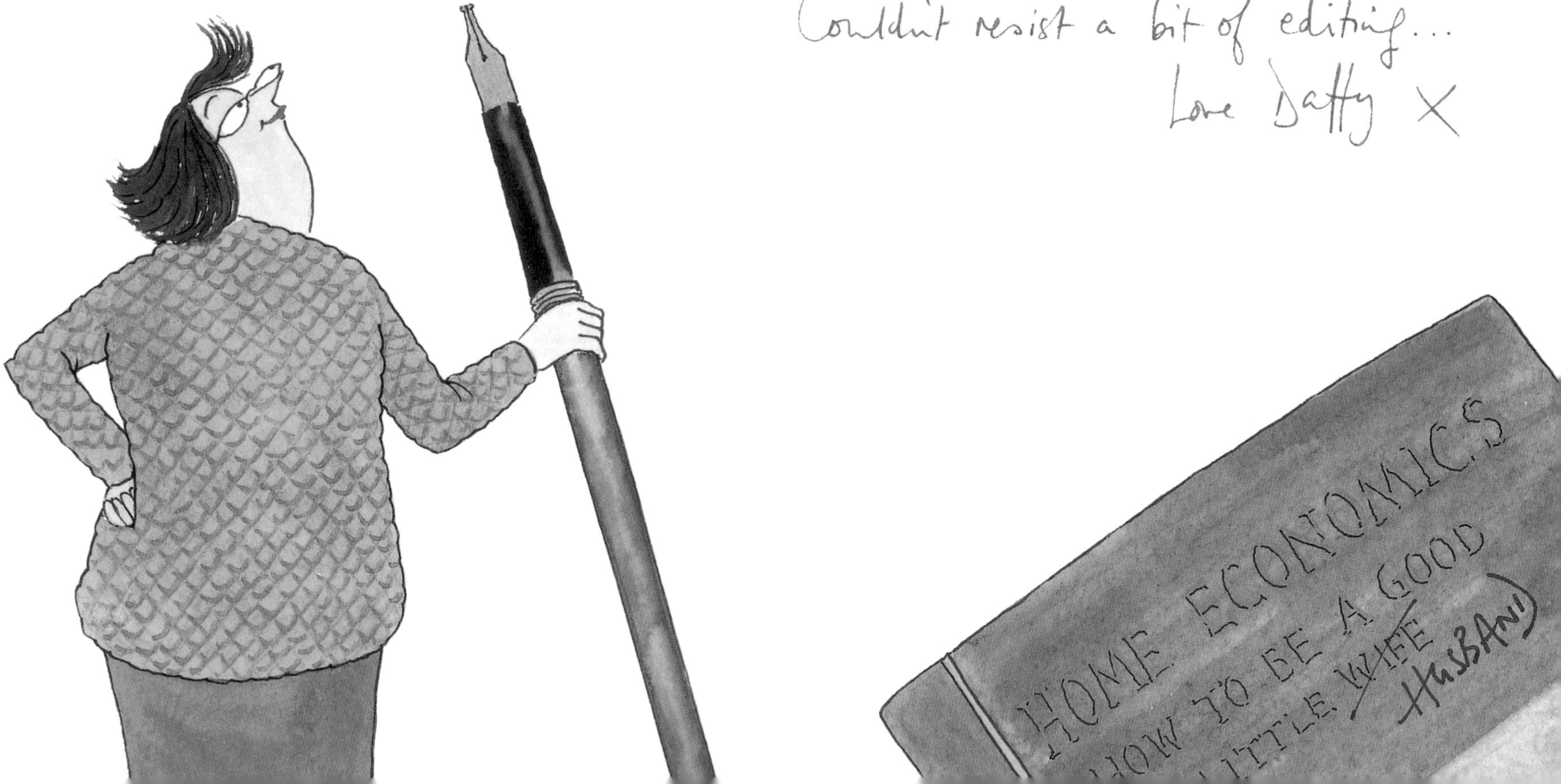
HOME ECONOMICS
TO BE A GOOD
~~WIFE~~ HUSBAND

M ARCH

16

17

18

19

20

21

Spring has Sprung

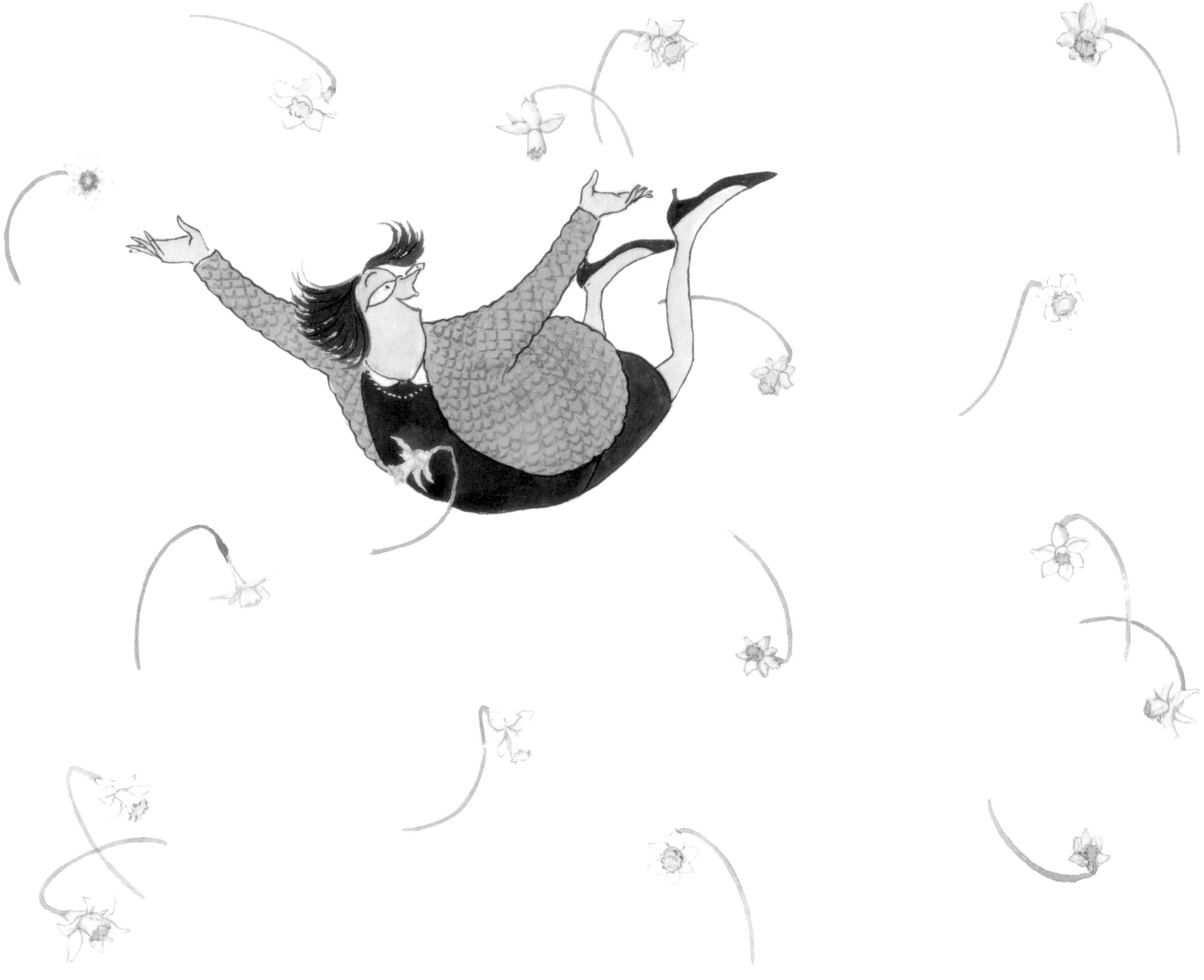

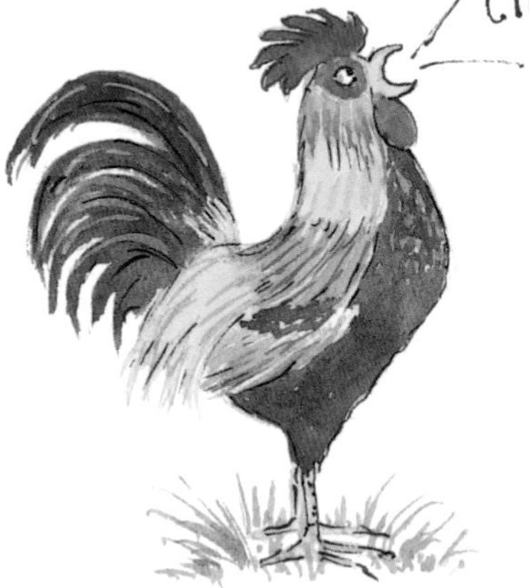
Clucks forward onto British Summertime...

MARCH

22

23 Tom Rodgers Birthday

24

25

26

27

28

29

30

31

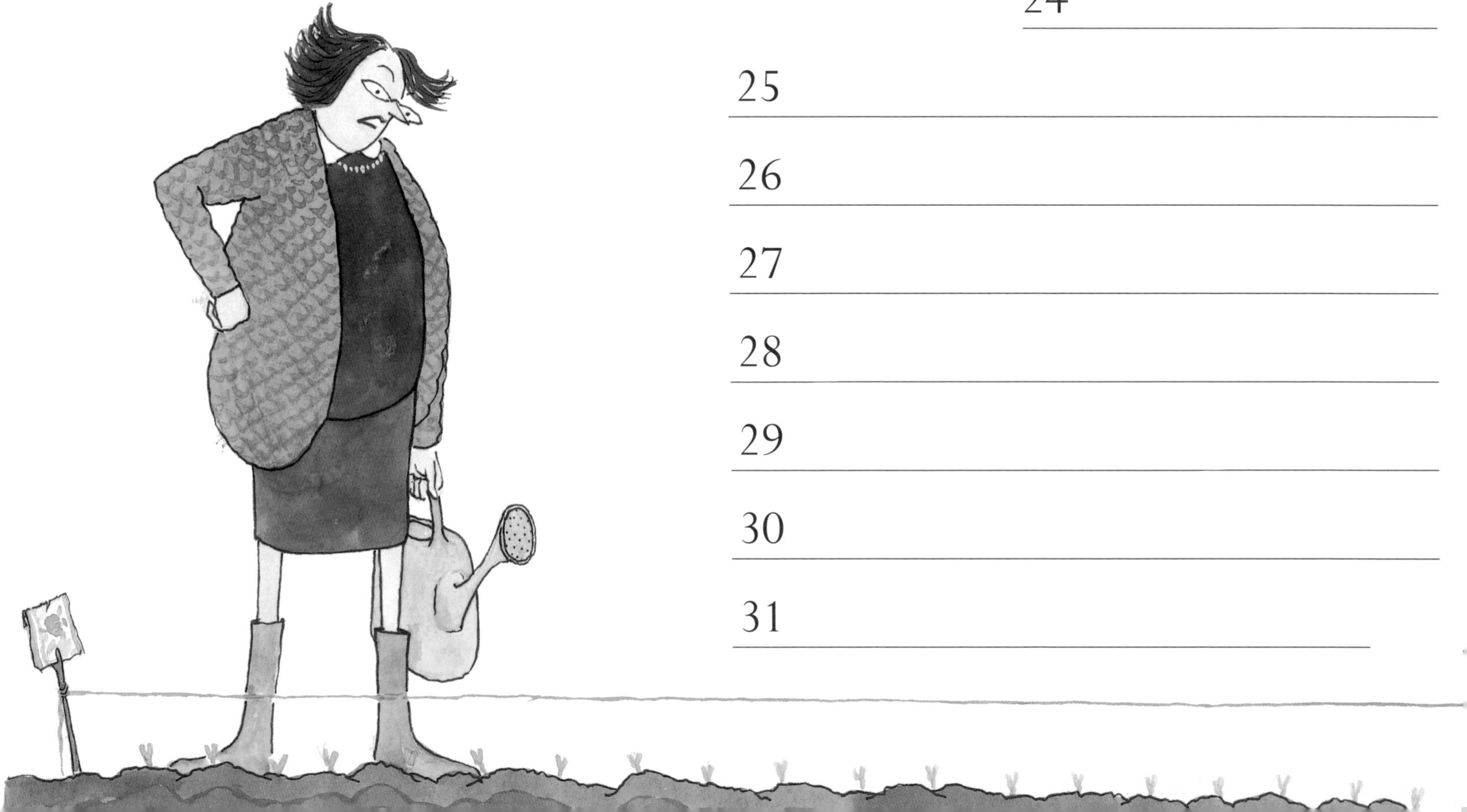
I do think that on Mother's Day you lot might have made a bit more effort for me...

APRIL

1   *April Fools day*

2

3

4

5   *End of Income Tax year*

6   Gill Welch

7

April Fool

4 to 6 green sink sponges cut into 1cm thick slices
grated rind of 2 Edam cheeses
grated rind of 1 Imperial leather soap bar
25-50g Growmore Granular
300mls Danish Oil
Yew chippings or shavings to decorate.

1. Use the sink sponges to line the bottom & half way up the sides of a deep dish or bowl. 2. Mix the Edam and Imperial leather rinds and lather with the Growmore Granular and stir until dissolved. 3. In another dish whip the Danish Oil until it starts to thicken and combine with above. 4 Pour the mixture over the sponges and refrigerate for at least two hours. Decorate with Yew chippings or shavings.

(POISONS 4-6 PEOPLE)

JOKER

JOKER

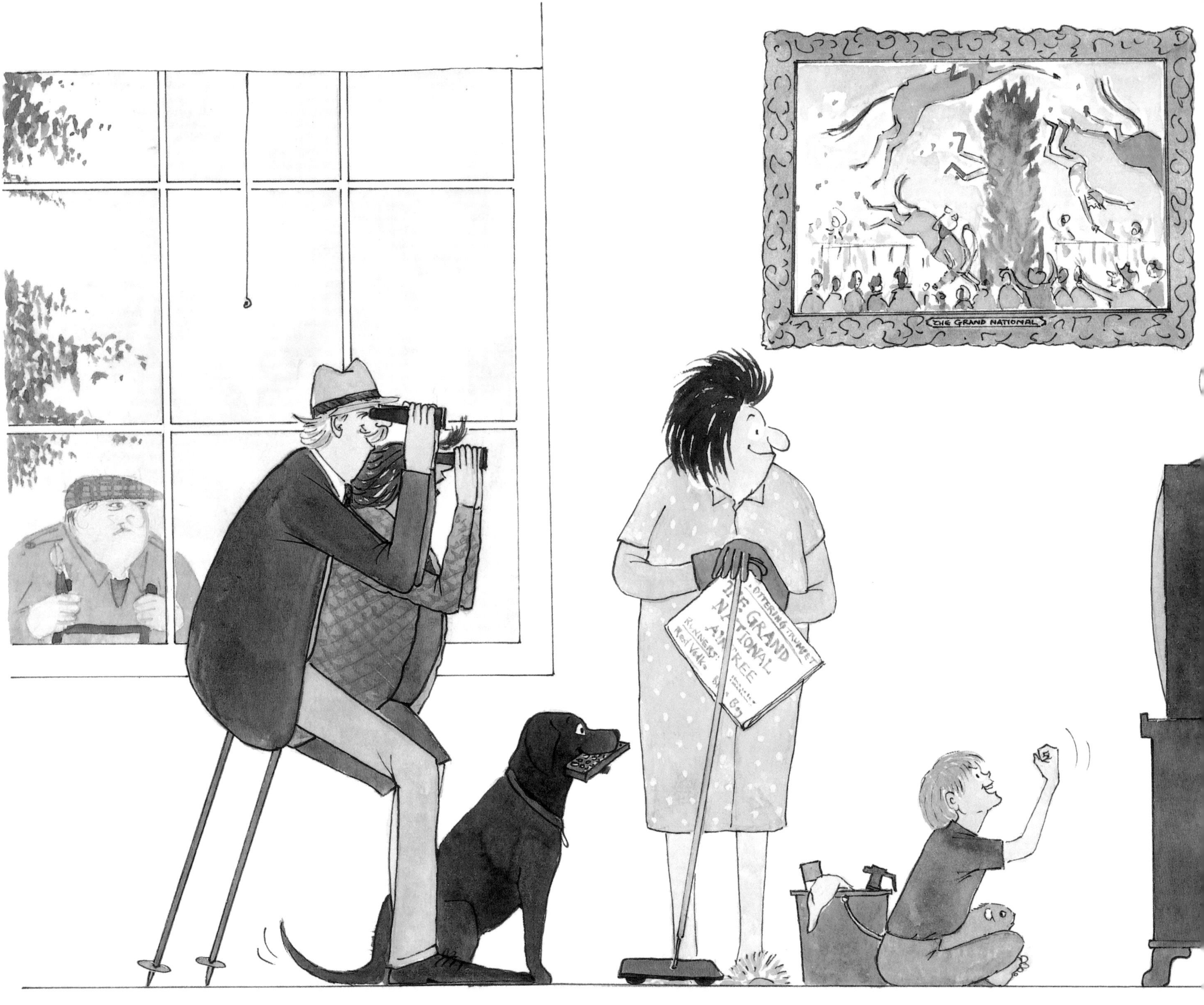
THE GRAND NATIONAL
THE GRAND NATIONAL
AINTREE
TRUMPET
RUNNERS:
Red Vodka

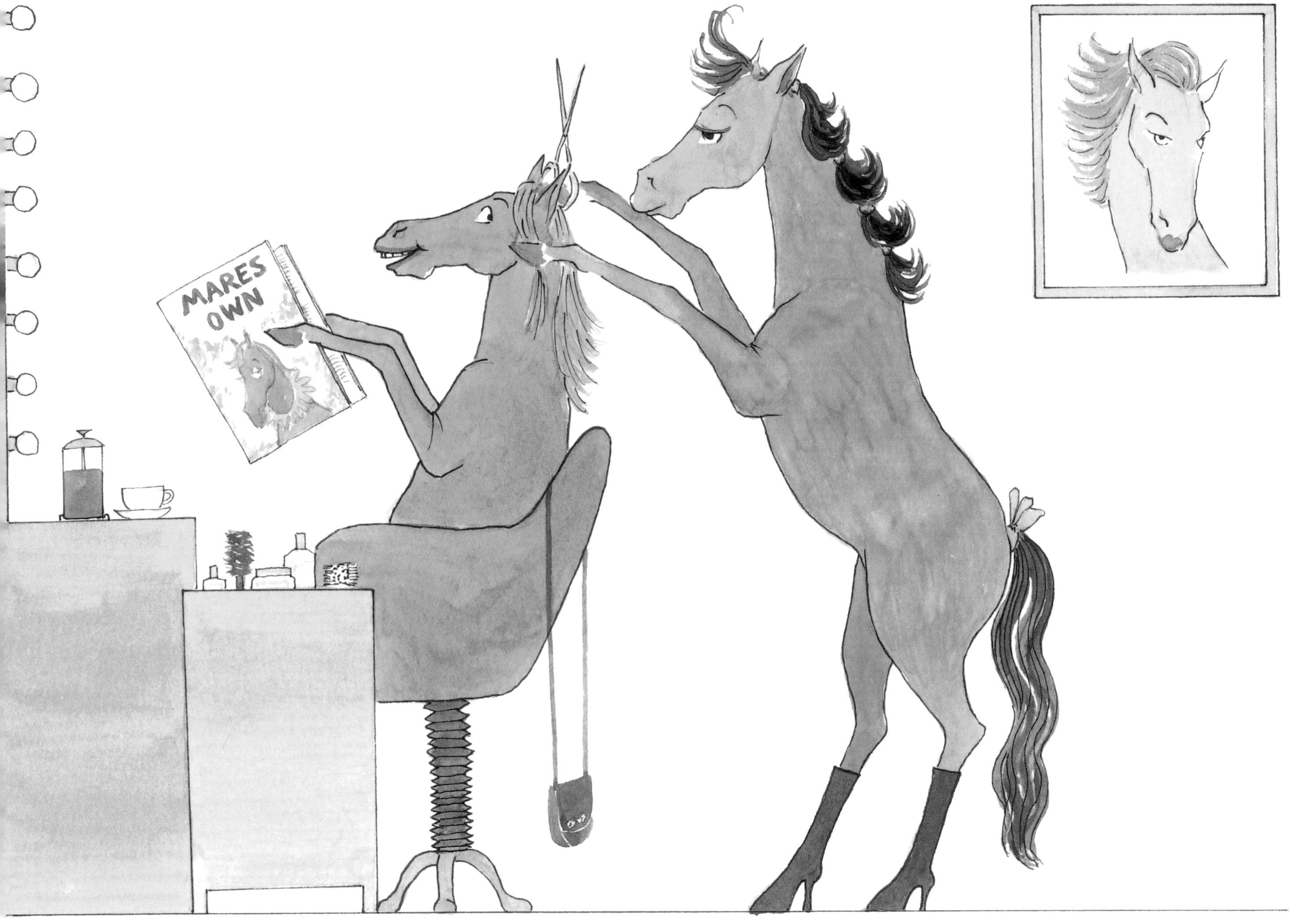
MARES
OWN

Can you keep it for me – I'm trying to grow my own sofa ...

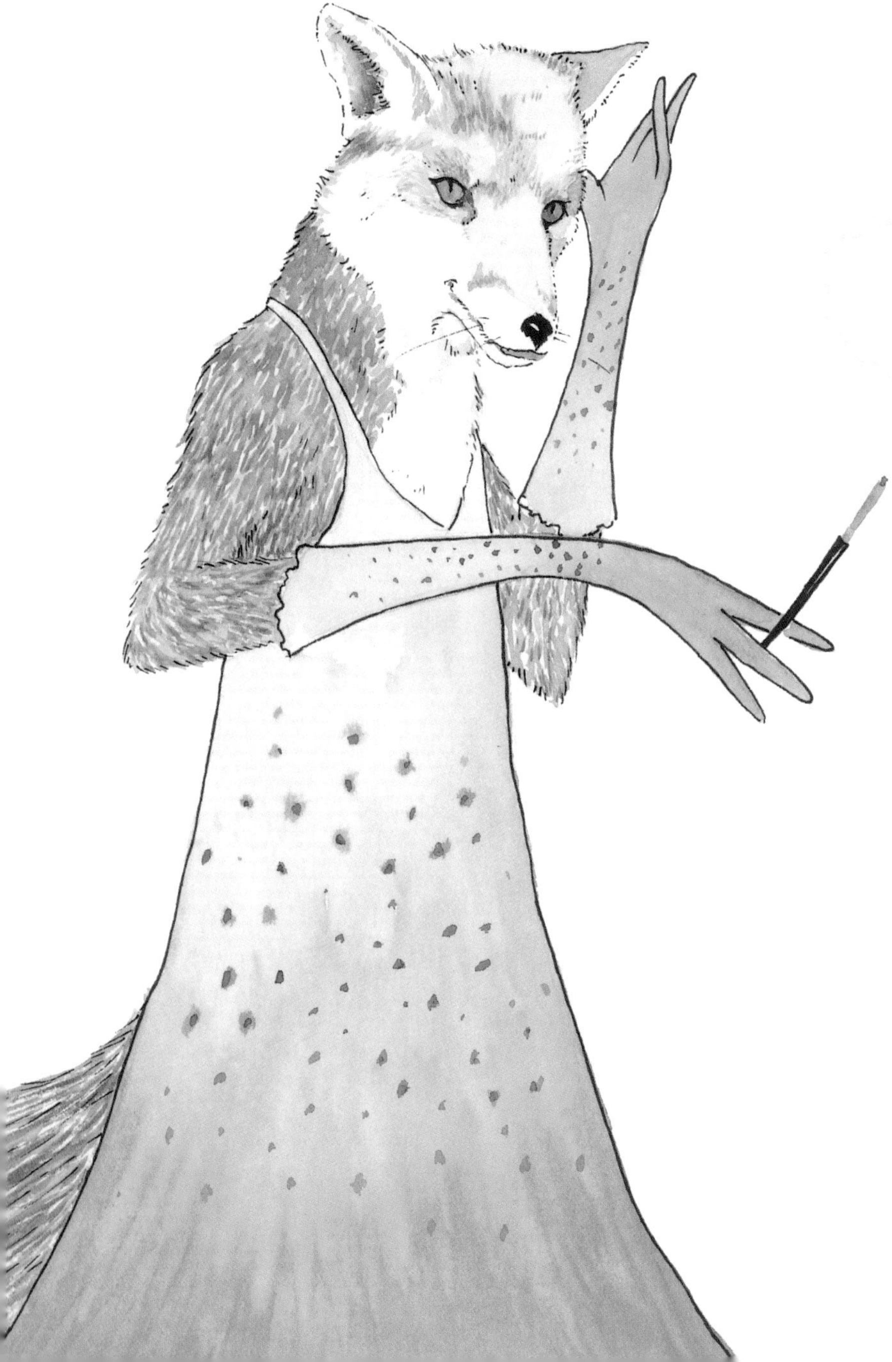

April

8

9

10

11

12

13

14

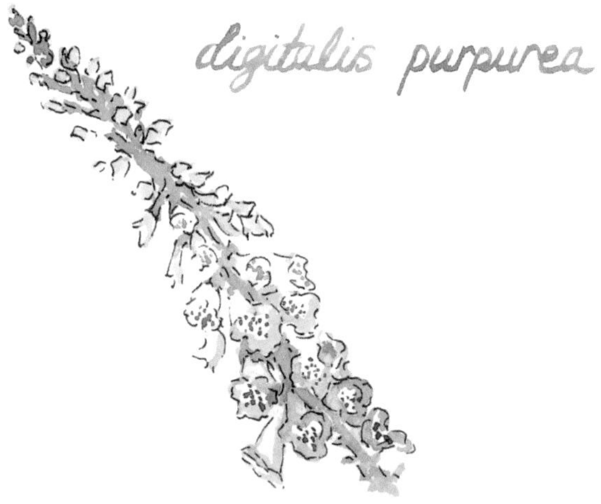
digitalis purpurea

foxy music

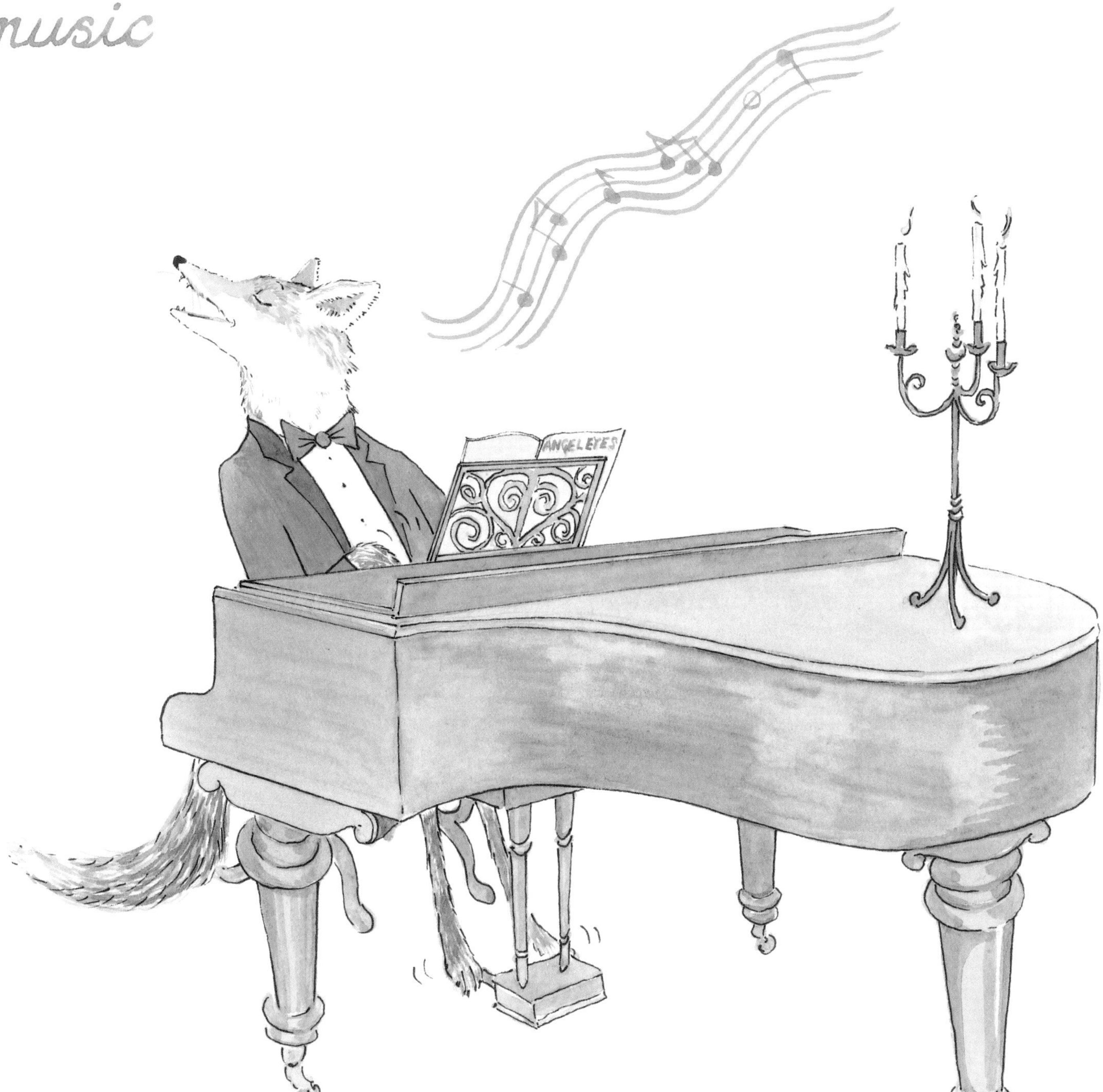
ANGEL EYES

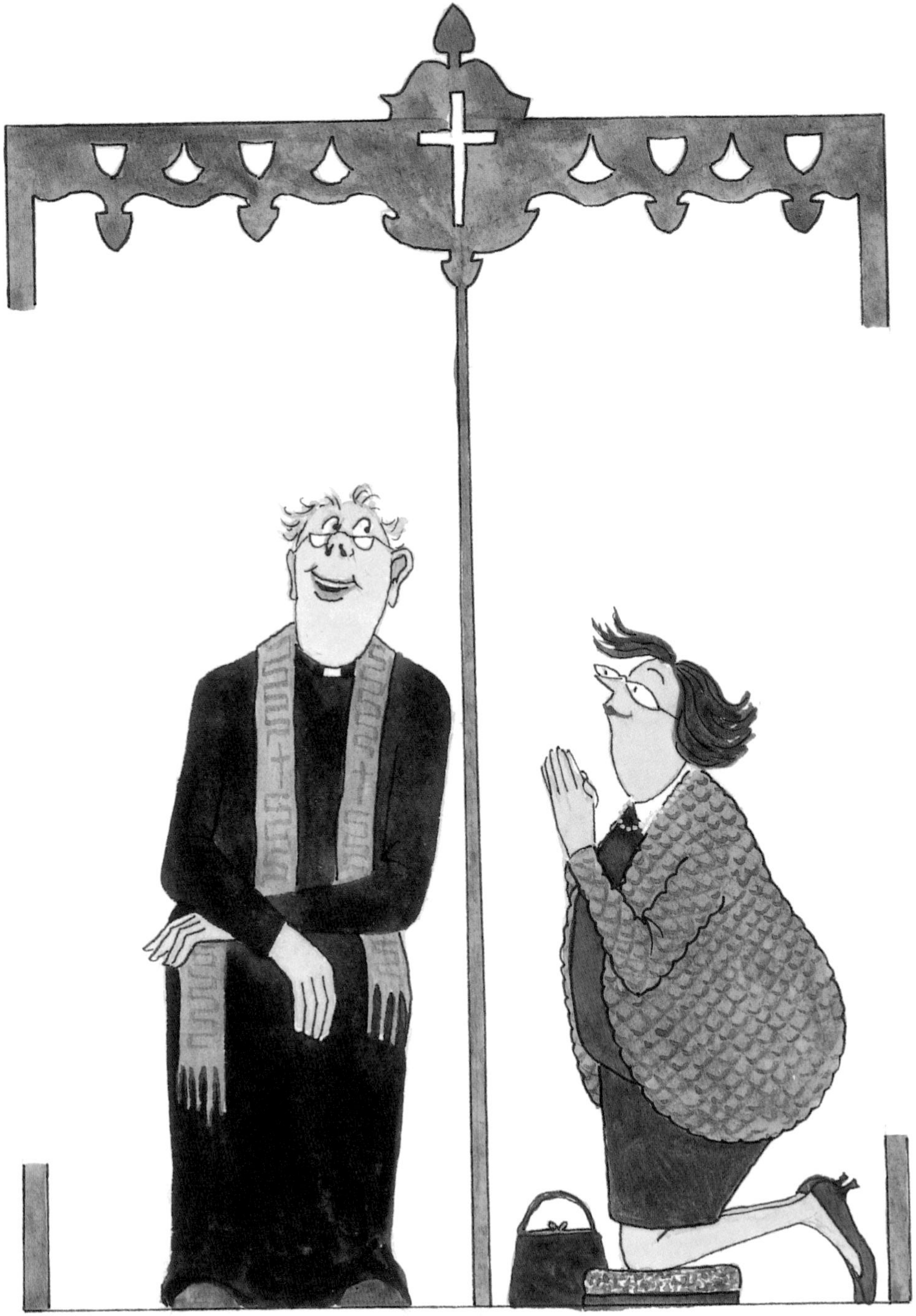

"I think the good Lord would forgive your greed if he knew they were Fauchon Easter eggs..."

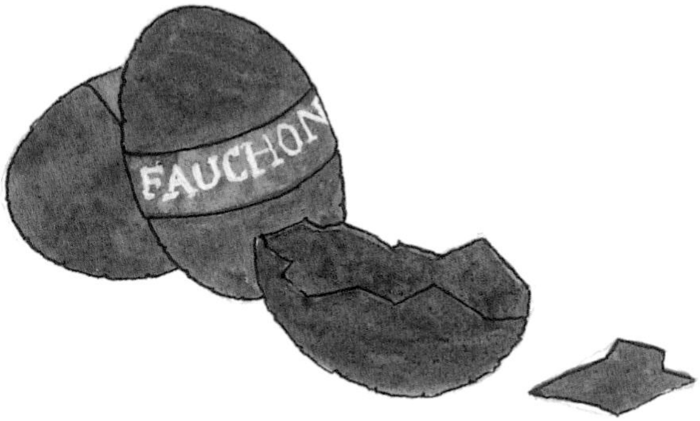
FAUCHON

APRIL

15

16

17

18

19 National primrose day

20

21

POST EASTER USEFUL TIP

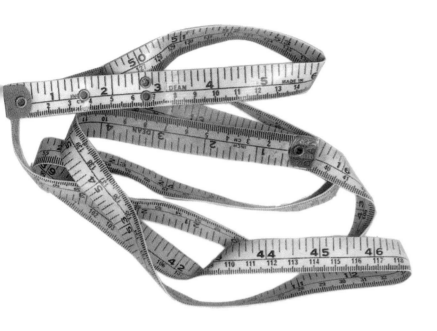

Eaten too many choccies over Easter?
Just take your tape measure and Tippex
out all the numbers.
Now mark every 2 inches as 1 inch (as shown below)

When you measure yourself now, you will
find you have a perfect 24 inch waist.

So you can eat all those left over choccies after all.

INCH
CM
1
DEAN
2
MADE IN
3
ENGLAND
7
8
FIBREGLASS
9
13 14 15 16 17 18 19 20 21 22

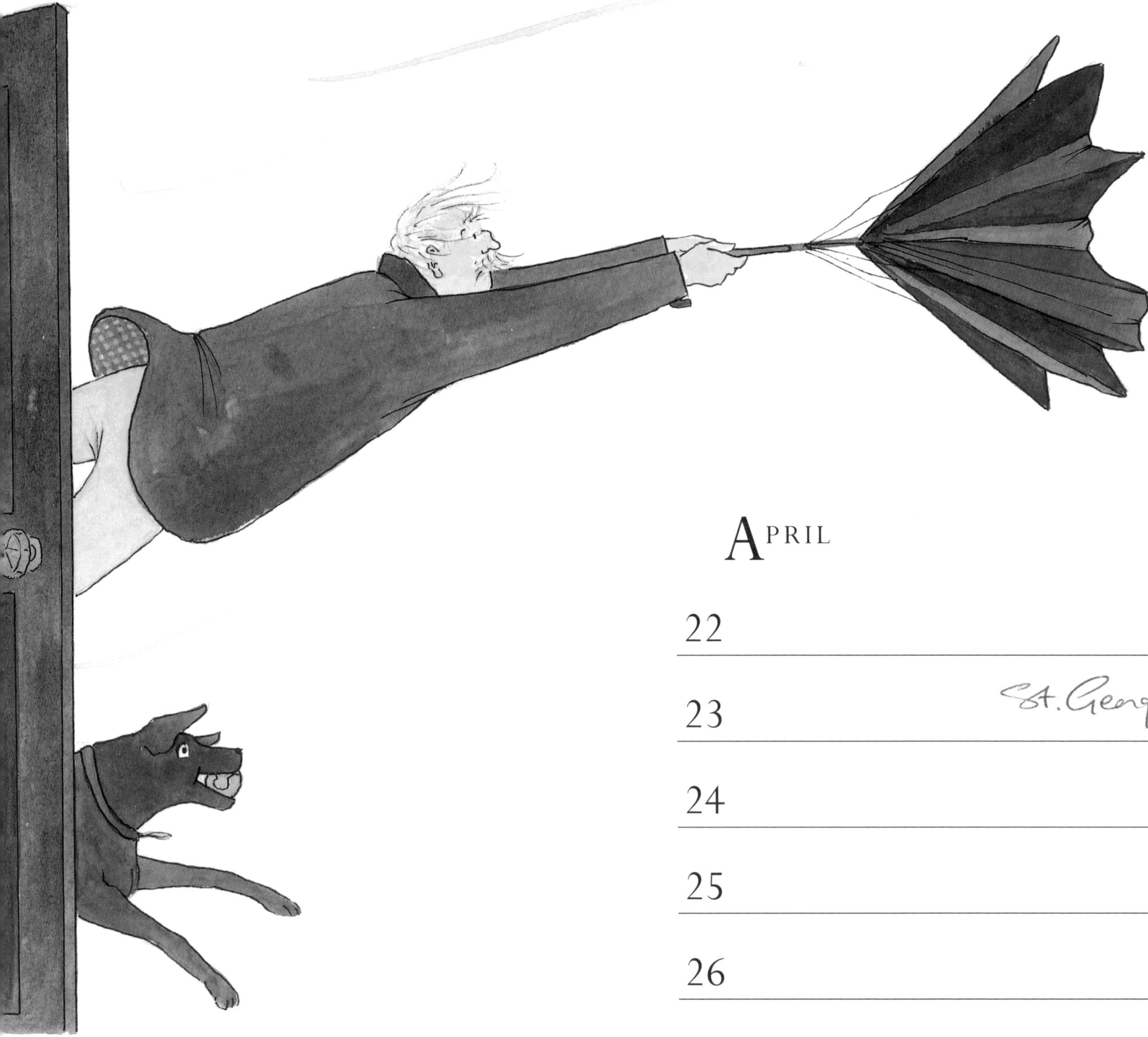

April

22

23 St. George's day

24

25

26

"I take it the weather still hasn't improved, Dicky..."

APRIL

27
_____

28
_____

29
_____

30
_____

'Arguing with a woman is like trying to fold the airmail edition of, THE TIMES in a high wind.'

LORD MANCROFT

'To my deafness I'm accustomed,
  To my dentures I'm resigned,
I can manage my bifocals,
  But Oh! How I miss my mind...'

(CAN'T REMEMBER WHO WROTE THIS...)

Tottering Hall,
Tottering-by-Gently,
Rottingbeam,
North Pimmshire

Dear ....,

It was so { nice / unexpected / revealing / amusing } *to* { make your acquaintance. / see you again. / endure the pleasure of your company. / realise that we have nothing in common. } *I/we haven't had more* { small talk / stress / entertainment / disruption }

for a long time and hope that I/we can { do it again soon. / forgive and forget. / persuade you to emigrate. / impose on YOU someday. } *May I/we say what* { a delight / an insight / a drudge }

it was for me/us to have you { to help consume my/our vintage reserves. / to stay. / to wait on hand and foot. } *Please do feel free to* { come again / keep going / petition in vain }

if you're ever { in the area. / divorced. / prepared to restock my/ our cellars. } *I will assume you meant to leave* { your teeth / nothing / your wallet / your............ }

unless I hear to the contrary.

Yours,

Tottering Hall,
Tottering-by-Gently,
Rottingbeam,
North Pimmshire

Dear………….,

Thank you so much for the
- unorthodox
- interesting
- infinite
- delightful

weekend at your
- enchanting
- unusual
- impressive
- spartan

house. I/we feel
- toxic
- invigorated
- exhausted
- rested

after the break. You cannot imagine how
- blissful
- interminable
- unexpected
- ghastly

it was returning home after the
- stomach pump.
- excess of hospitality.
- traffic jams.
- expense.

I/we greatly look forward to coming again
- should you invite me/us.
- when you have fixed the heating.
- when you employ a kitchen hand.
- your family problems are resolved.

I'm afraid I omitted to pack
- our child
- your monogrammed towels
- my…………………………

and would be grateful if you could return it/them by
- Tuesday.
- post.

Yours,

M<small>AY</small>

1

2

3

4

5

6

7

Motley Hall   23rd

Dearest Daffy,

With love to invite you and
..... to join our party for the 3rd
..... Caledonian Ball on the 3rd
..... arranged to have dinner
..... the Connaught.
..... let me know
..... cocoa and
..... pair

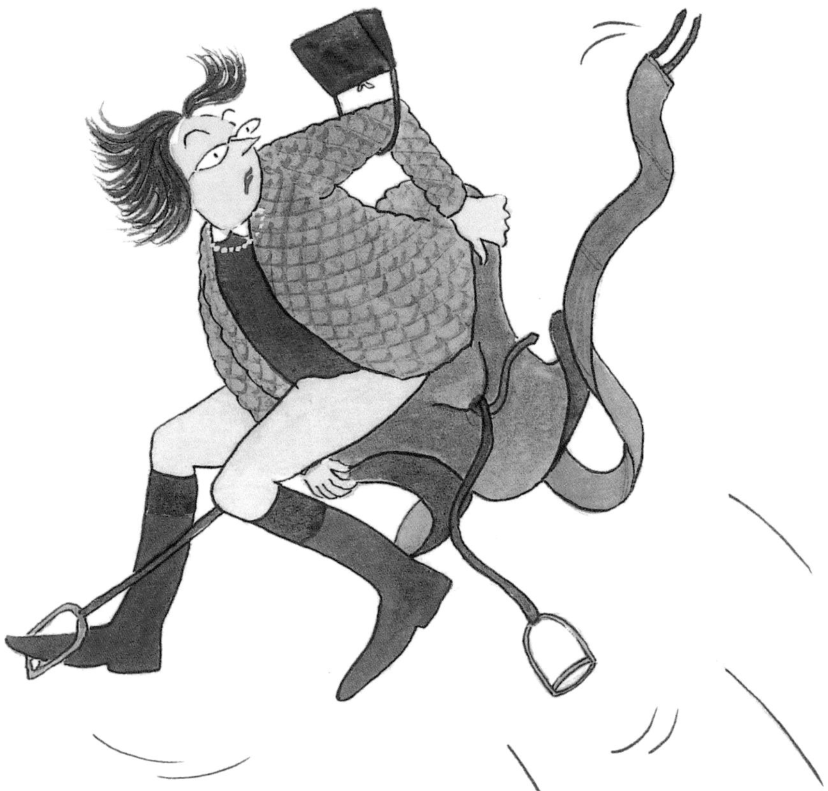

May

8

9

10

11

12

13

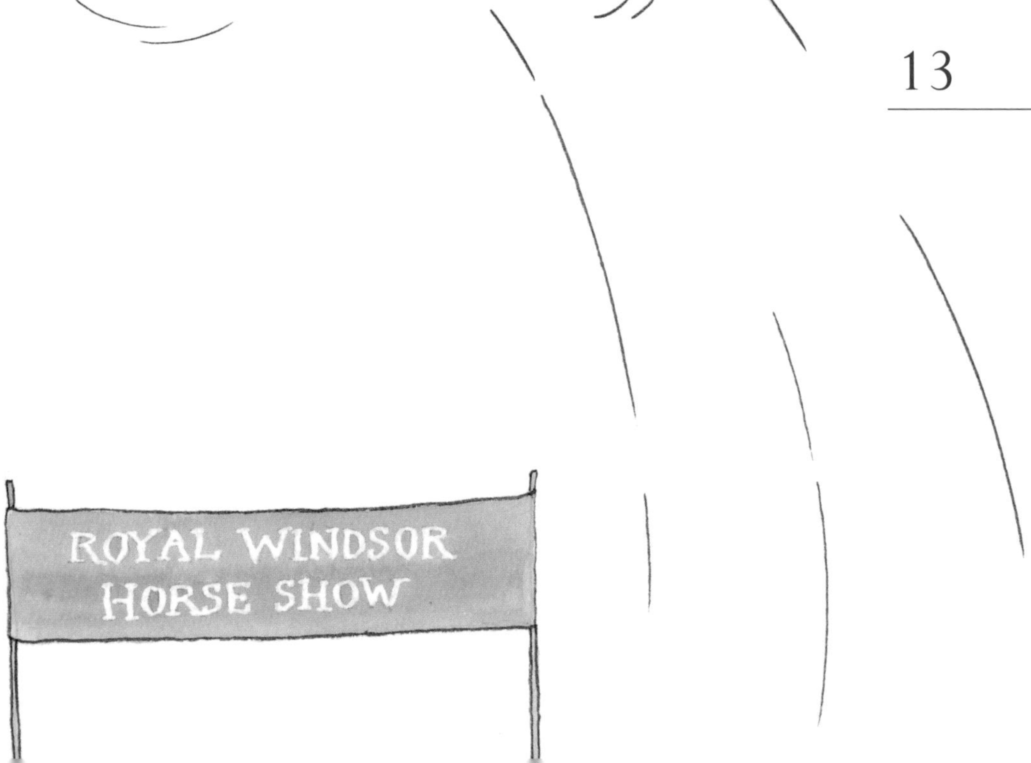
ROYAL WINDSOR
HORSE SHOW

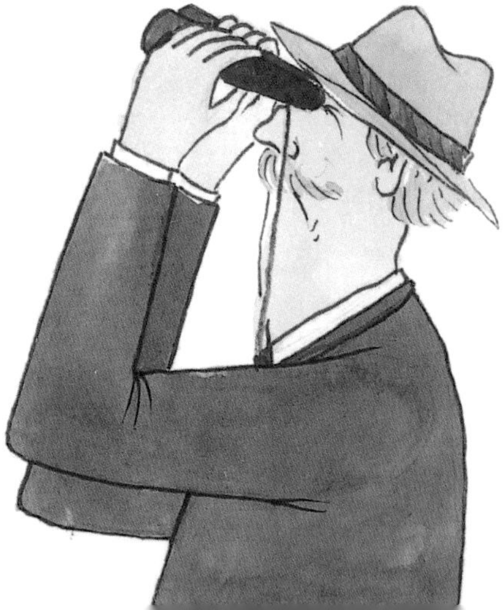

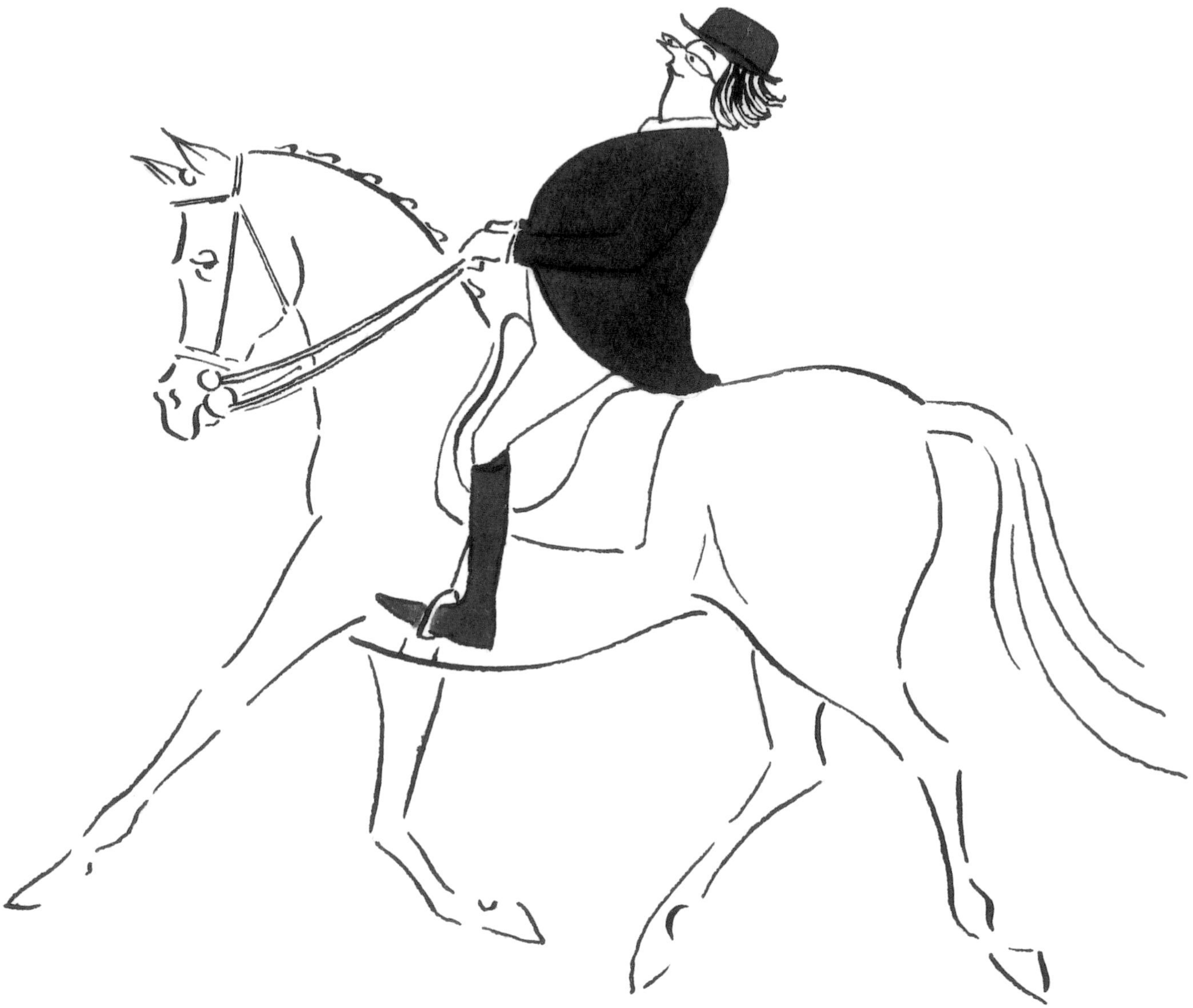

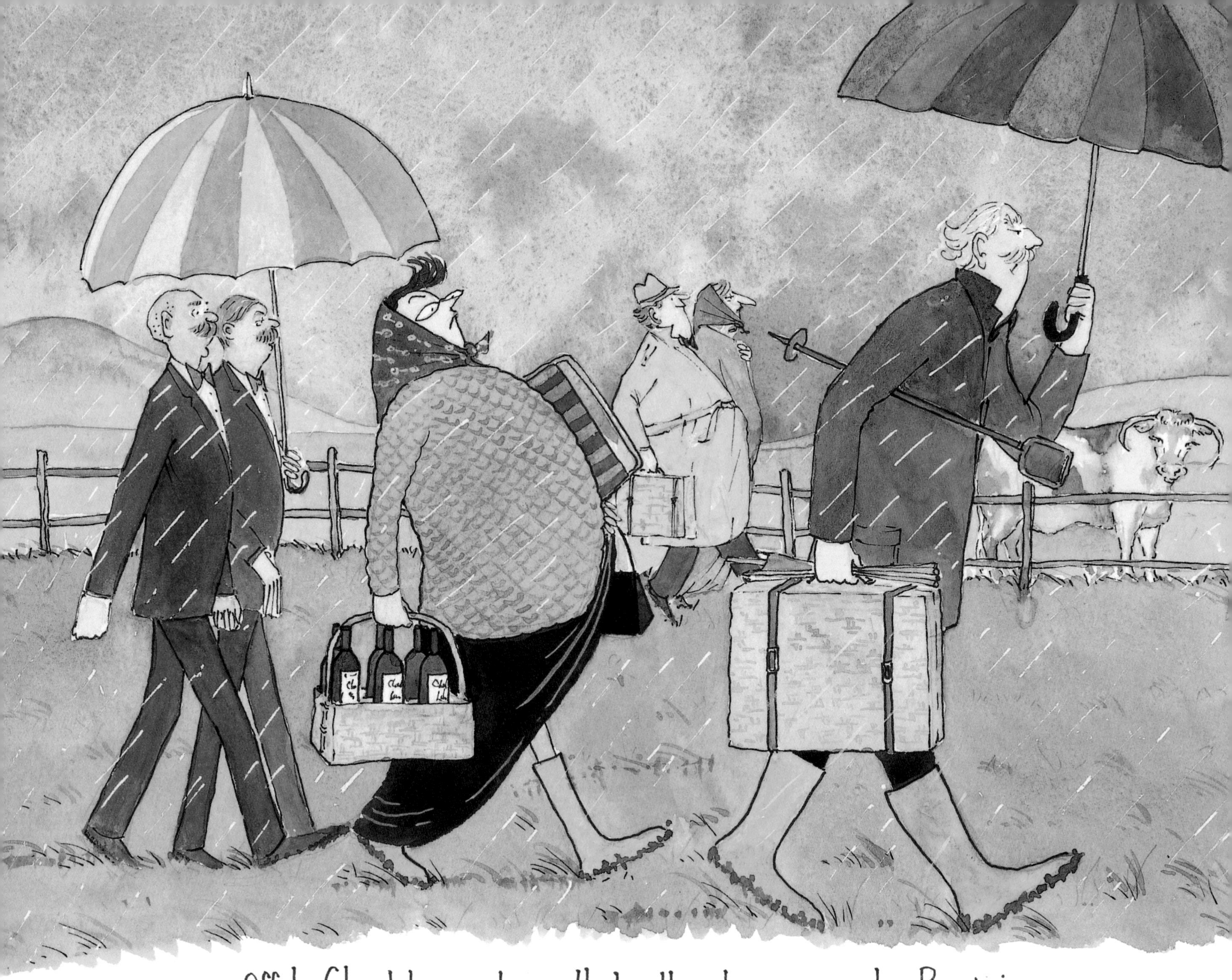

Off to Glyndebourne to see that rather dreary opera by Rossini ...

M^{AY}

14
_____

15
_____

16
_____

17
_____

18
_____

19
_____

20
_____

21
_____

"Hi! Can you hear me? Yup - I'm in the middle of an opera at Glyndebourne - I'll call you back in the interval ..."

Weeping standard...

Tub or pot...

A small shrub of loose, open habit— origin uncertain...

MAY

22

23

24

25

26

27

28

HORTI-TYPES

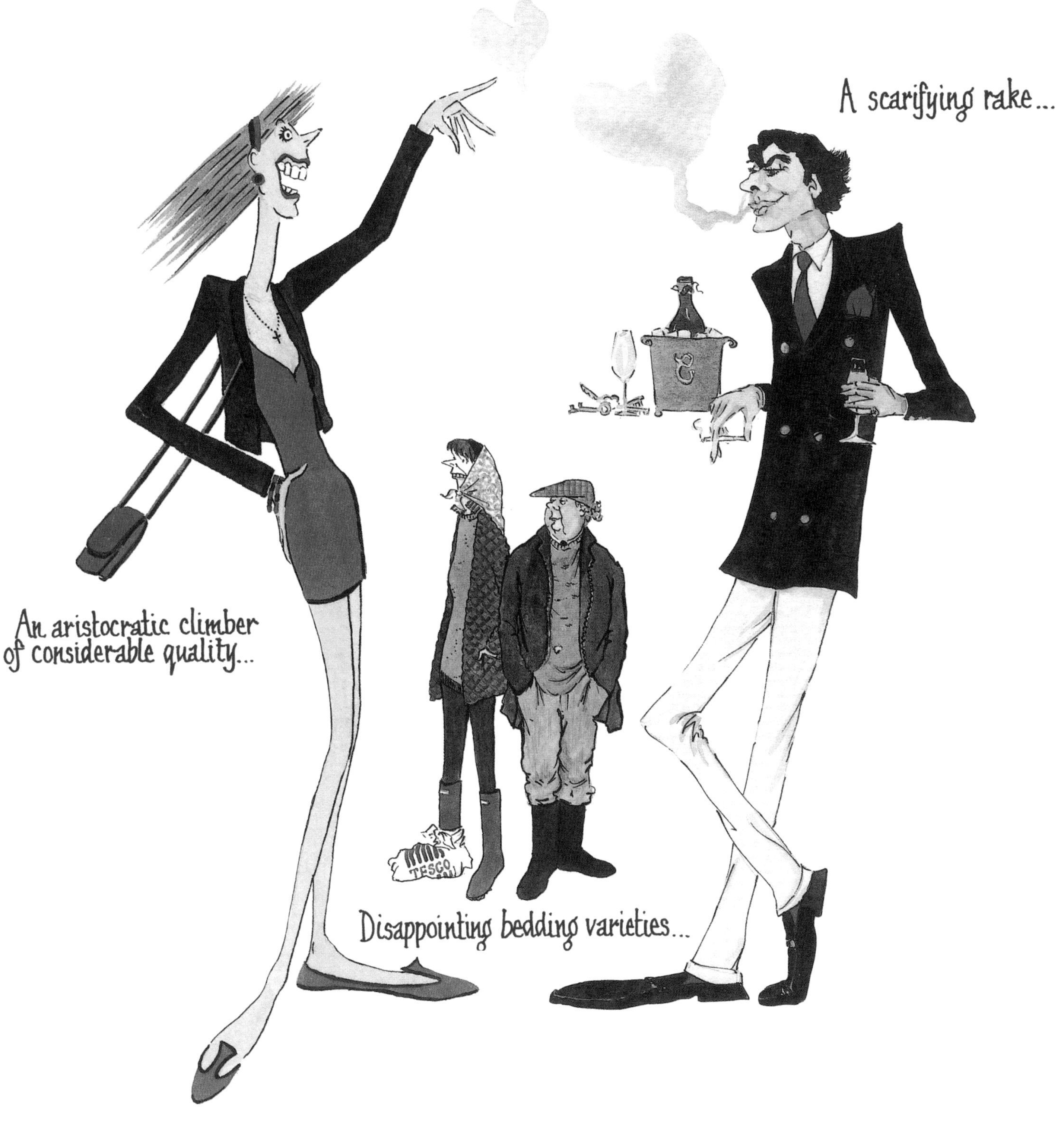
A scarifying rake...
An aristocratic climber of considerable quality...
TESCO
Disappointing bedding varieties...

May

29

30

31

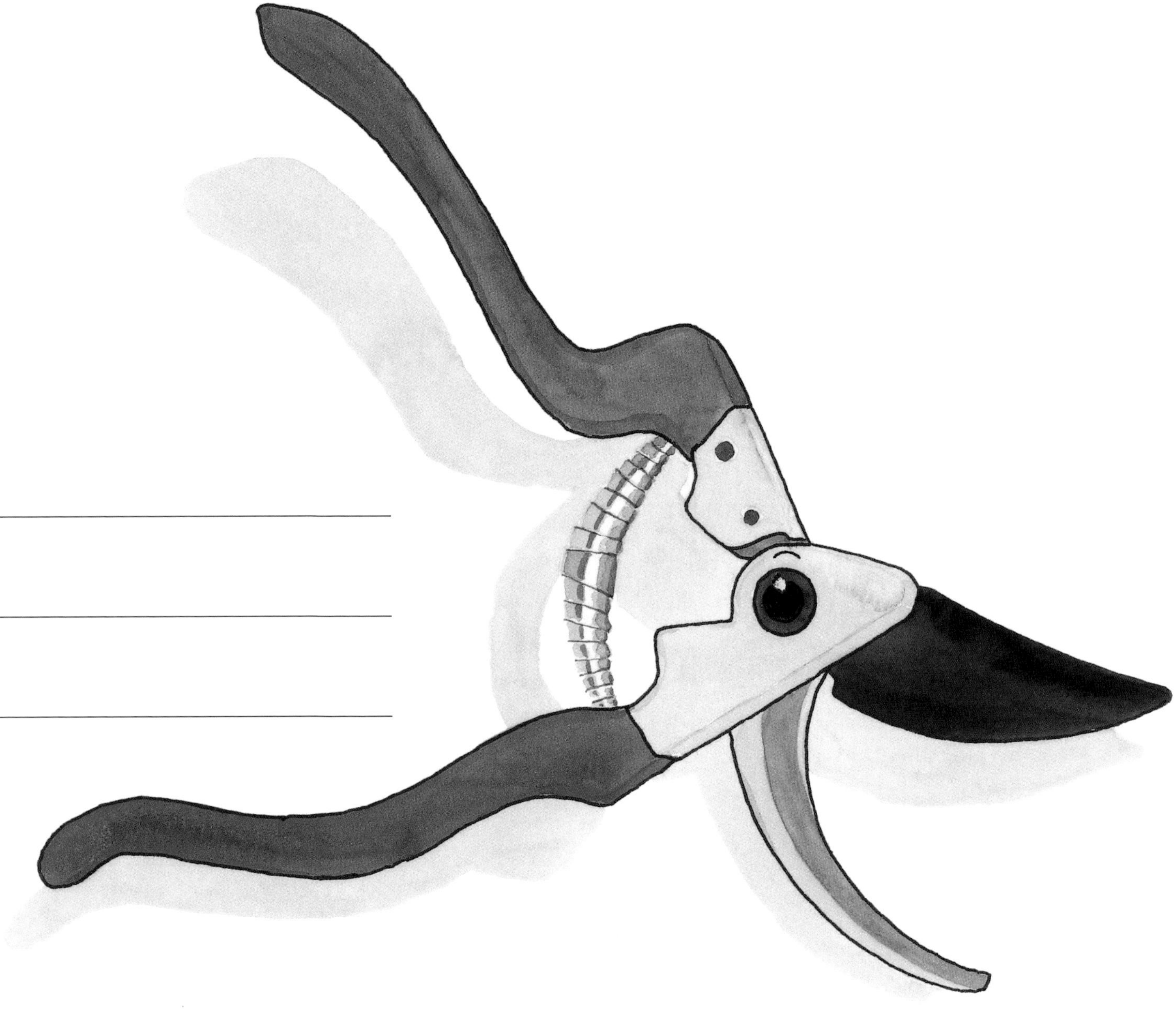

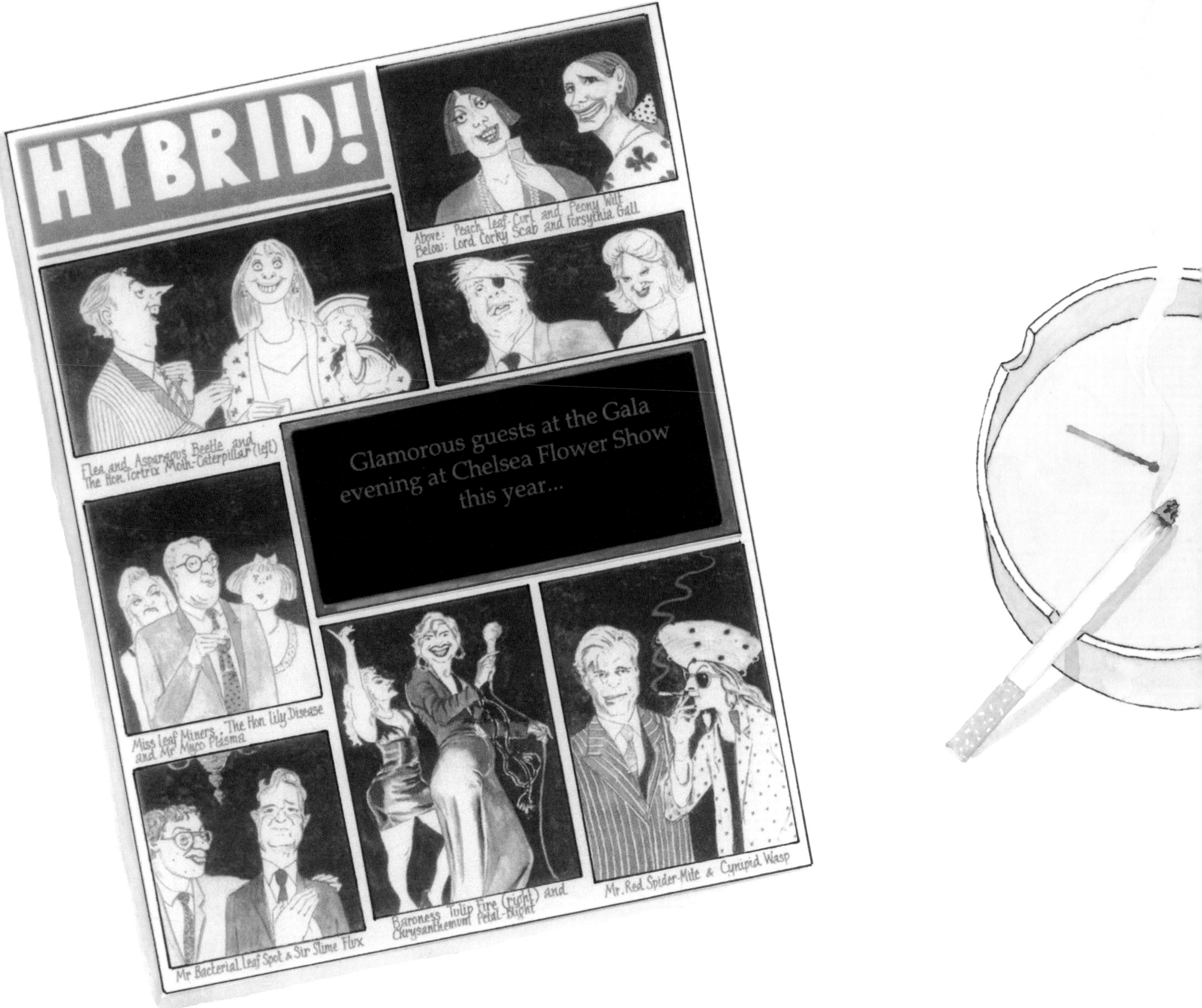
HYBRID!
Above: Peach Leaf-Curl and Peony Wilt
Below: Lord Corky Scab and forsythia Gall
Flea and Asparagus Beetle and The Hon Tortrix Moth-Caterpillar (left)
Glamorous guests at the Gala evening at Chelsea Flower Show this year...
Miss Leaf Miners, The Hon Lily Disease and Mr Myco Plasma
Mr Bacterial Leaf Spot & Sir Slime Flux
Baroness Tulip Fire (right) and Chrysanthemum Petal-Blight
Mr. Red Spider-Mite & Cynipid Wasp

JUNE

1

2

3

4

5

6

7

Would you give me some batting practice, Grandpa?

I'm afraid my bowling's pretty rusty, Freddy, but I'll give it a try...

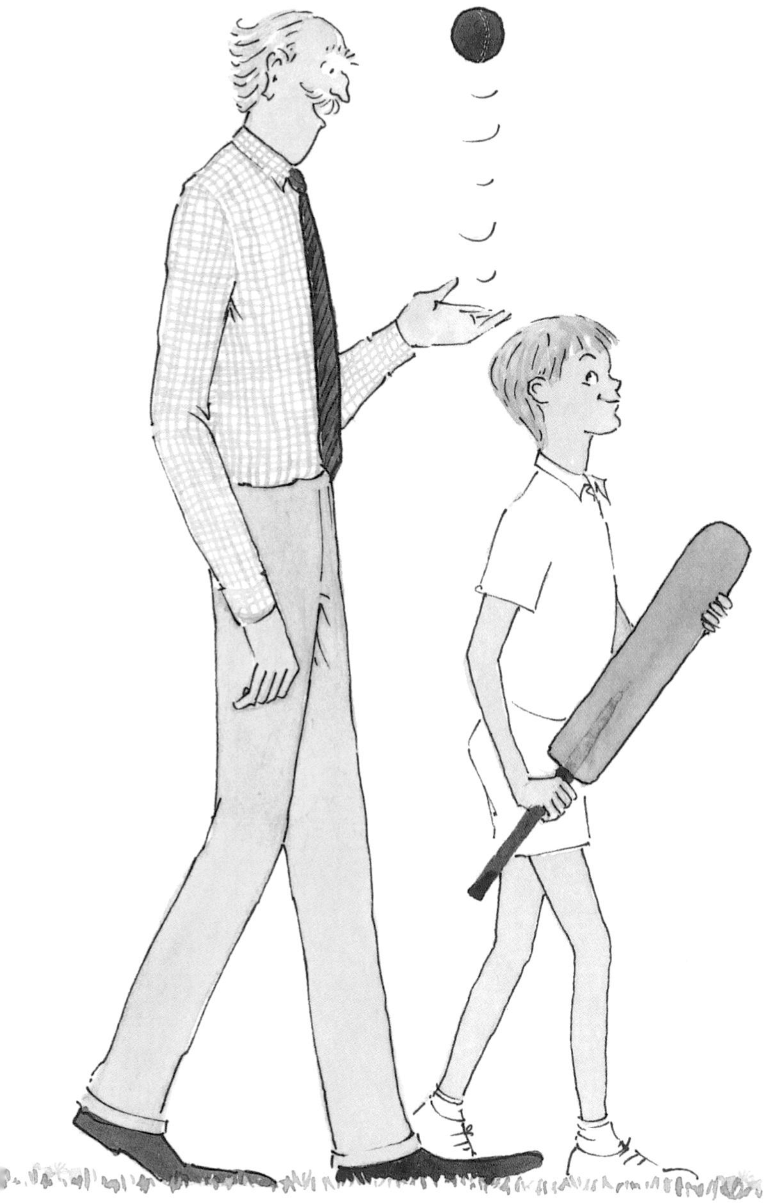

Just stick to underarm then – I won't tell your friends...

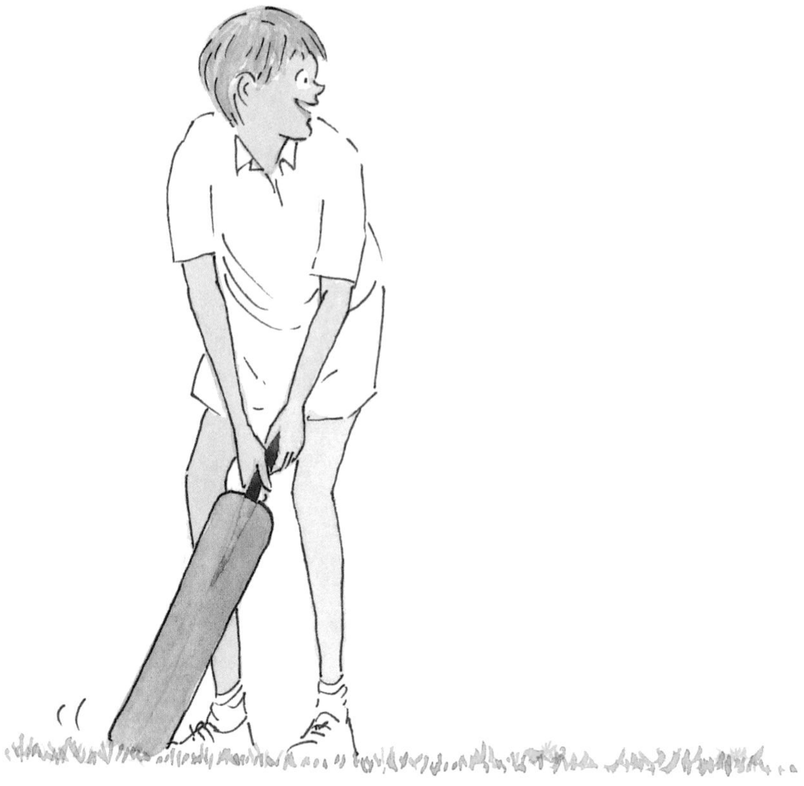

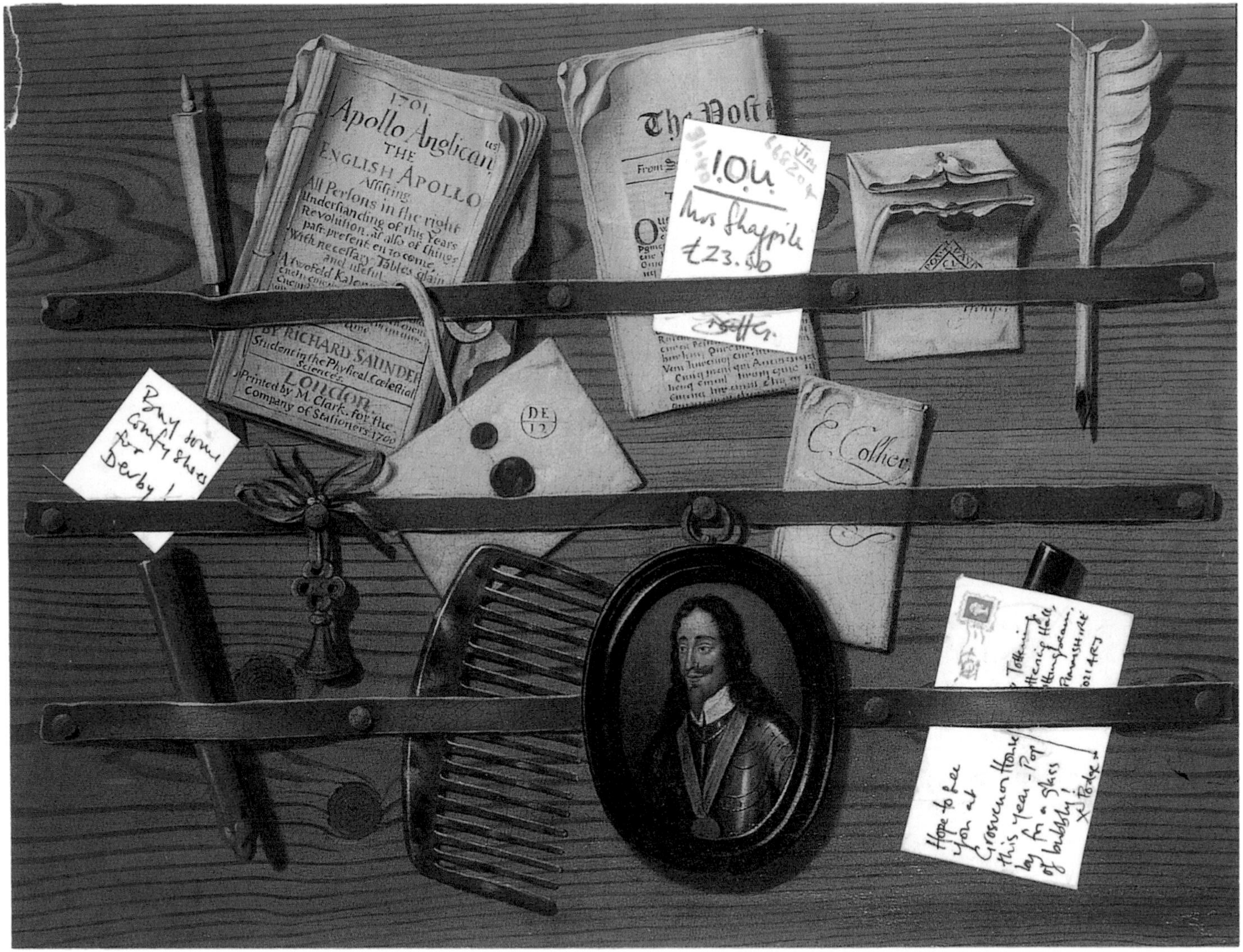

1701.
Apollo Anglican
THE
ENGLISH APOLLO
Assisting
All Persons in the right
Understanding of this Years
Revolution, as also of things
past, present, en to come,
With necessary Tables and useful
BY RICHARD SAUNDER
Student in the Physical Cœlestial Sciences.
London.
Printed by M. Clark, for the
Company of Stationers 1700
I.O.U.
Mrs Shappik
£23.00
Buy some comfy shoes for Derby!
DE 12
C. Collier
Hope to see you at Grosvenor House this year - Pop by for a glass of bubbly!

June

8

9

10

11

A STRIKING PAIR WITH SPLENDID PROVENANCE...

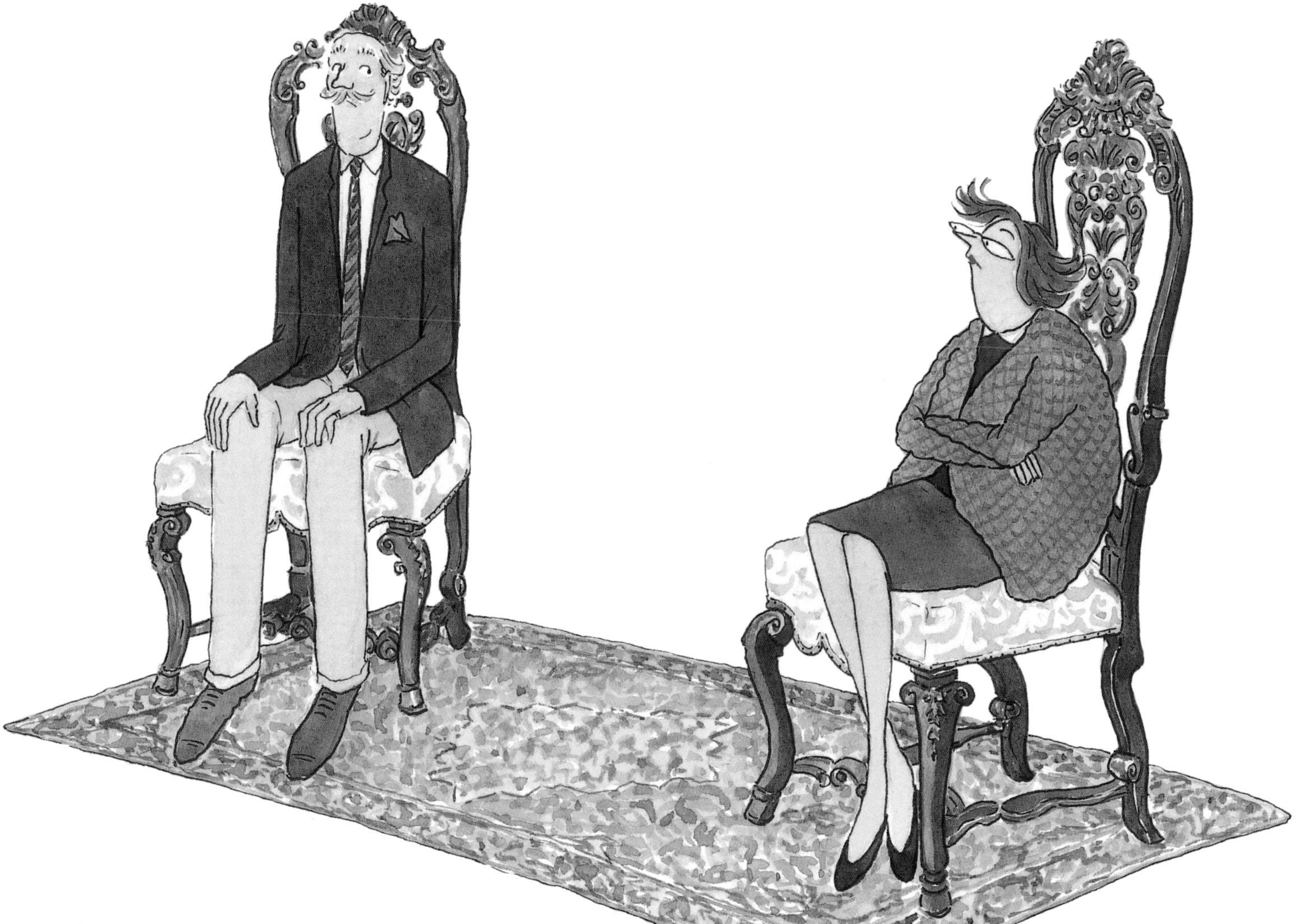

This tallboy with dentil cornice and fully fitted interior has one or two later additions. Condition average for the period. Supported on original club legs and pad feet.

A large bow-fronted chest with slightly over-stuffed seat and tapering block feet. Difficult to age. Excellent value.

Six weeks after the daffs have finished - your work* begins...

(* getting in touch with your inner terminator..)

J UNE

12 _____

13 _____

14 _____

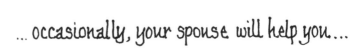

... occasionally, your spouse will help you...

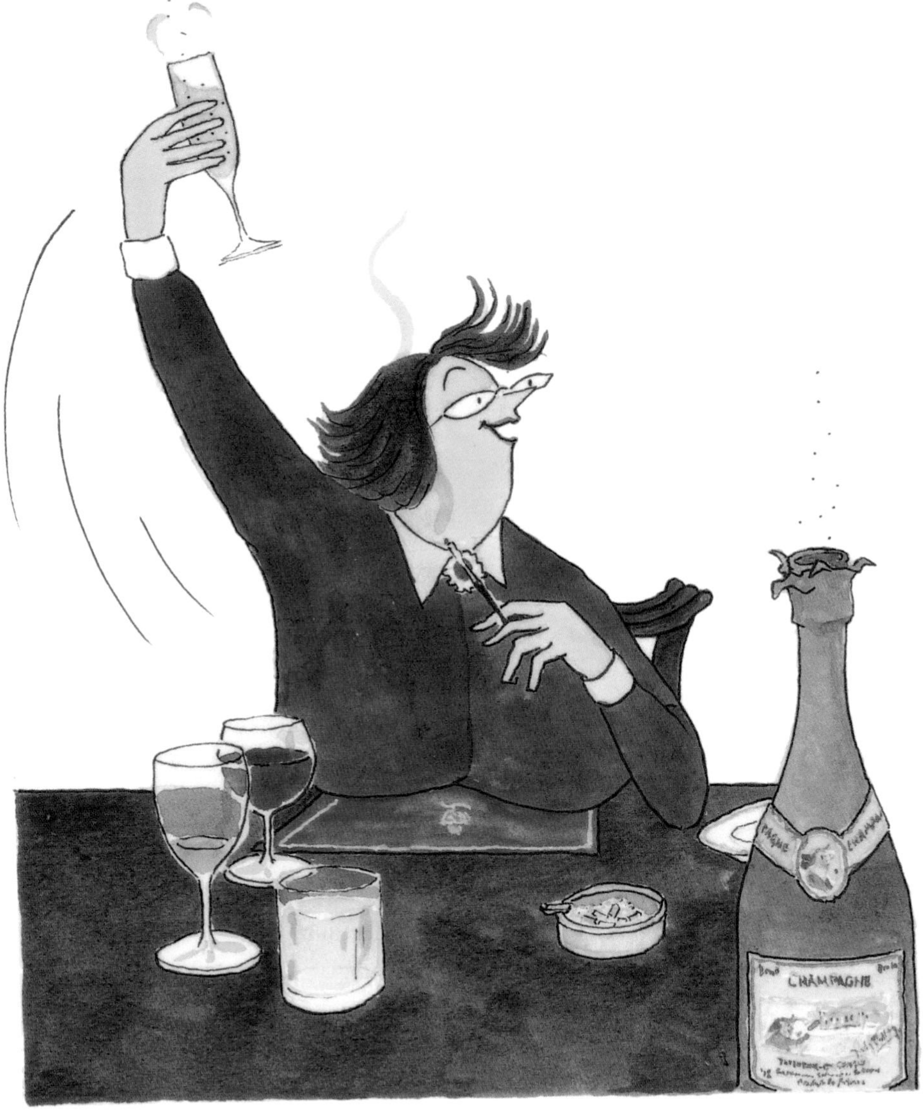
CHAMPAGNE

" TO THE QUEER OLD DEAN..."

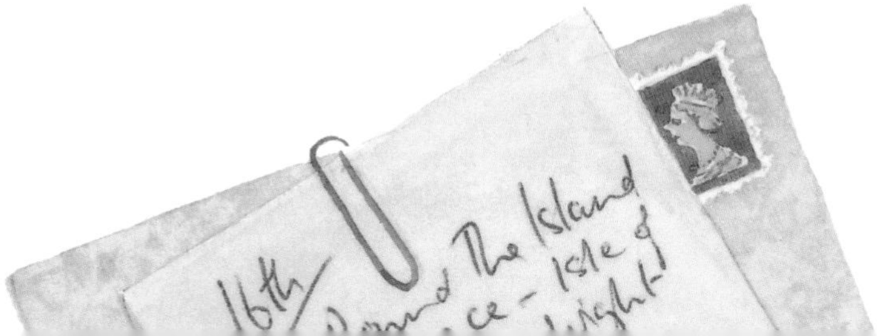
16th
The Island
Isle of

JUNE

15

16 Queen's official b'day

17

18

19

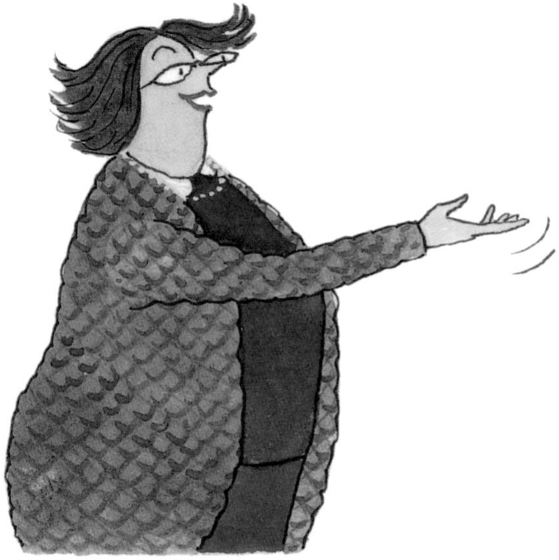

Can I have some money to buy you some flowers for Father's Day..?

" I'm not writing a thank you letter for dinner – I'm writing a letter of complaint…"

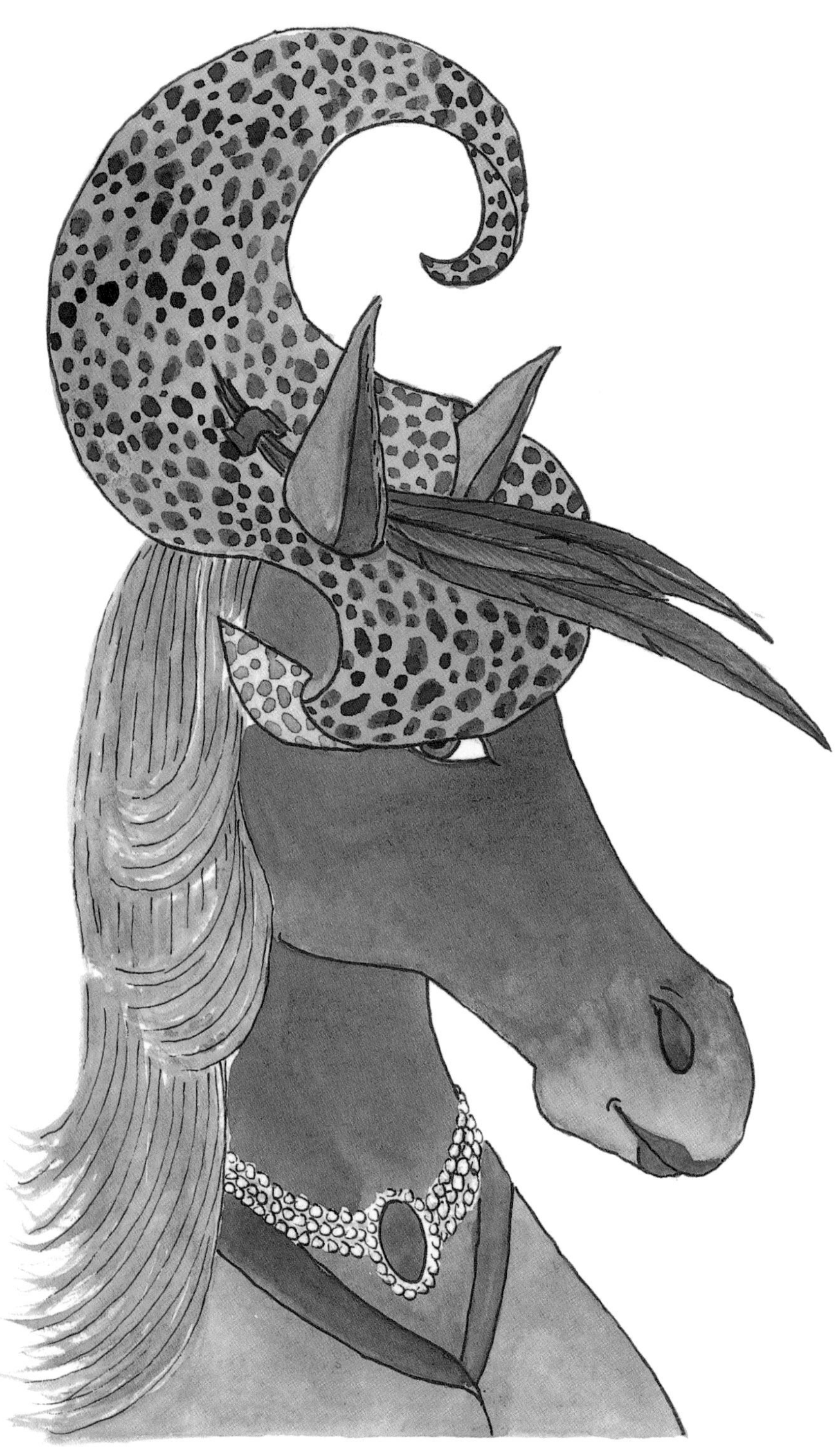

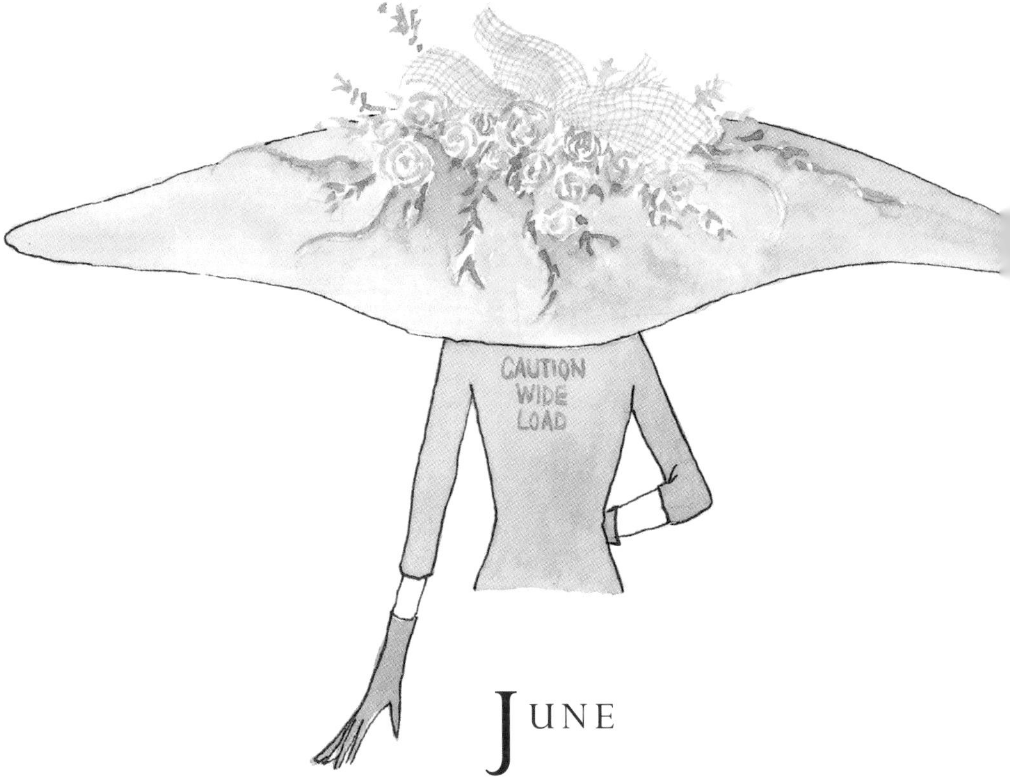
CAUTION
WIDE
LOAD

JUNE

20

21

22

23

Royal Ascot - Ladies day

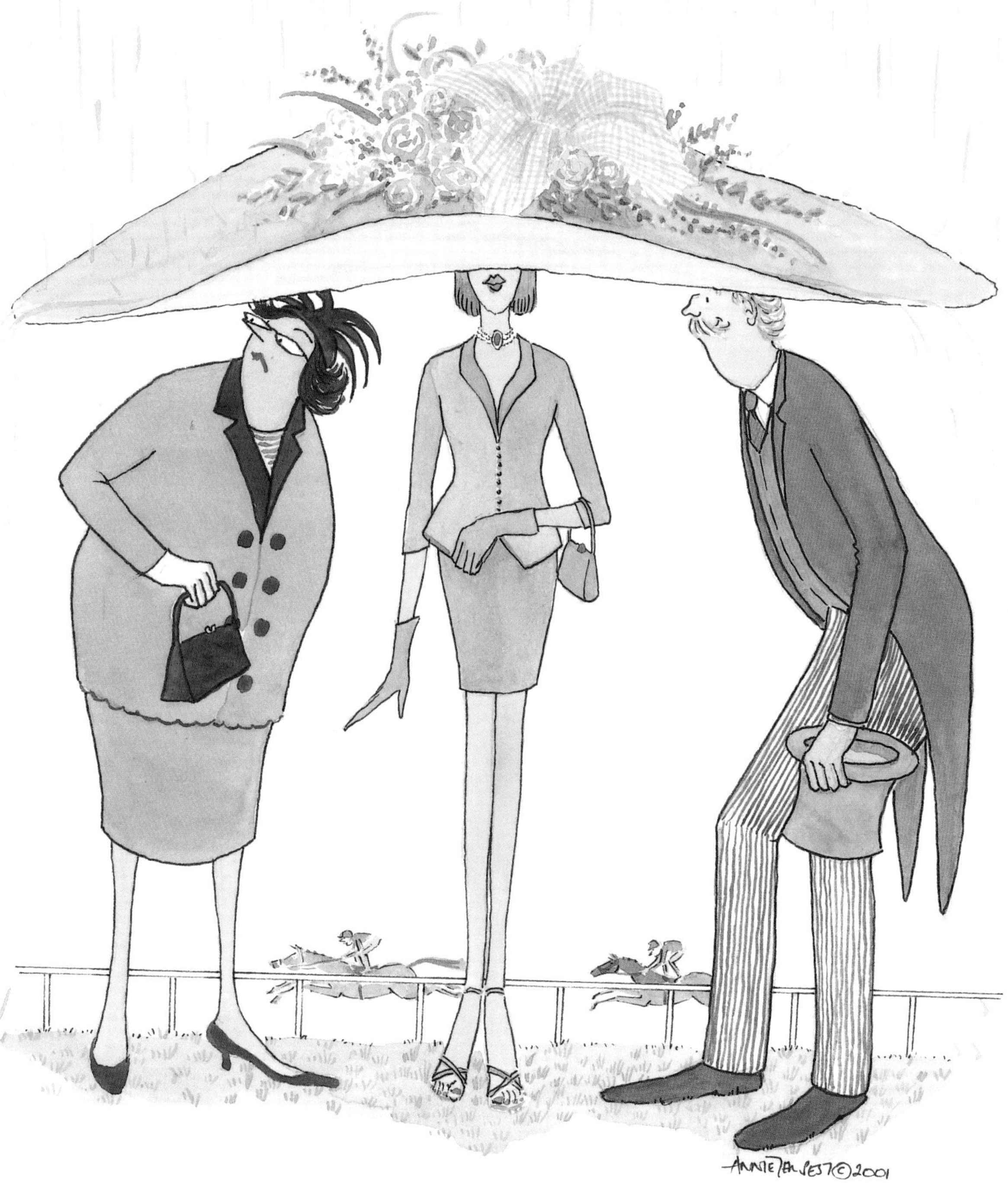
ANNIE TEMPEST ©2001

ANY PORT IN A STORM...

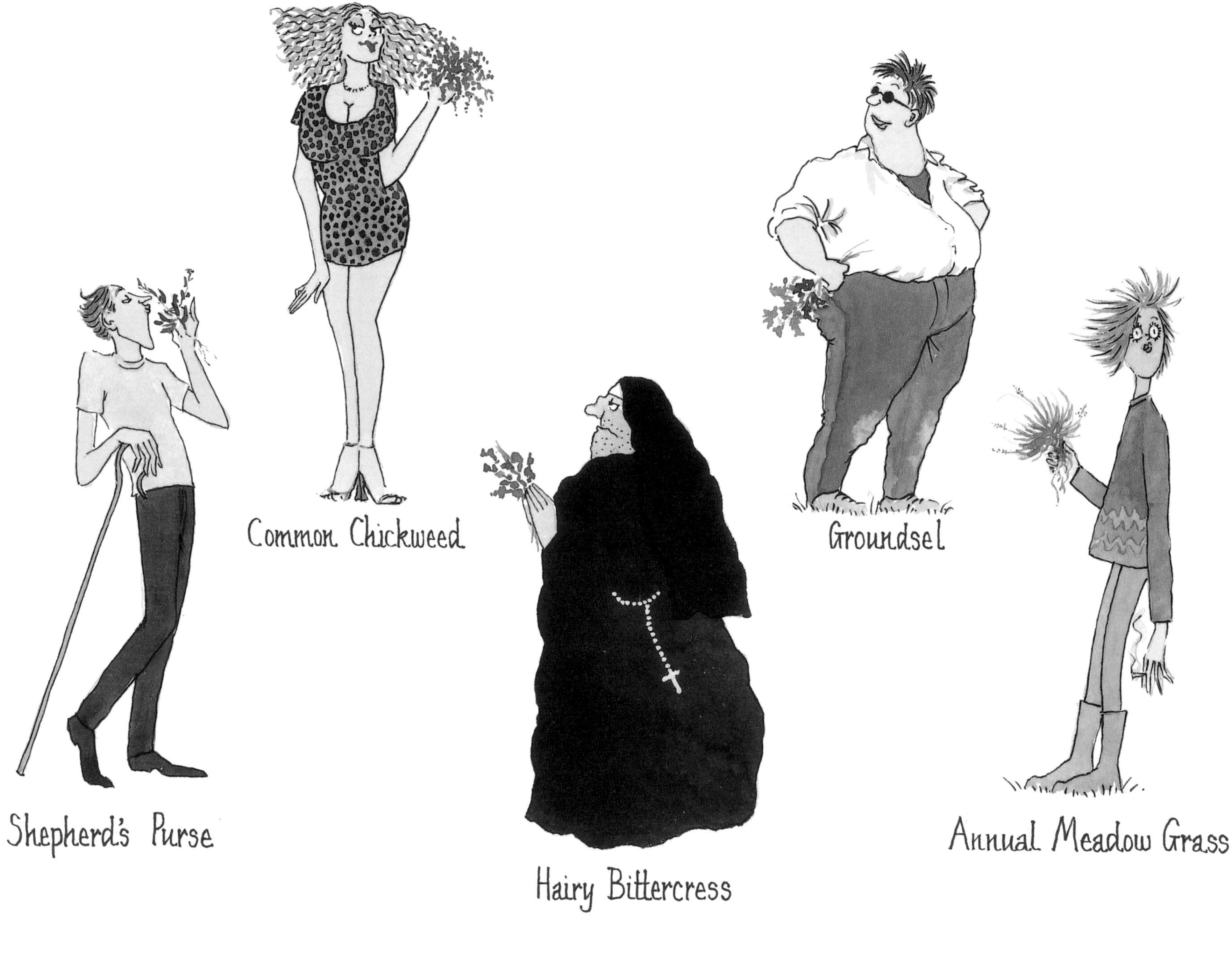
Common Chickweed
Groundsel
Shepherd's Purse
Hairy Bittercress
Annual Meadow Grass

COMMON ANNUAL WEEDS...

J UNE

24
_____

25
_____

26
_____

27
_____

28
_____

29
_____

30
_____

Annual Nettle

NOTHING CONFUSES
A MAN MORE THAN
A WOMAN DRIVER WHO
DOES EVERYTHING RIGHT...

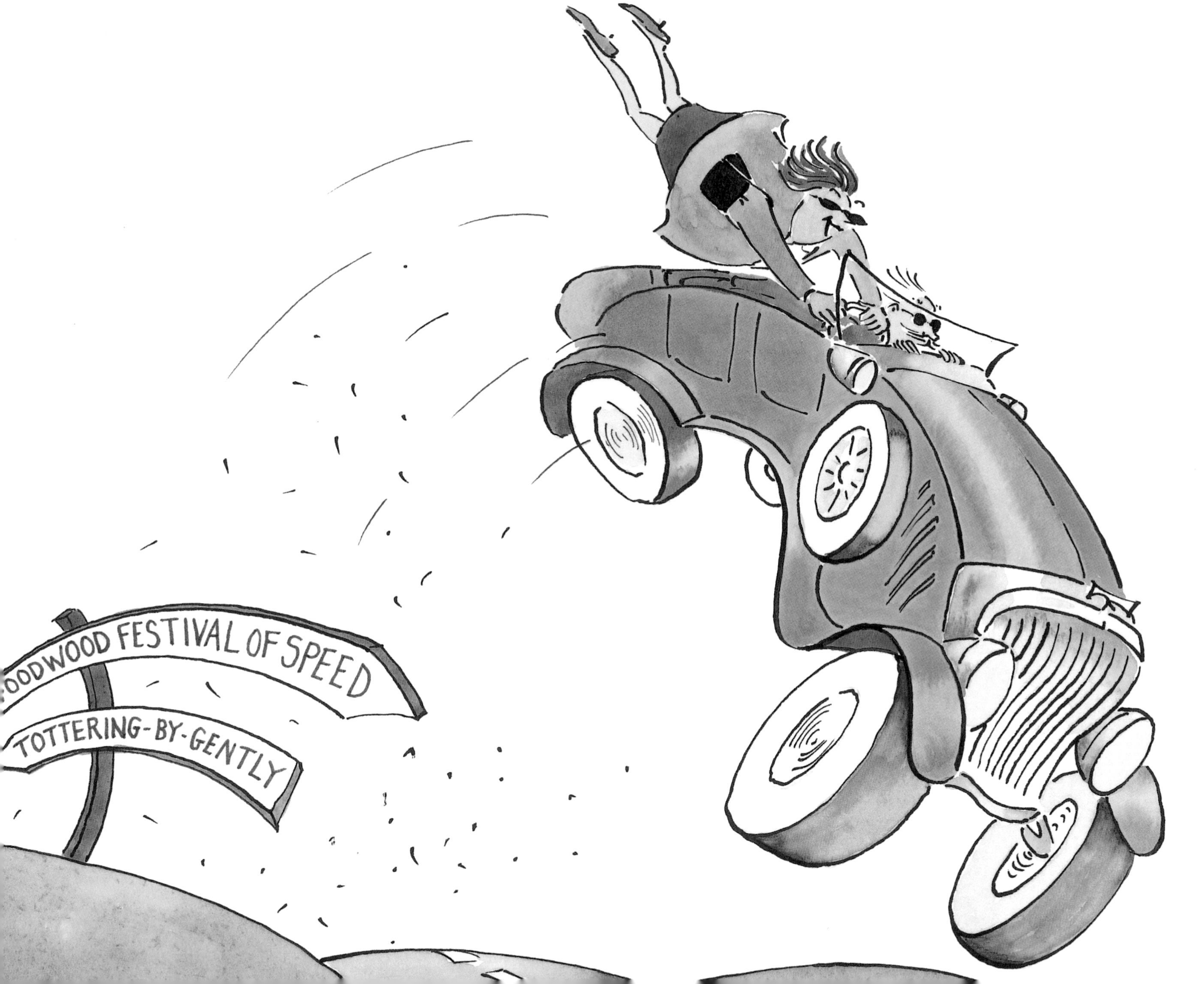
OODWOOD FESTIVAL OF SPEED
TOTTERING-BY-GENTLY

JULY

1
_____

2
_____

3 Piers Websters Birthday
_____

4
_____

5
_____

6
_____

7
_____

fruit, fruit and more fruit...

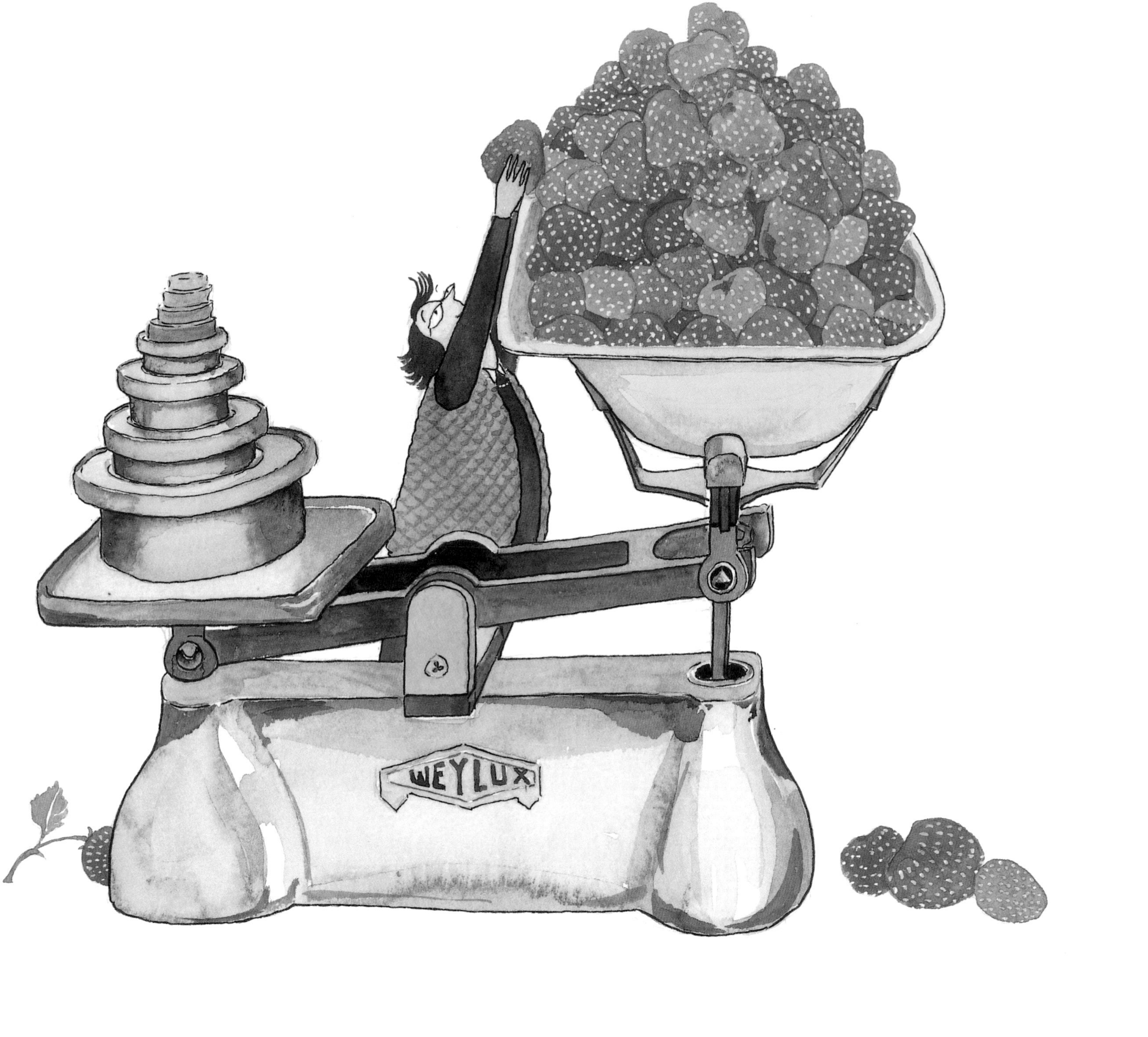
WEYLUX

JULY Wimbledon

8

9

You're supposed to hit them back, Grandpa...

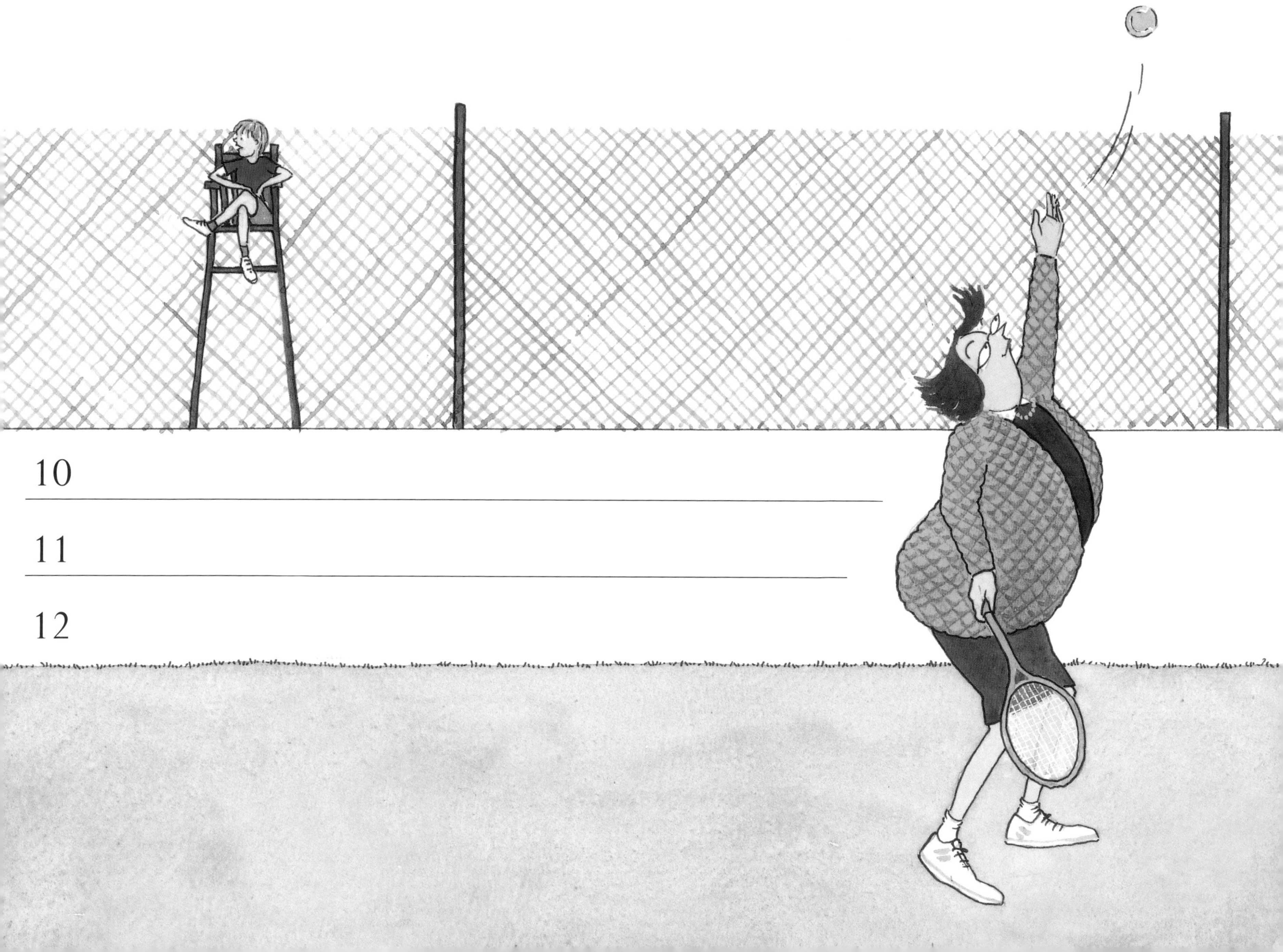

10

11

12

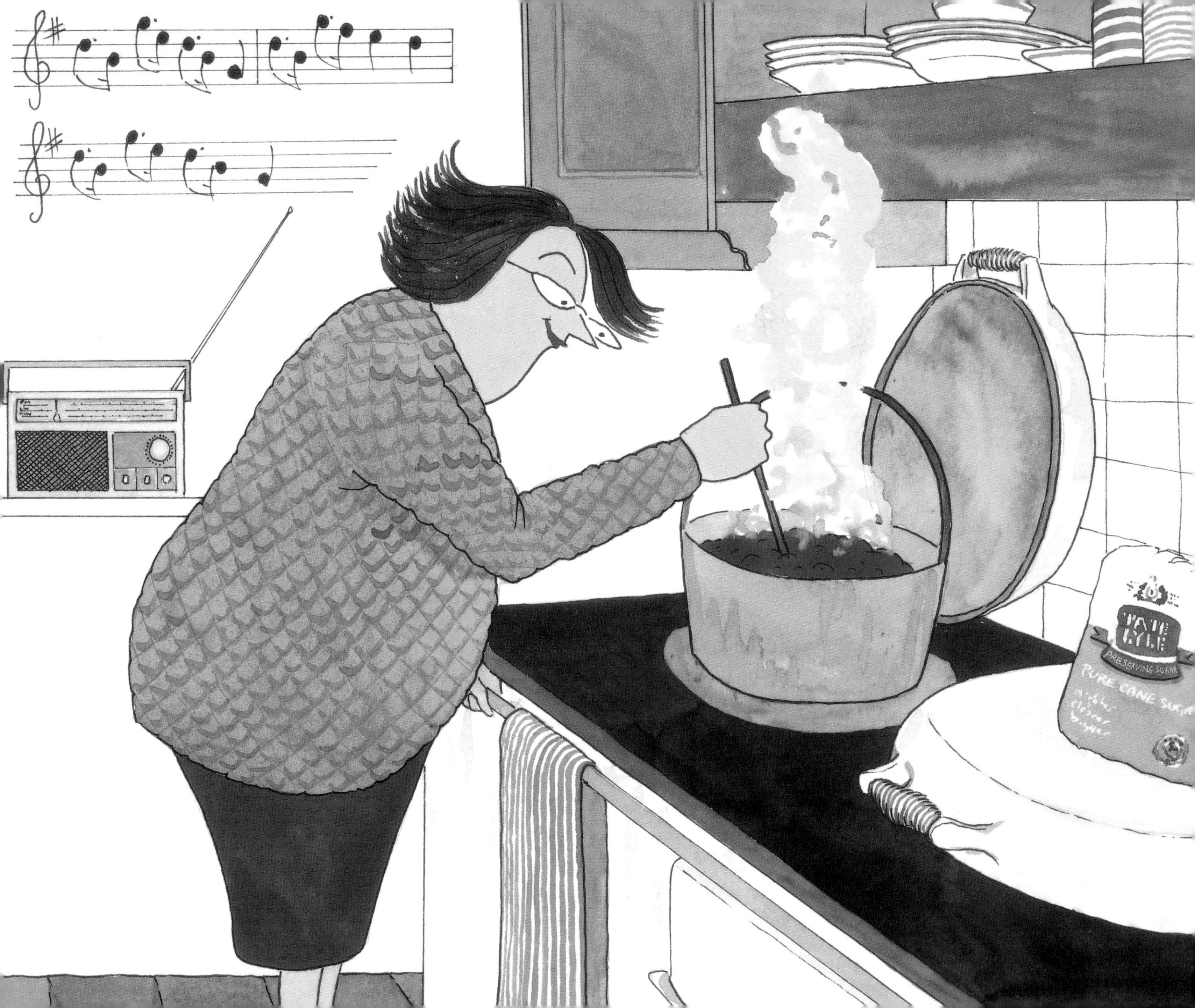
TATE LYLE
PRESERVING SUGAR
PURE CANE SUGA

JULY

13

14

Tottering Hall Jam

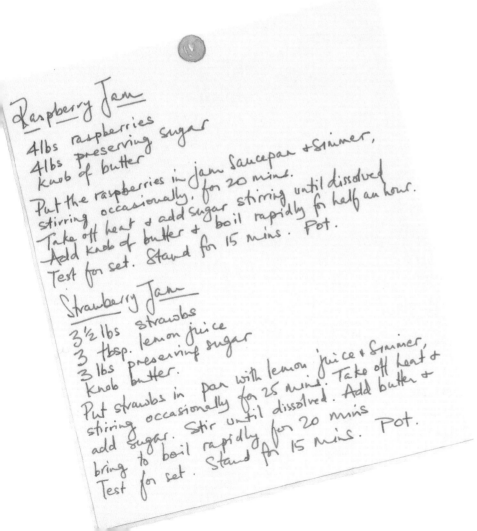

Raspberry Jam

4lbs raspberries
4lbs preserving sugar
knob of butter

Put the raspberries in jam saucepan & simmer, stirring occasionally, for 20 mins.
Take off heat & add sugar stirring until dissolved
Add knob of butter & boil rapidly for half an hour.
Test for set. Stand for 15 mins. Pot.

Strawberry Jam

3½ lbs strawbs
3 tbsp. lemon juice
3 lbs preserving sugar
knob butter.

Put strawbs in pan with lemon juice & simmer, stirring occasionally for 25 mins. Take off heat & add sugar. Stir until dissolved. Add butter & bring to boil rapidly for 20 mins
Test for set. Stand for 15 mins. Pot.

Tottering Hall Jam

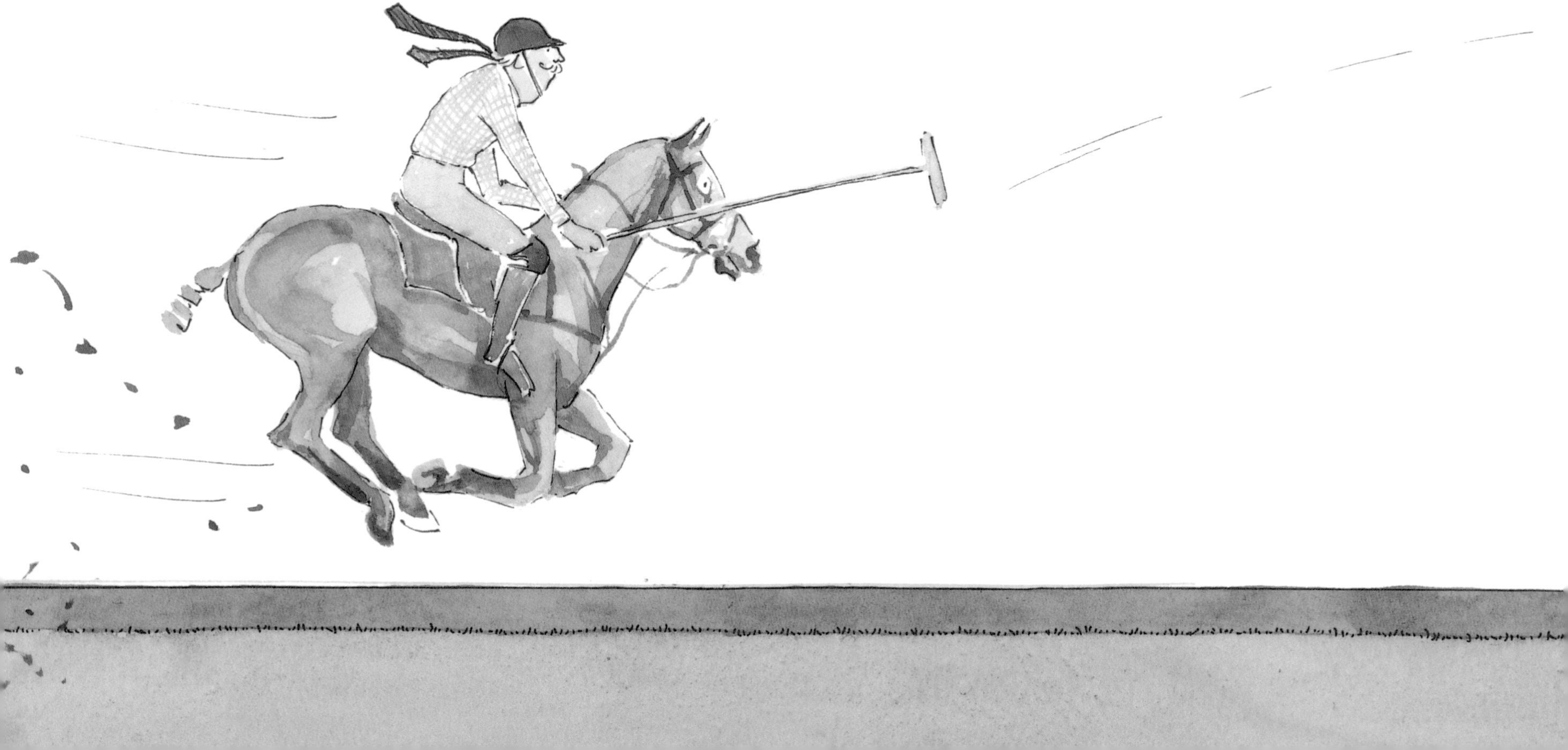

July

15

16

17

18

19 Polo at Cowdray- Veuve Clicquot's Gold Cup

20

21

22

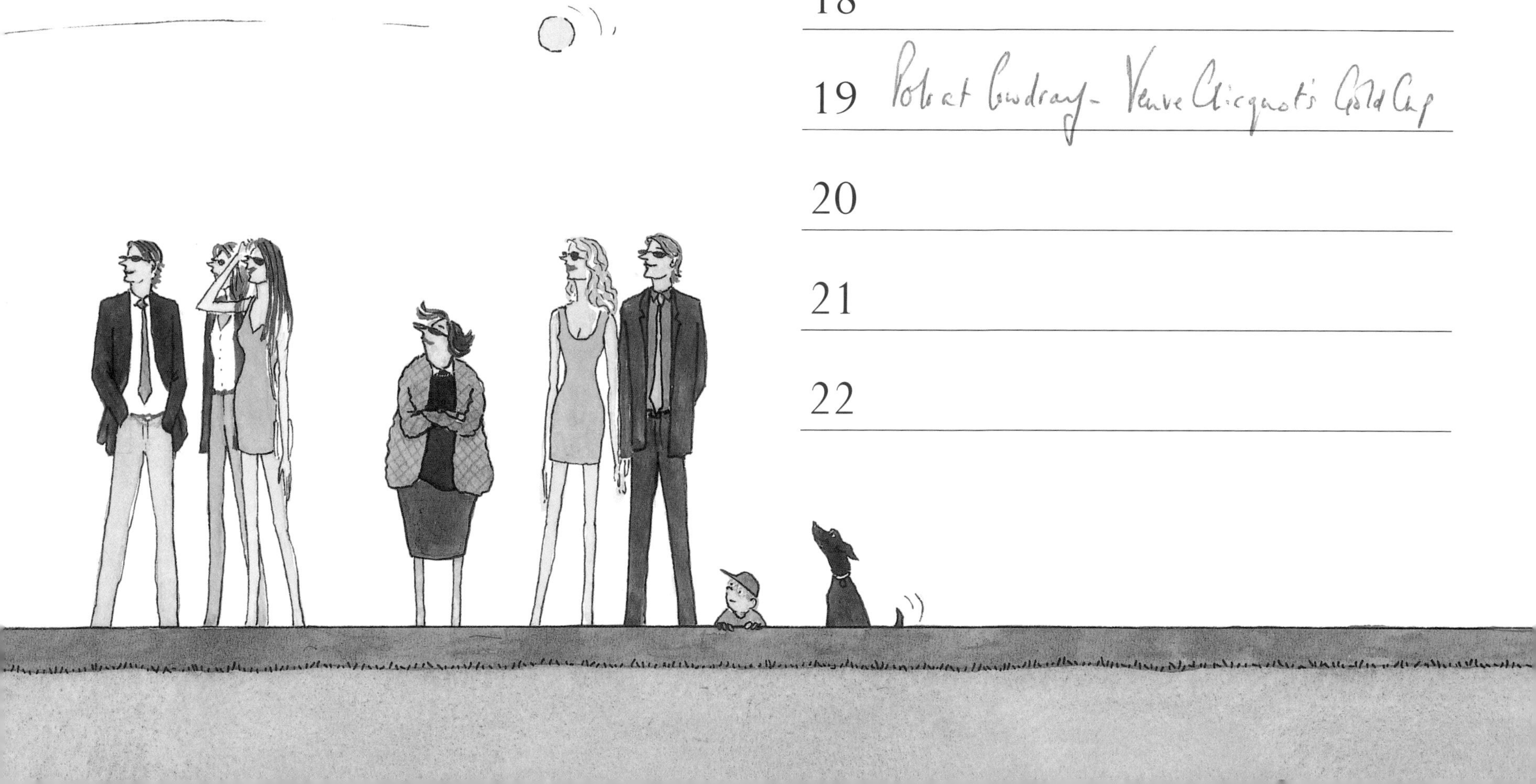

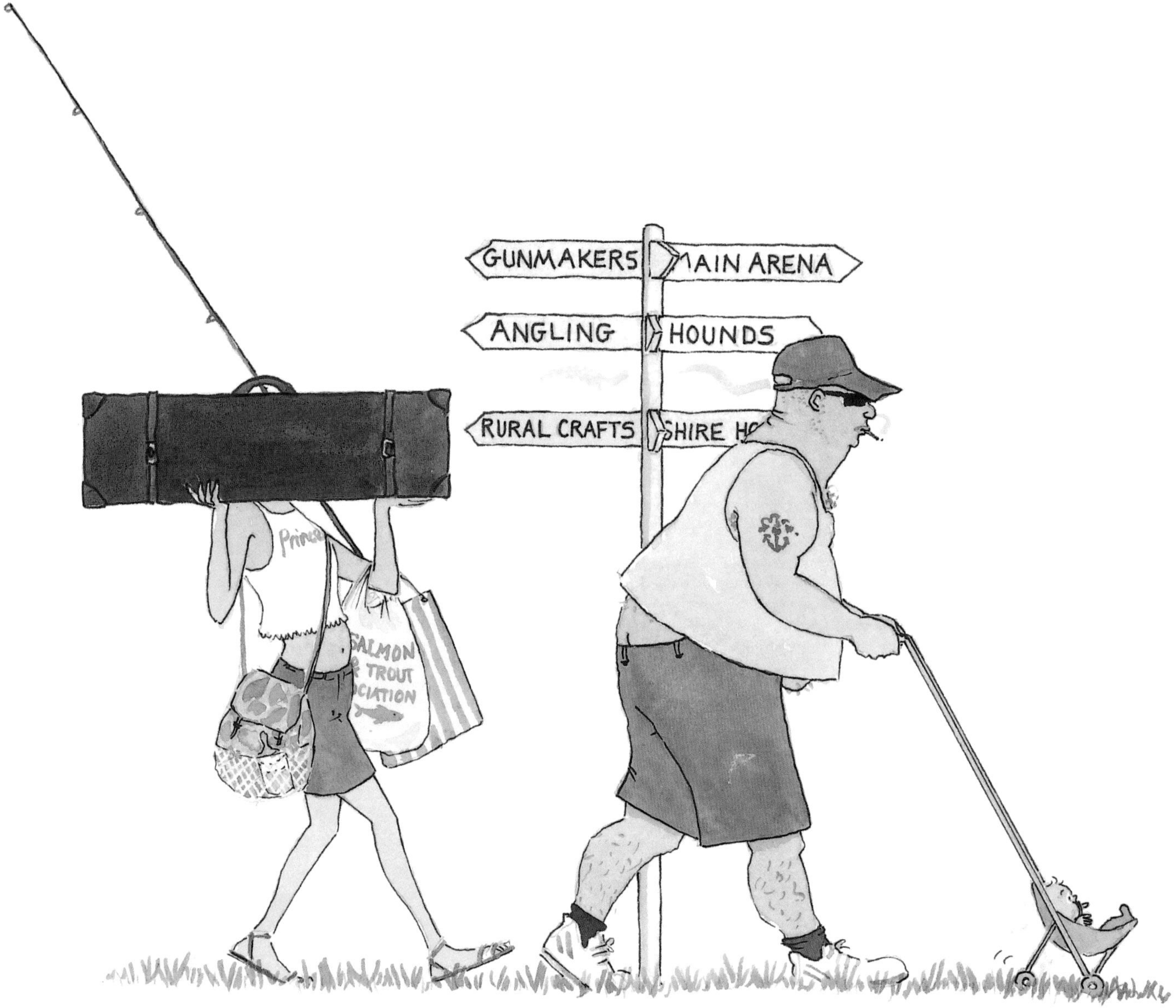
GUNMAKERS
MAIN ARENA
ANGLING
HOUNDS
RURAL CRAFTS
SHIRE HO
SALMON
TROUT

Countryside Alliance

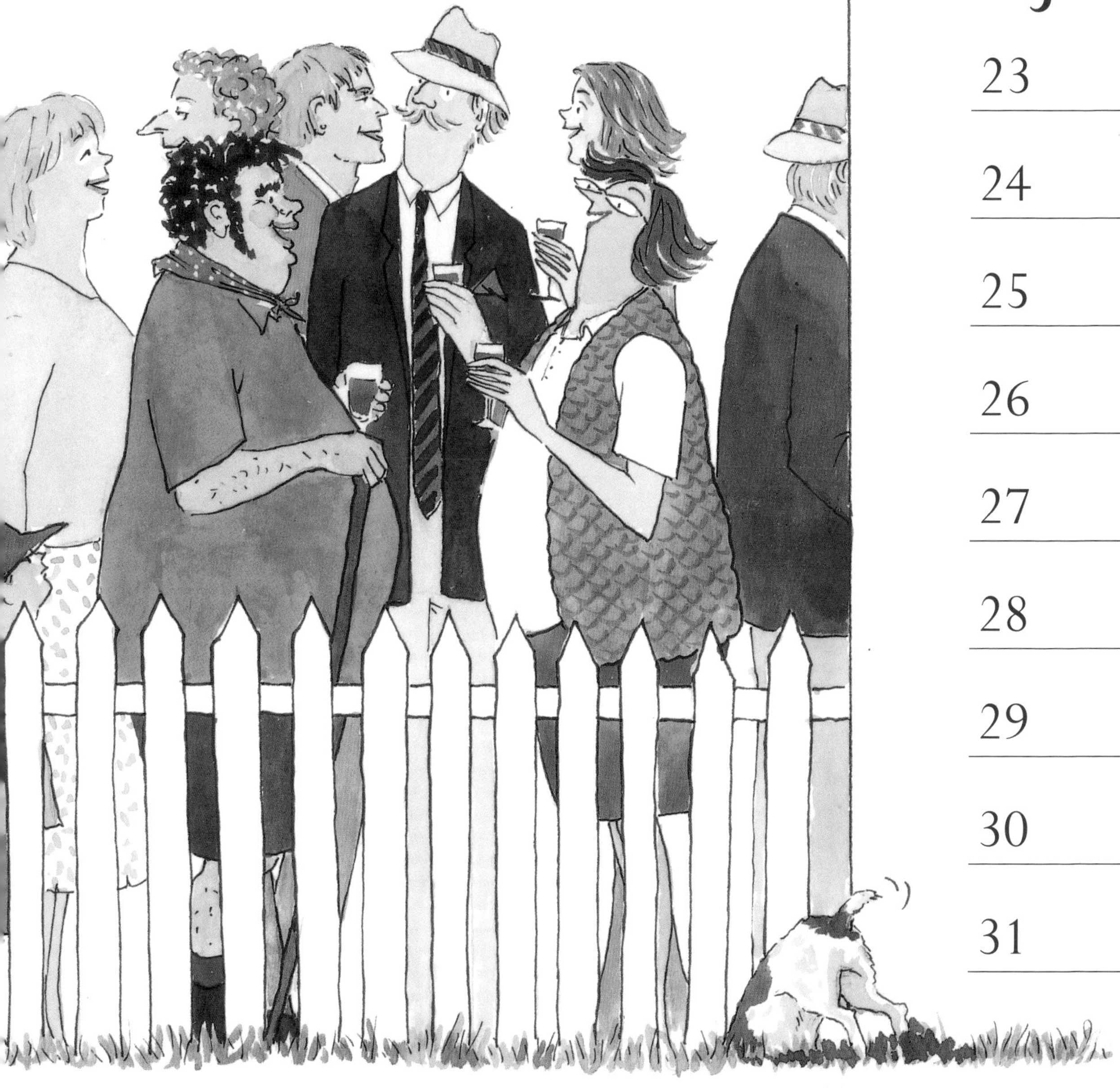

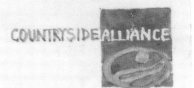

JULY

23

24

25

26

27

28 GAME FAIR!

29

30

31

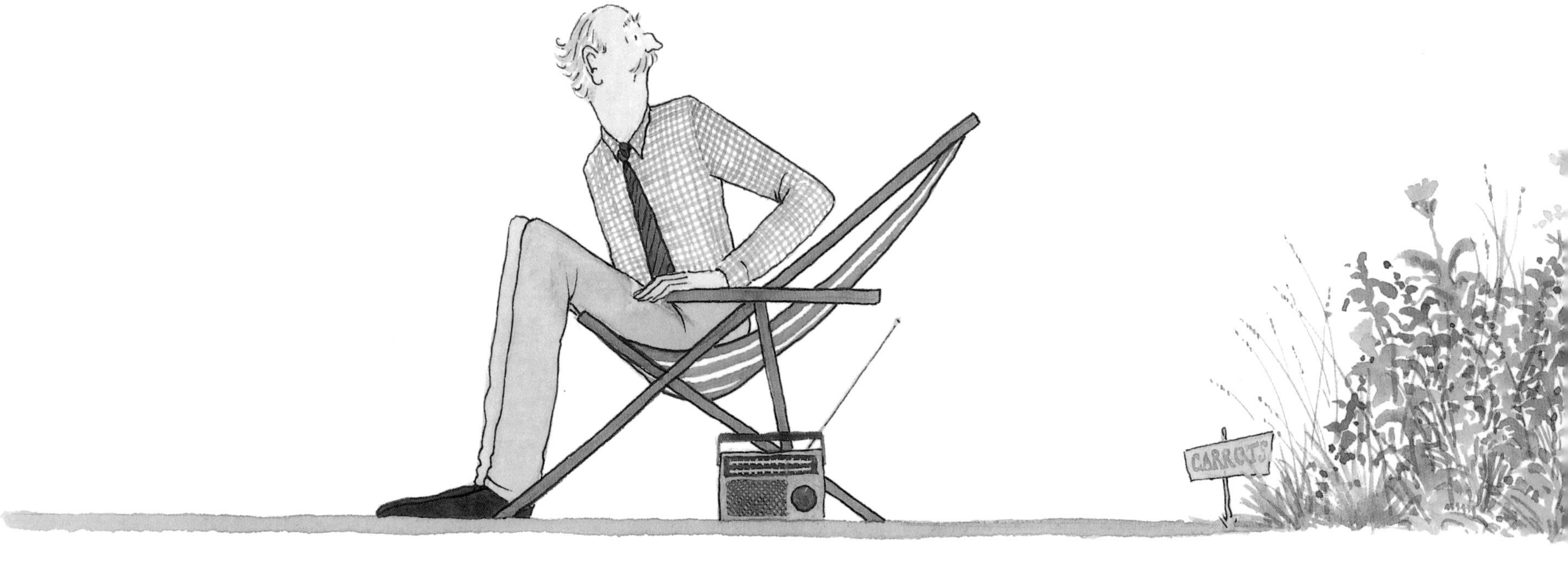
CARROTS

Our first organic carrot, Dicky...

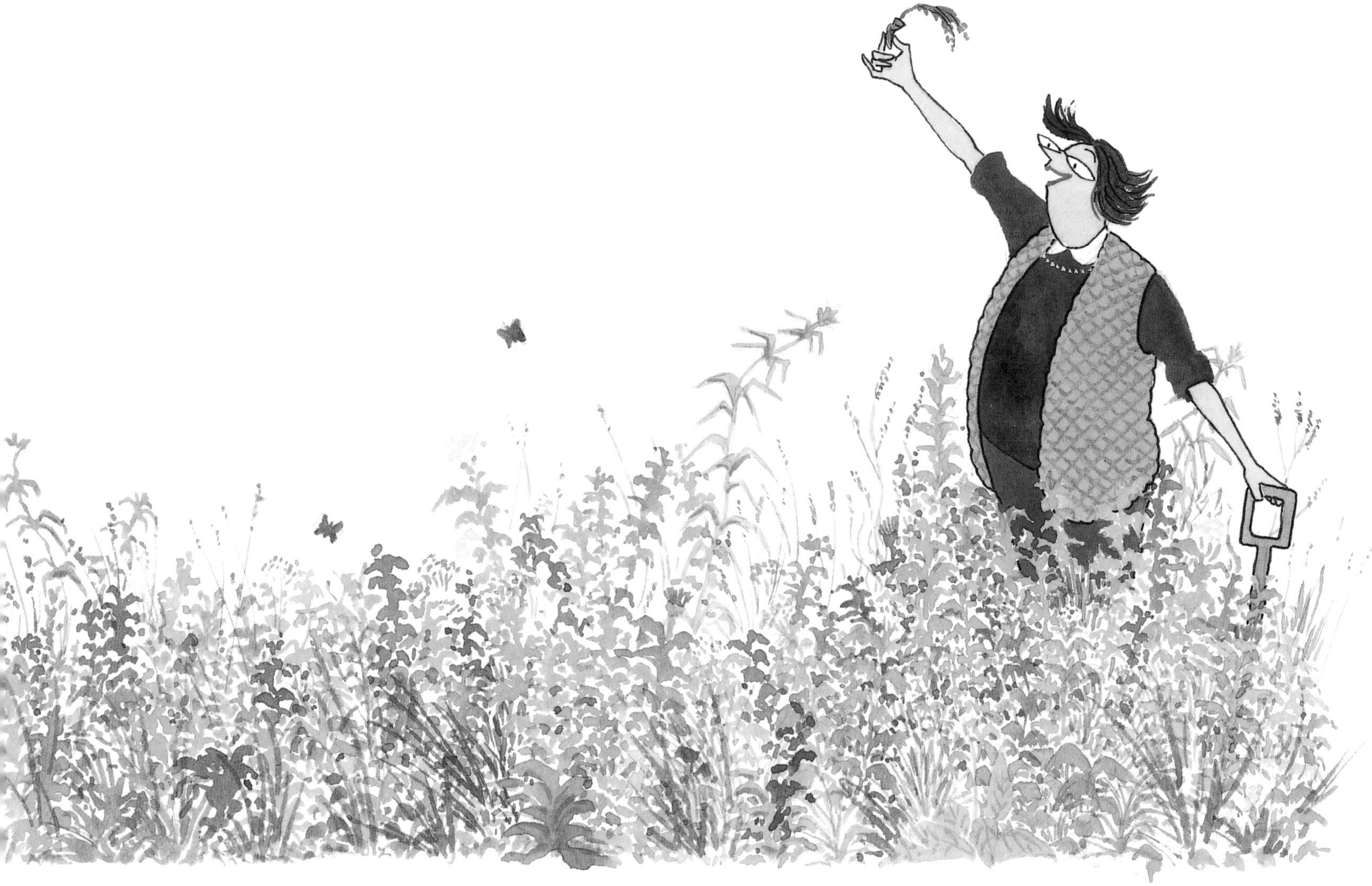

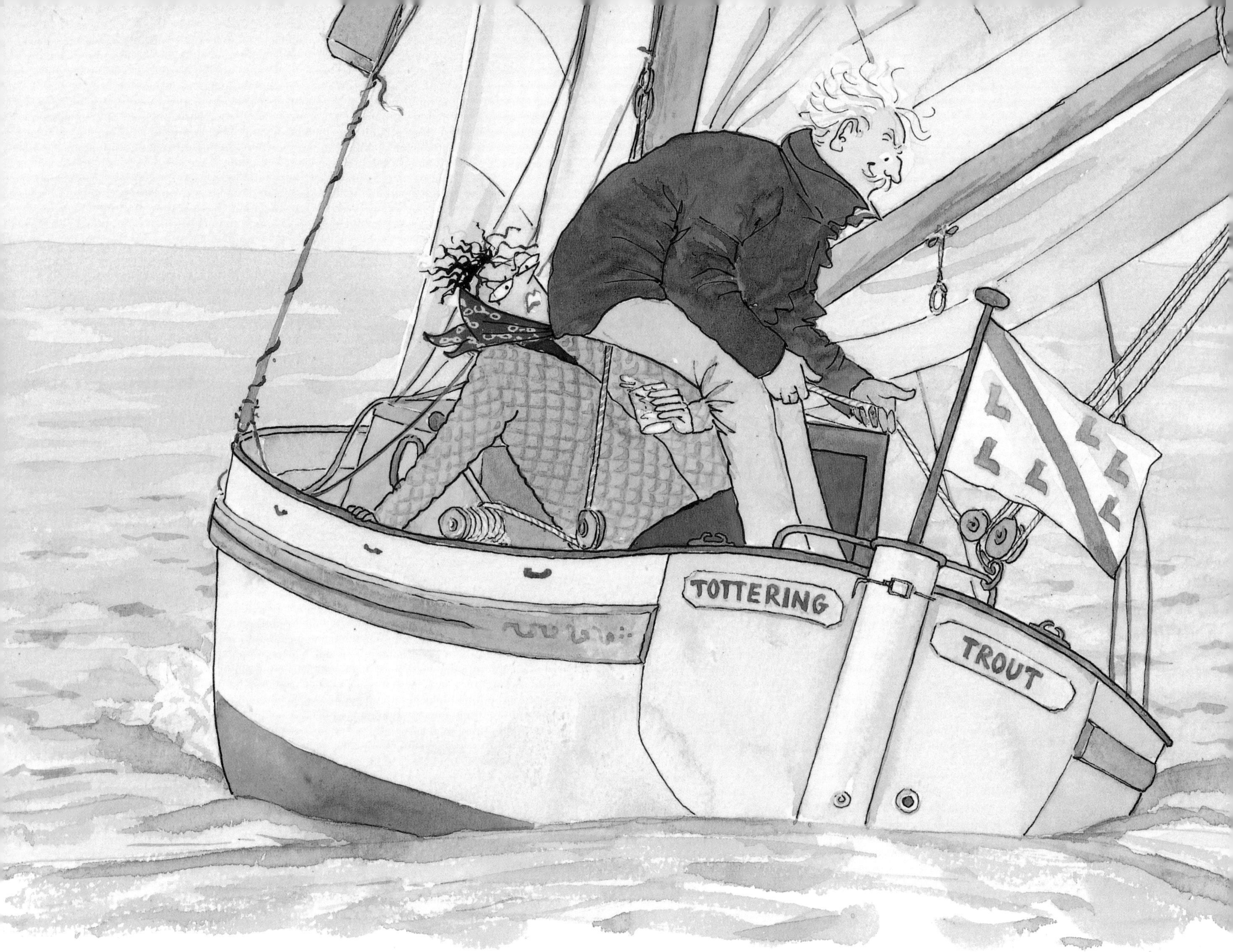
TOTTERING
TROUT

" What do you mean 'get a grip'? Your bum's in my face, you've spilt my gin and my hair's gone frizzy..."

Cow's Week? When's Pig's Week, then?

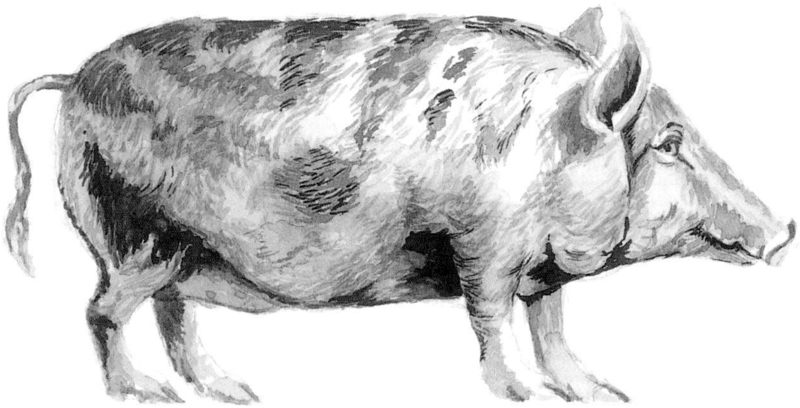

August

1

2

3

4 Cowes week

5

6

7

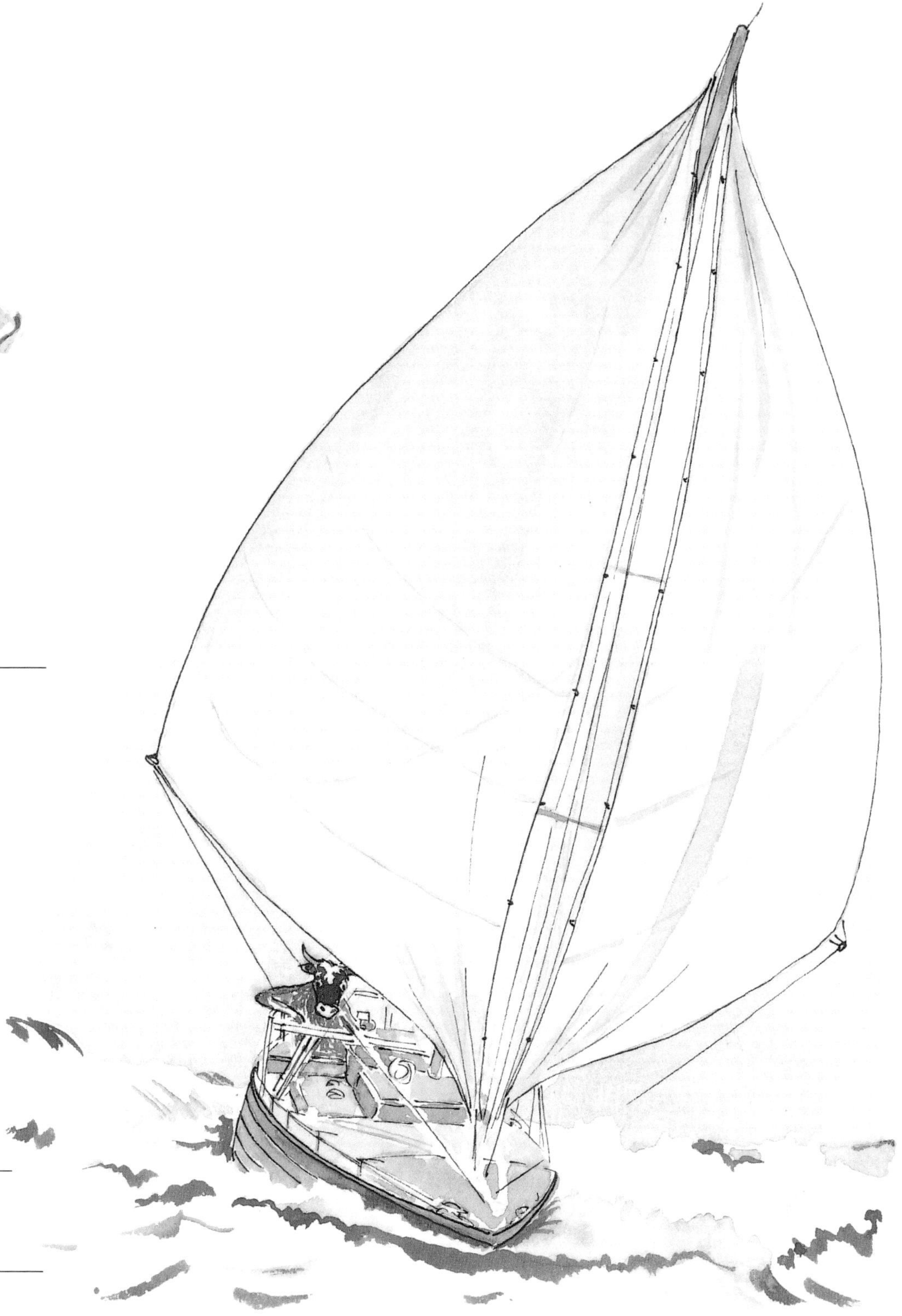

AUGUST

8
_____

9
_____

10
_____

11
_____

12
_____

13
_____

14
_____

15
_____

Edinburgh Festival
← Fringe theatre...

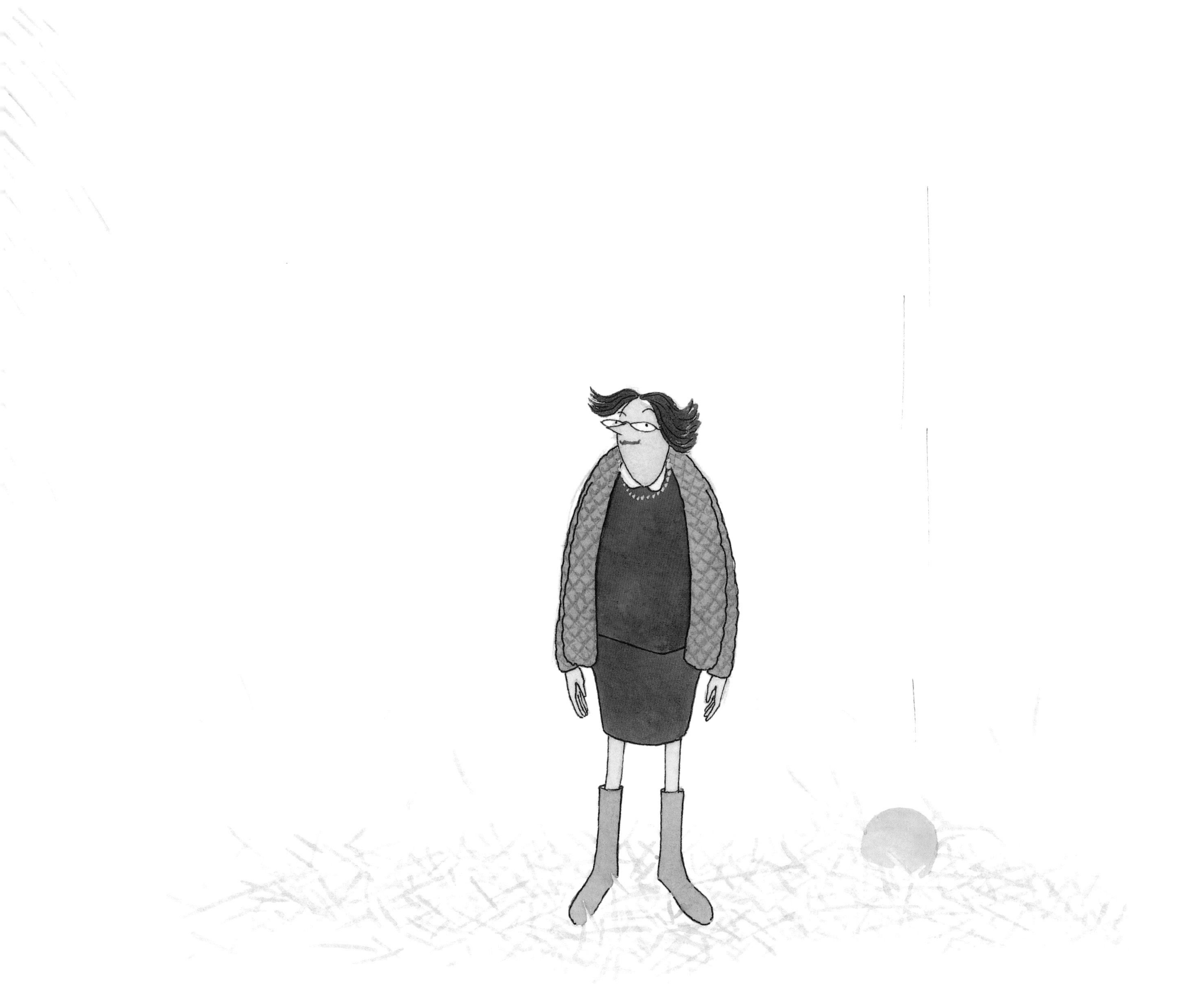

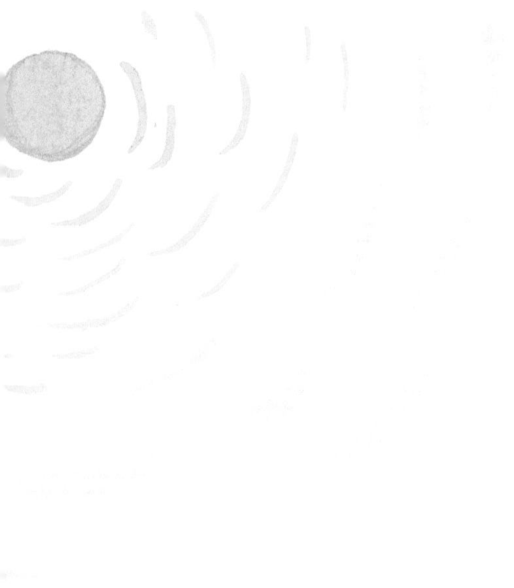

August

16

17

18

19

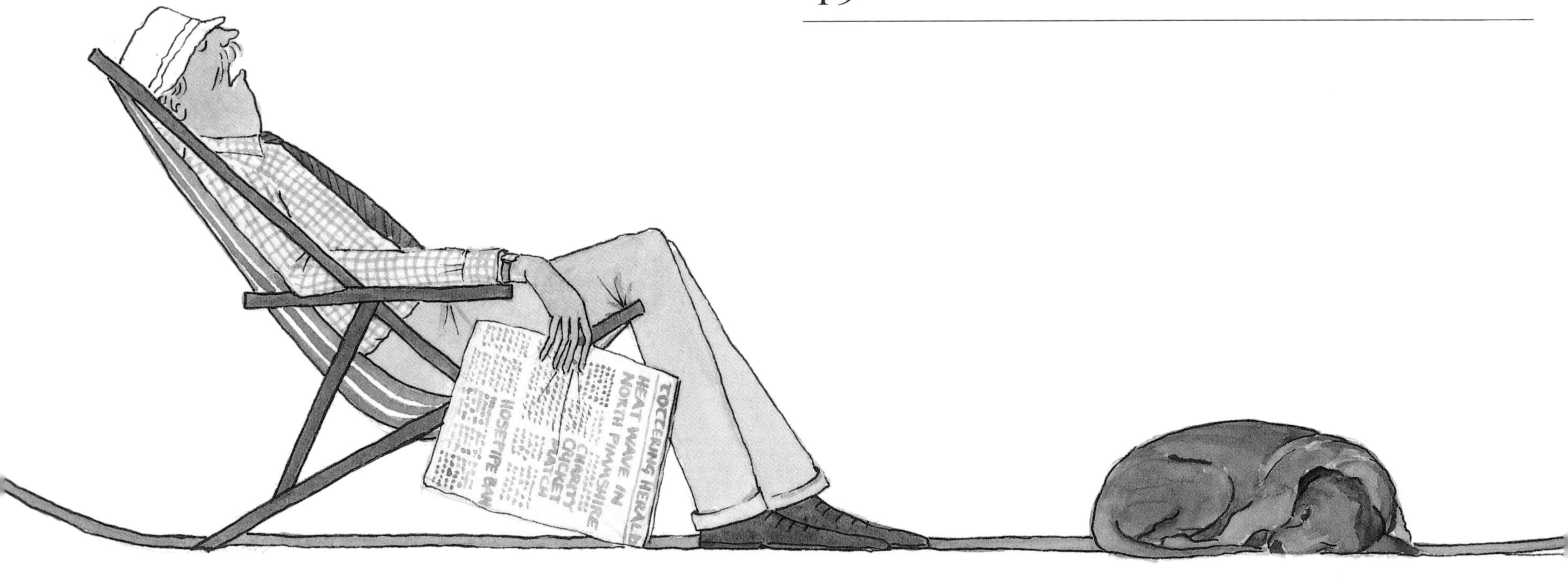

TOCCERING HERALD
HEAT WAVE IN NORTH PIMMSHIRE
CHARITY CRICKET MATCH
HOSEPIPE BAN

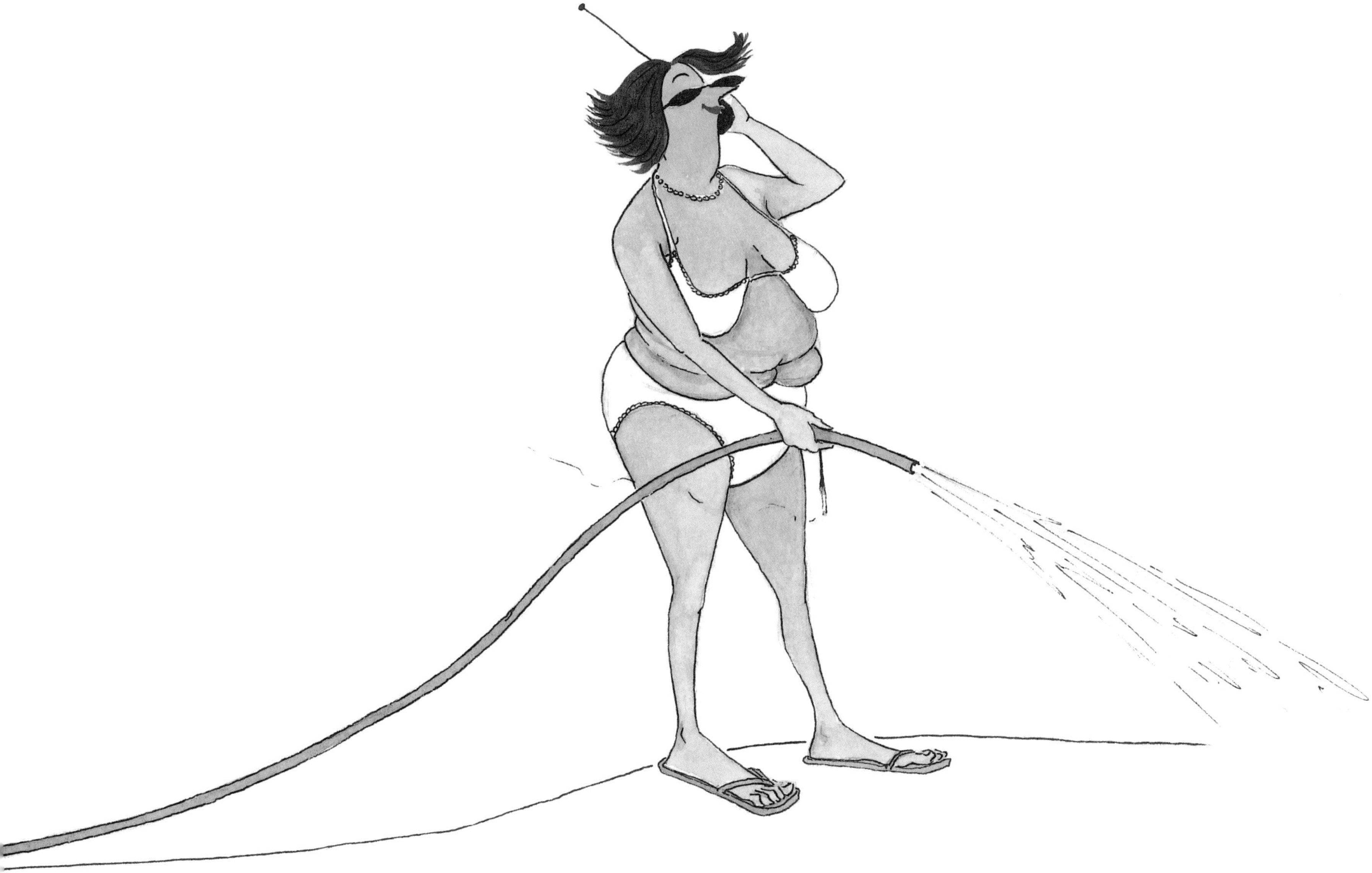

AUGUST

20
_____

21
_____

22
_____

23
_____

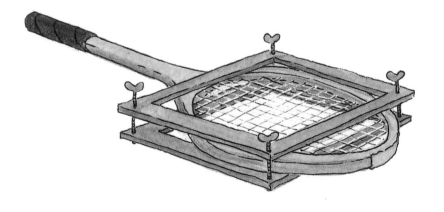

24
_____

25
_____

26
_____

27
_____

28
_____

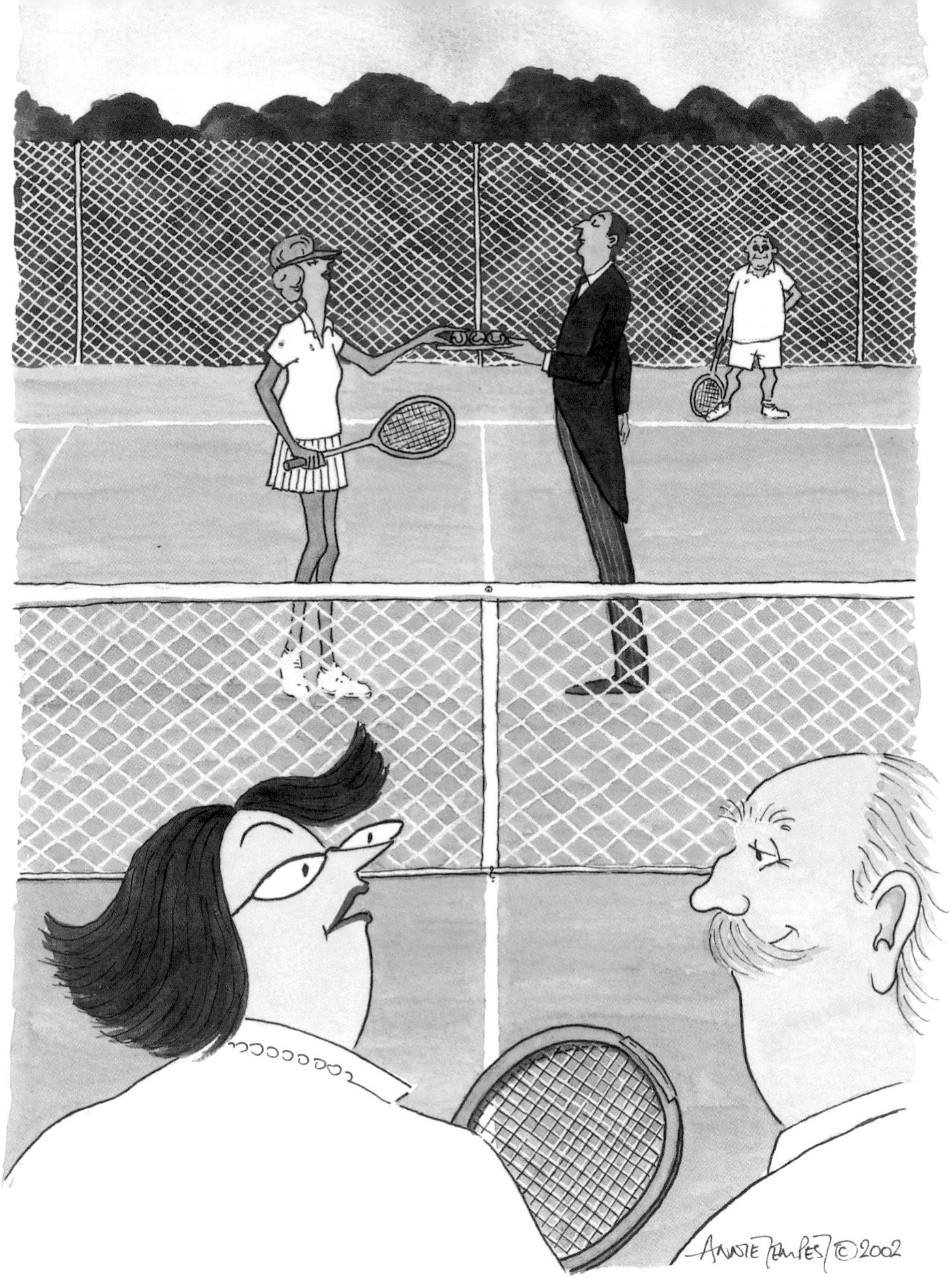
ANNIE TEMPEST ©2002

"I do think the Tissington-Tatlers overdo it a little..."

"Well of course they don't look like the ones in the Marshalls catalogue – those were posed by professional vegetables..."

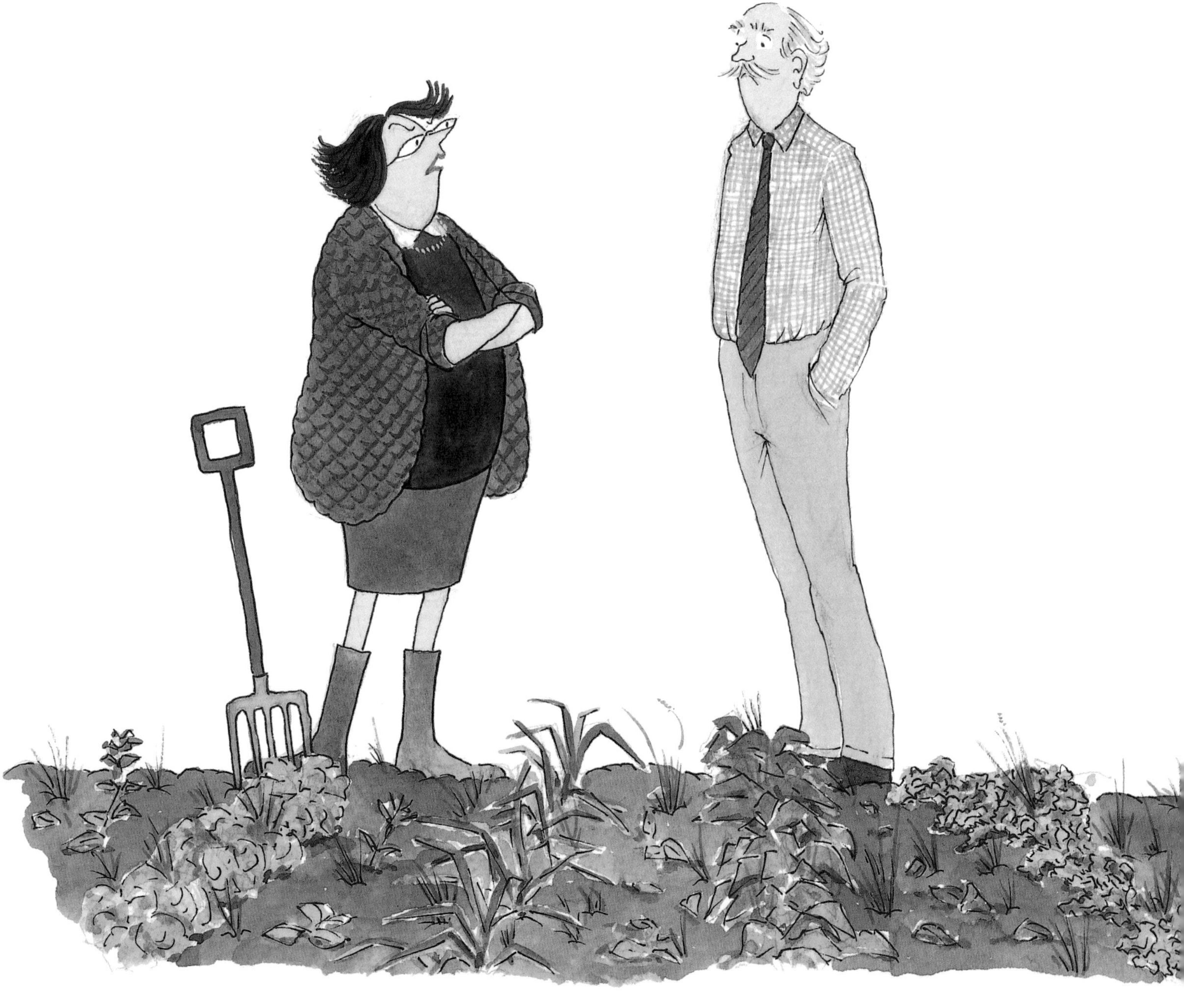

August

29

30

31

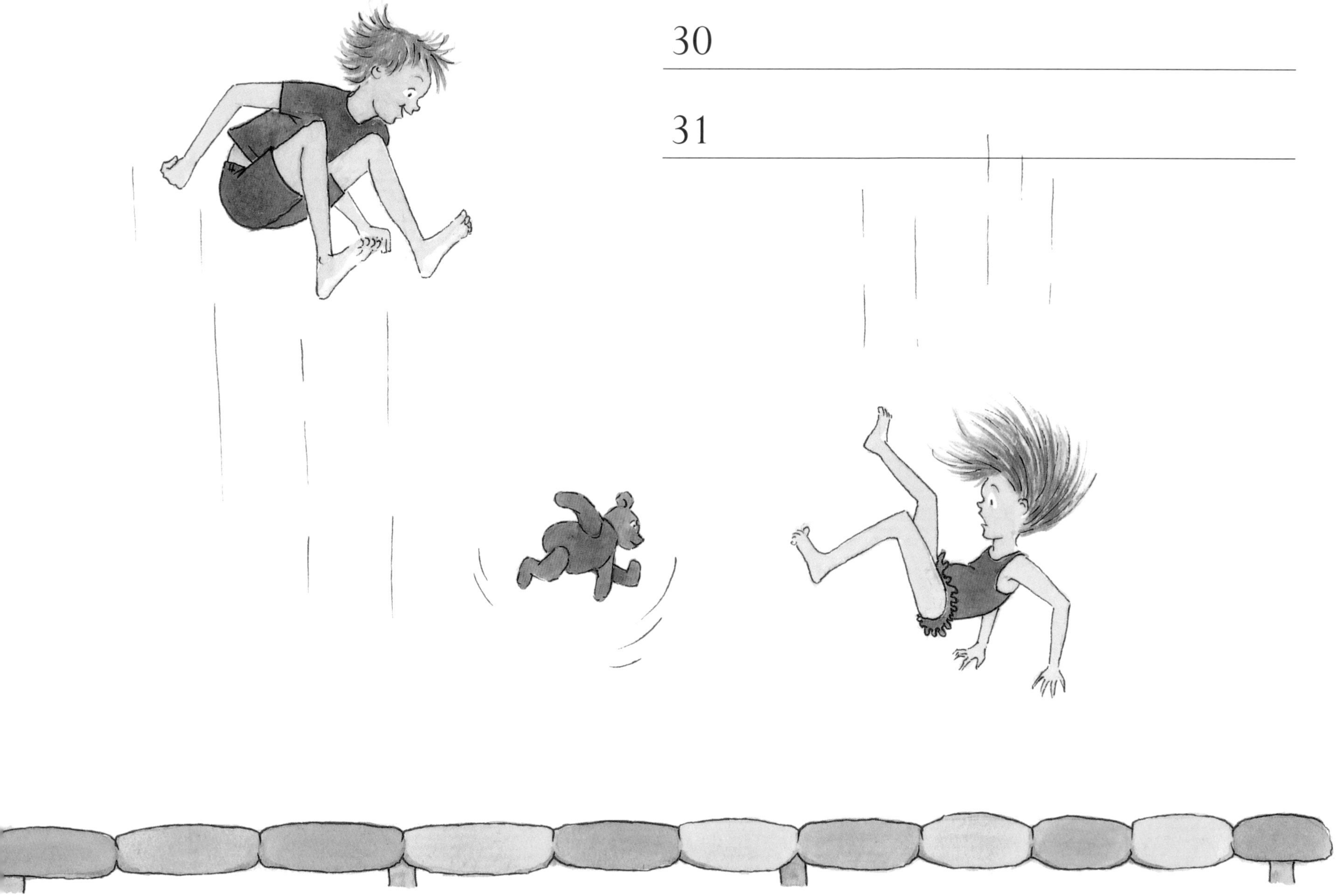

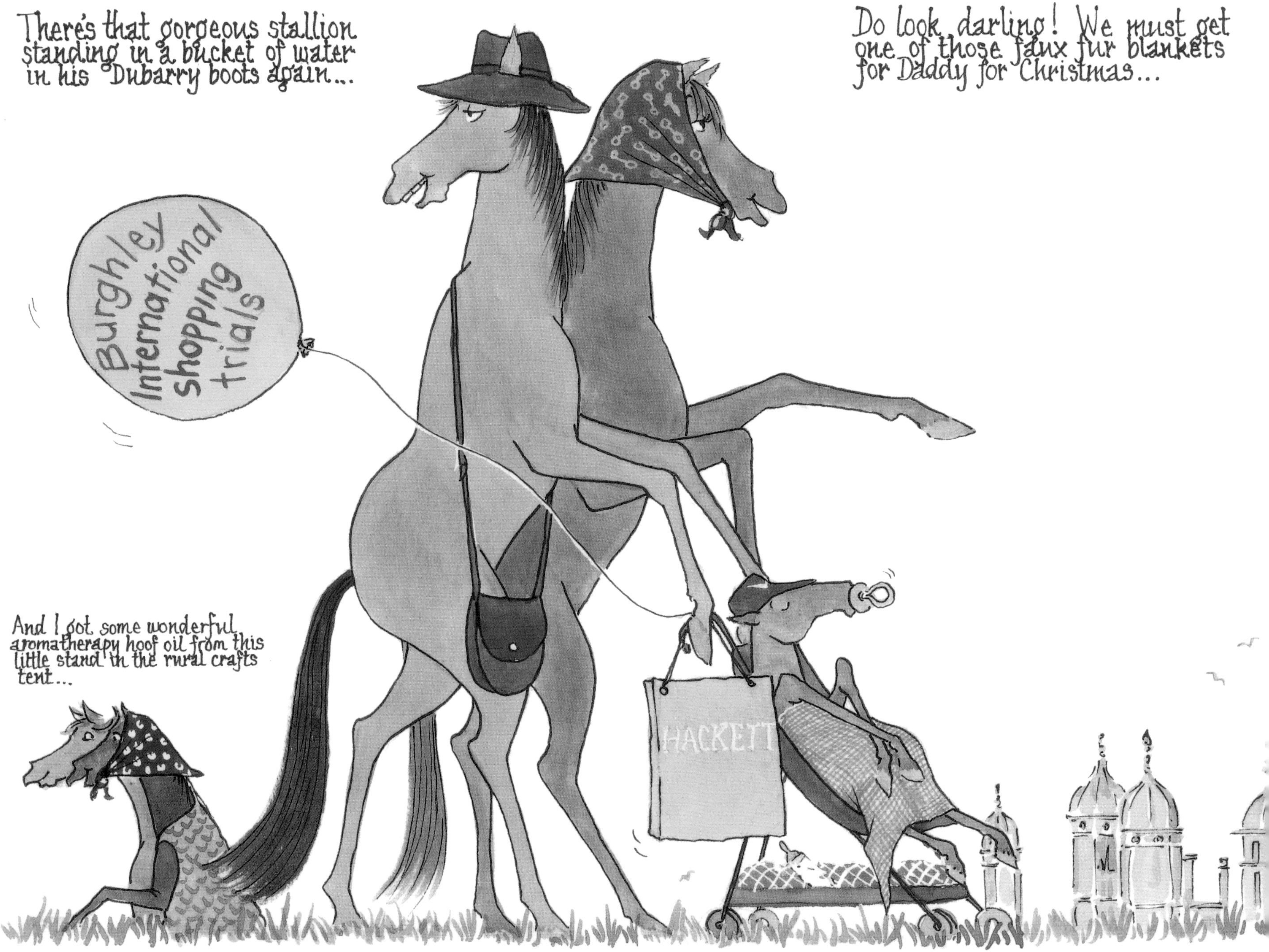
There's that gorgeous stallion standing in a bucket of water in his Dubarry boots again...
Do look darling! We must get one of those faux fur blankets for Daddy for Christmas...
Burghley International shopping trials
And I got some wonderful aromatherapy hoof oil from this little stand in the rural crafts tent...
HACKETT

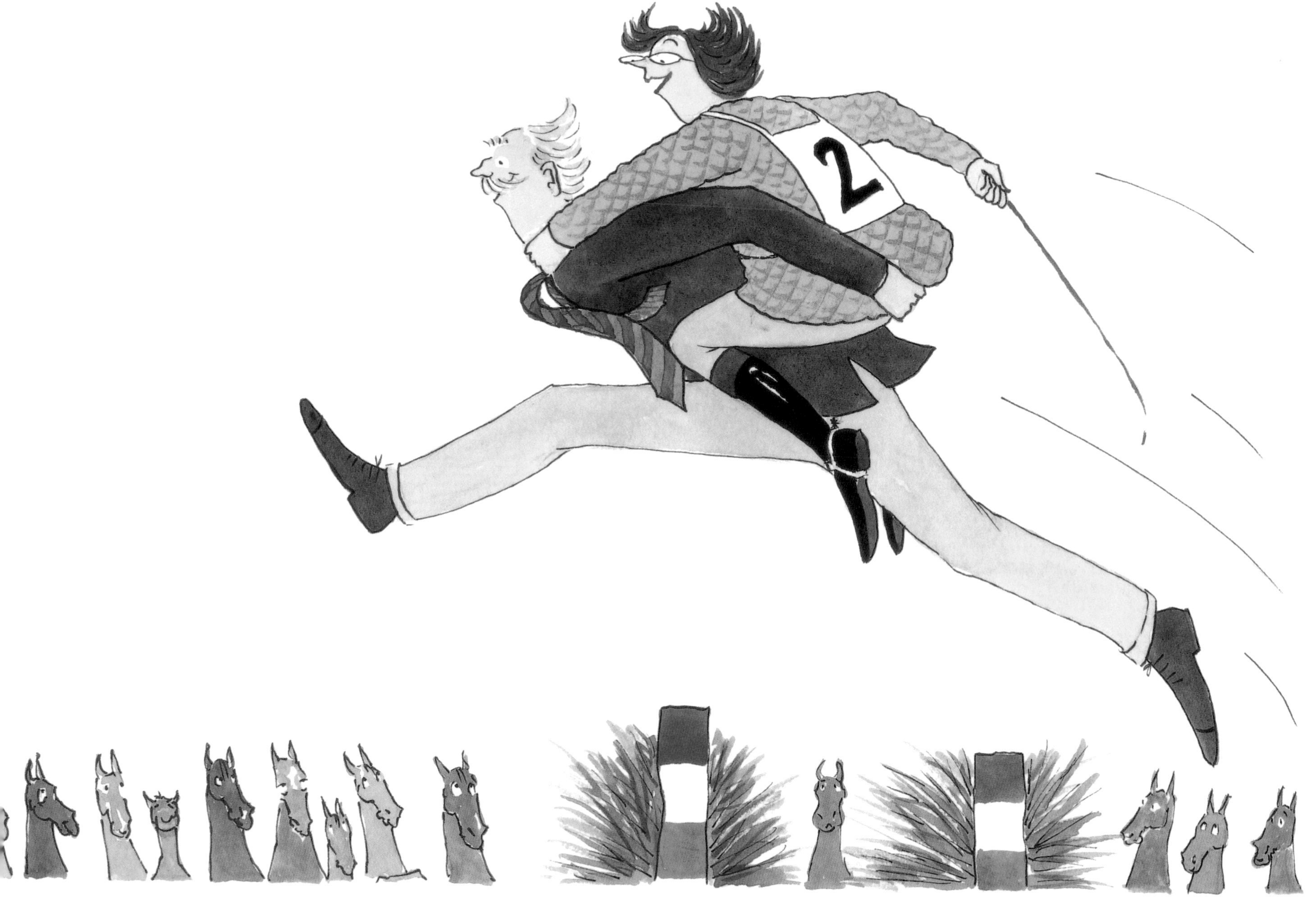

SEPTEMBER

1 _____

2 _____

3 _____

4 _____

5 _____

6 _____

7 _____ Braemar games

bloody
awful
racket!

"Well, Freddy – Today, we've been watching a lot of bearded men in skirts seeing how far they can lob cabers, stones and hammers..."

A mosquito visits the bedroom at midnight...
THE FEMALE APPROACH...

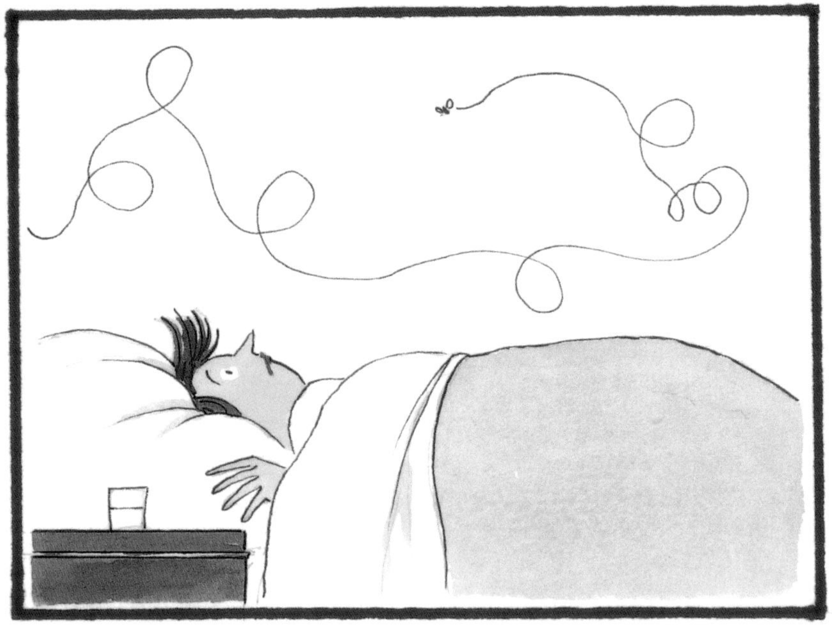

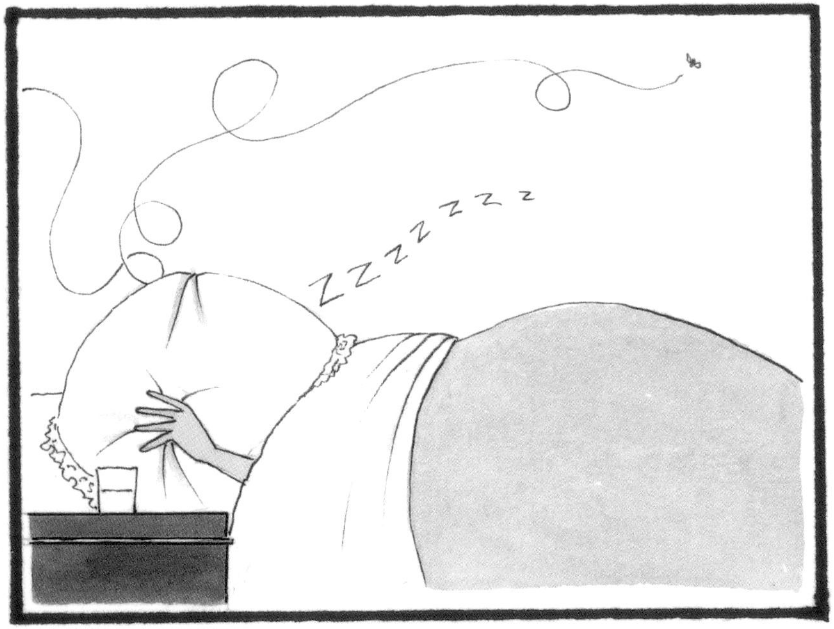
Z Z Z Z Z Z Z Z z

SEPTEMBER

8

9

10

11

12 Judy's Birthday

13

14

THE MOSQUITO FROM MZUZU

To all brunettes whom love has conned,
This comfort I repeat-oh;
If gentlemen prefer a blonde-
Then so does a mosquito...

(From Kit and The Widow's 'African Alphabet')

A mosquito visits the bedroom at midnight...
THE MALE APPROACH...

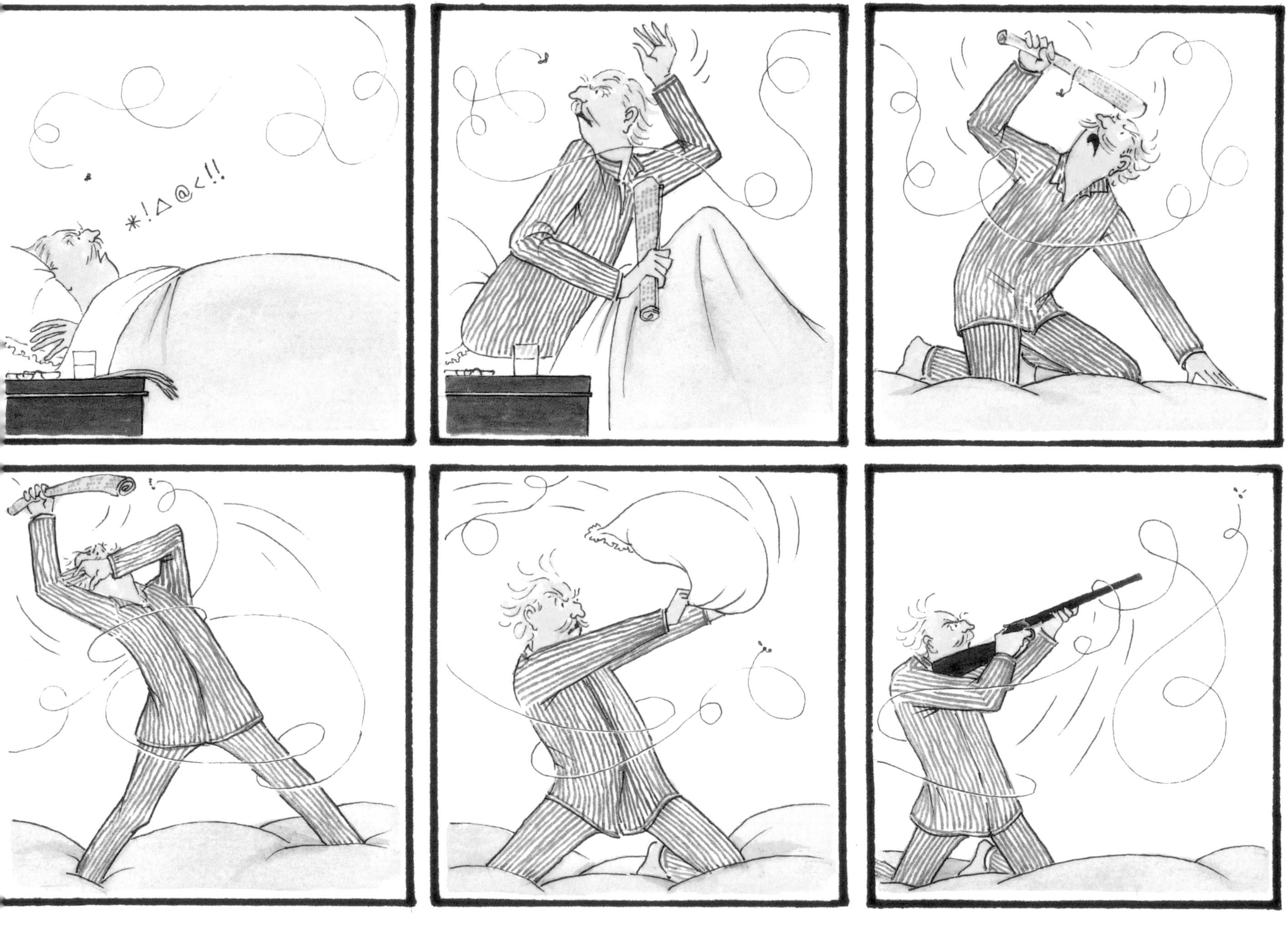
*!△@<!!

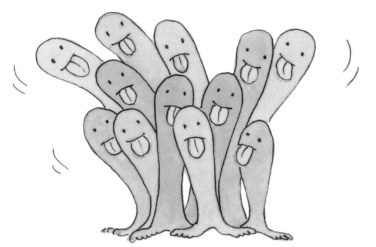

A ditty of hungry staves.

An appoggiatura humming in bee flats.

Sᴇᴘᴛᴇᴍʙᴇʀ

15   *last night of the proms.*
      Jules Websters Birthday

16

17

18

19

20

21

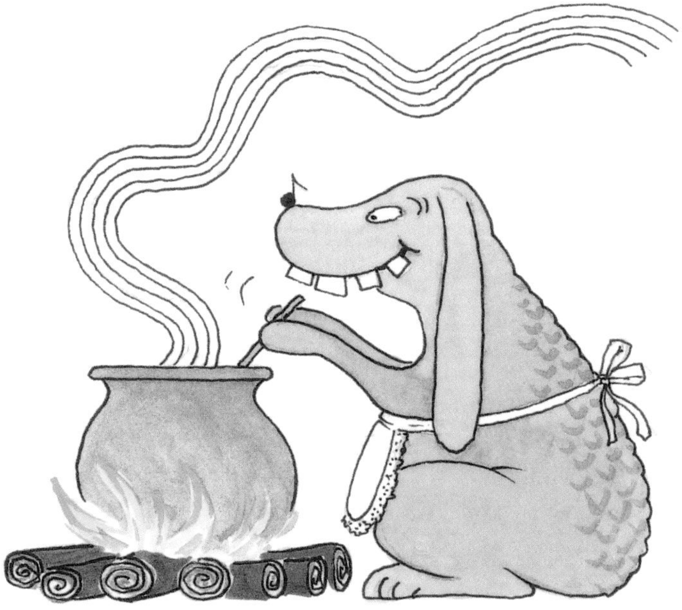

A xylophone minuetting his favourite rhapsody on the fugue.

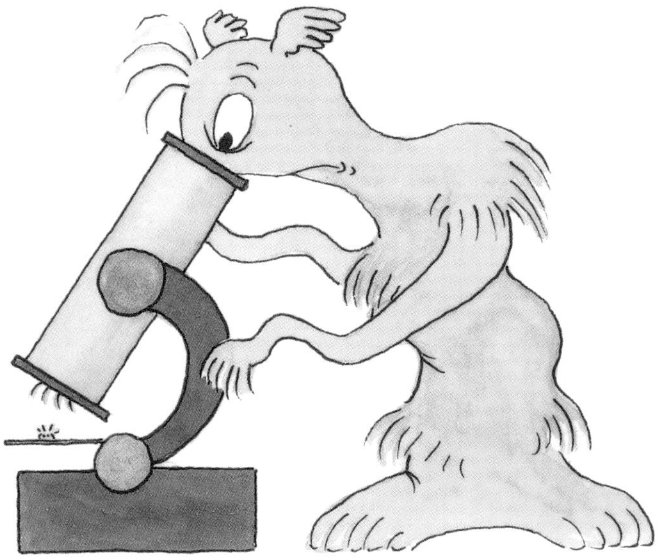

An arpeggio analysing the chromatic scales of a slur.

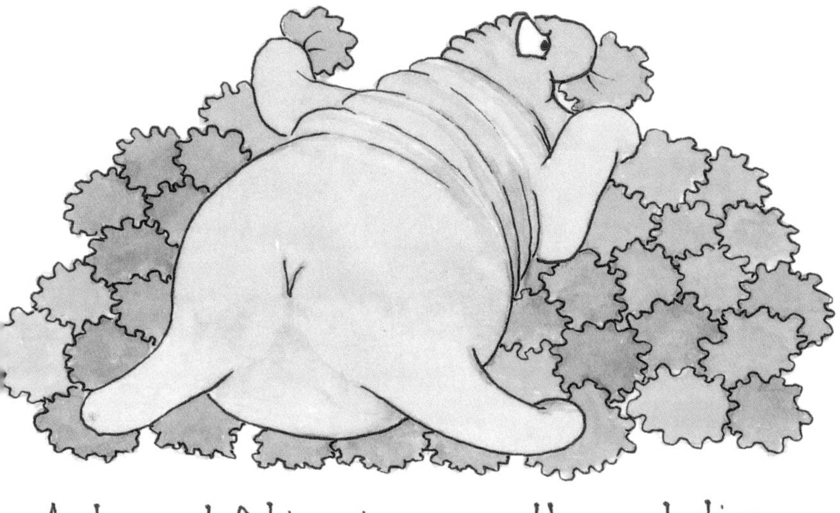

A base clef bingeing on rotten melodies.

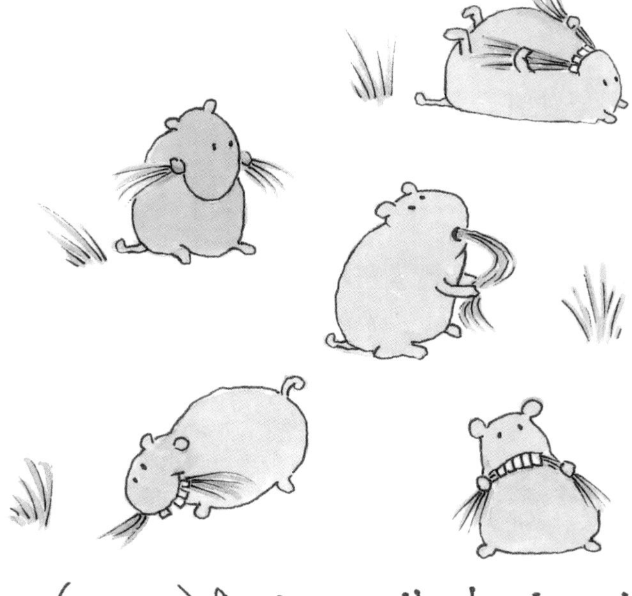

Stradi (various) feeding on the local verdi.

ME AND MY VITAMINS...
I take them to keep me young, thin and beautiful...

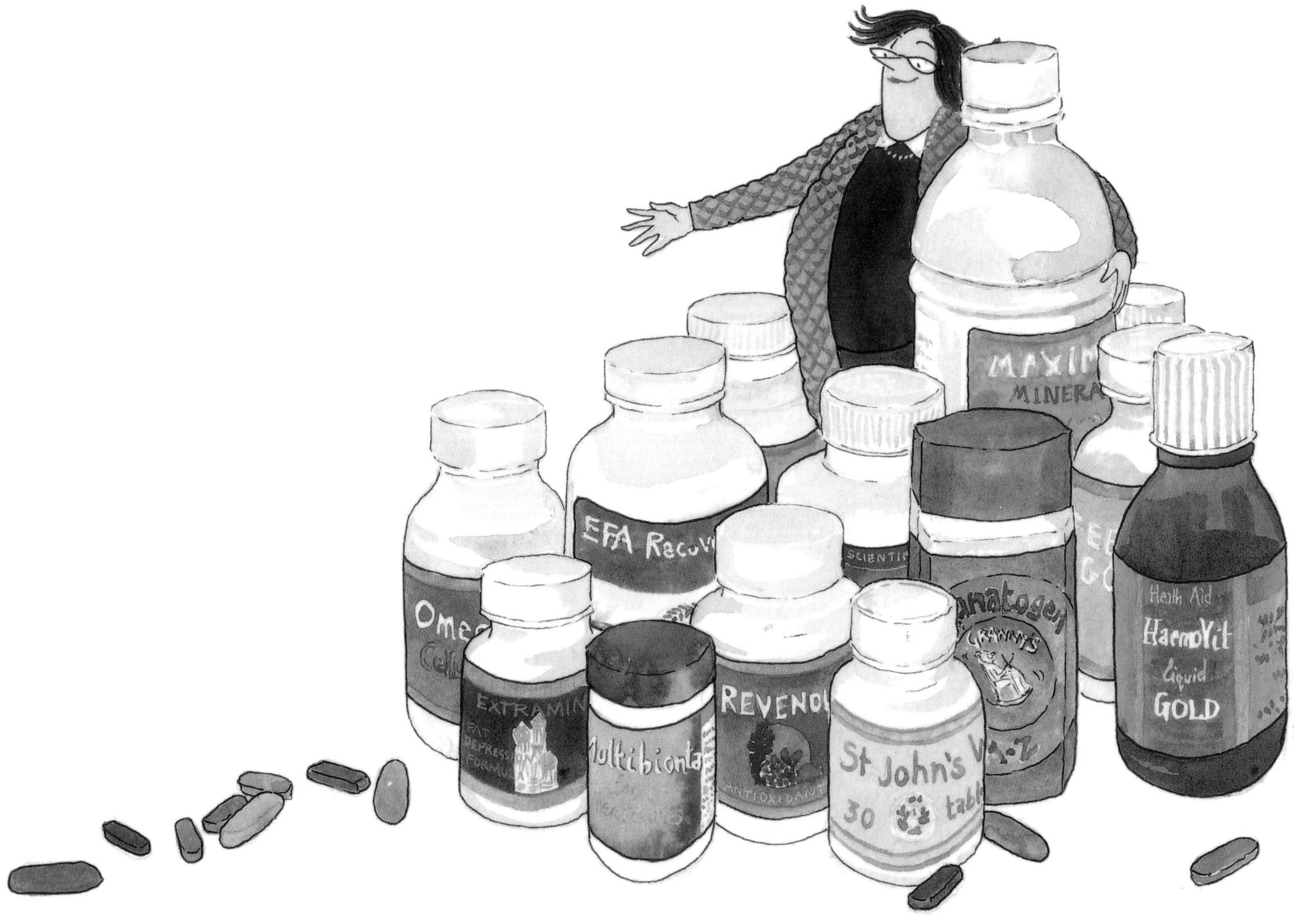

MAXIM
MINERA
Health Aid
HaemoVit
Liquid
GOLD
St John's
30
ANTIOXIDANT

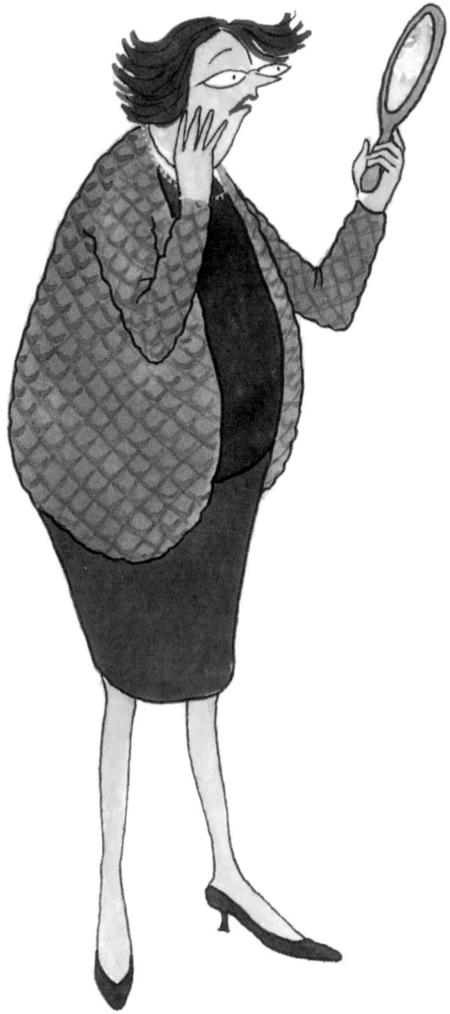

I expect they'll kick in any day now...

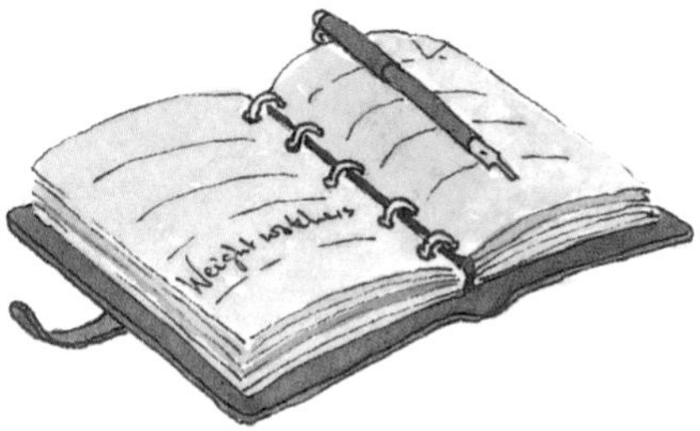
Weight watchers

SEPTEMBER

22

23

24

25

26 John welch

27

LADY TOTTERING
The English county Lady...

built for comfort, not for speed....

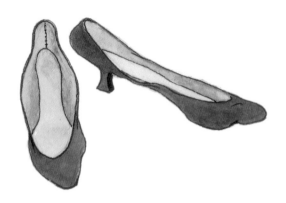

September

28 _____

29 _____

30 _____

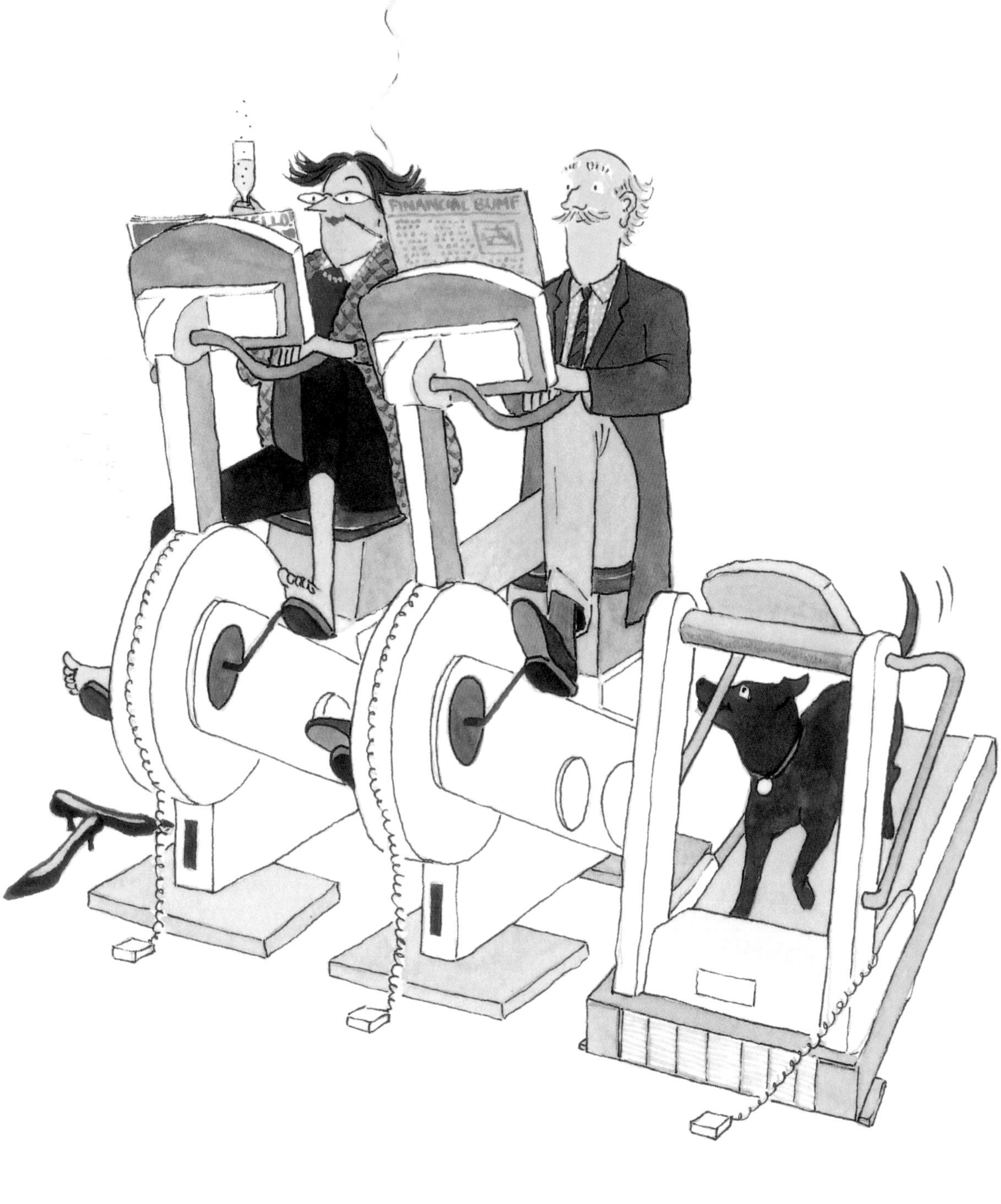
FINANCIAL BUMF

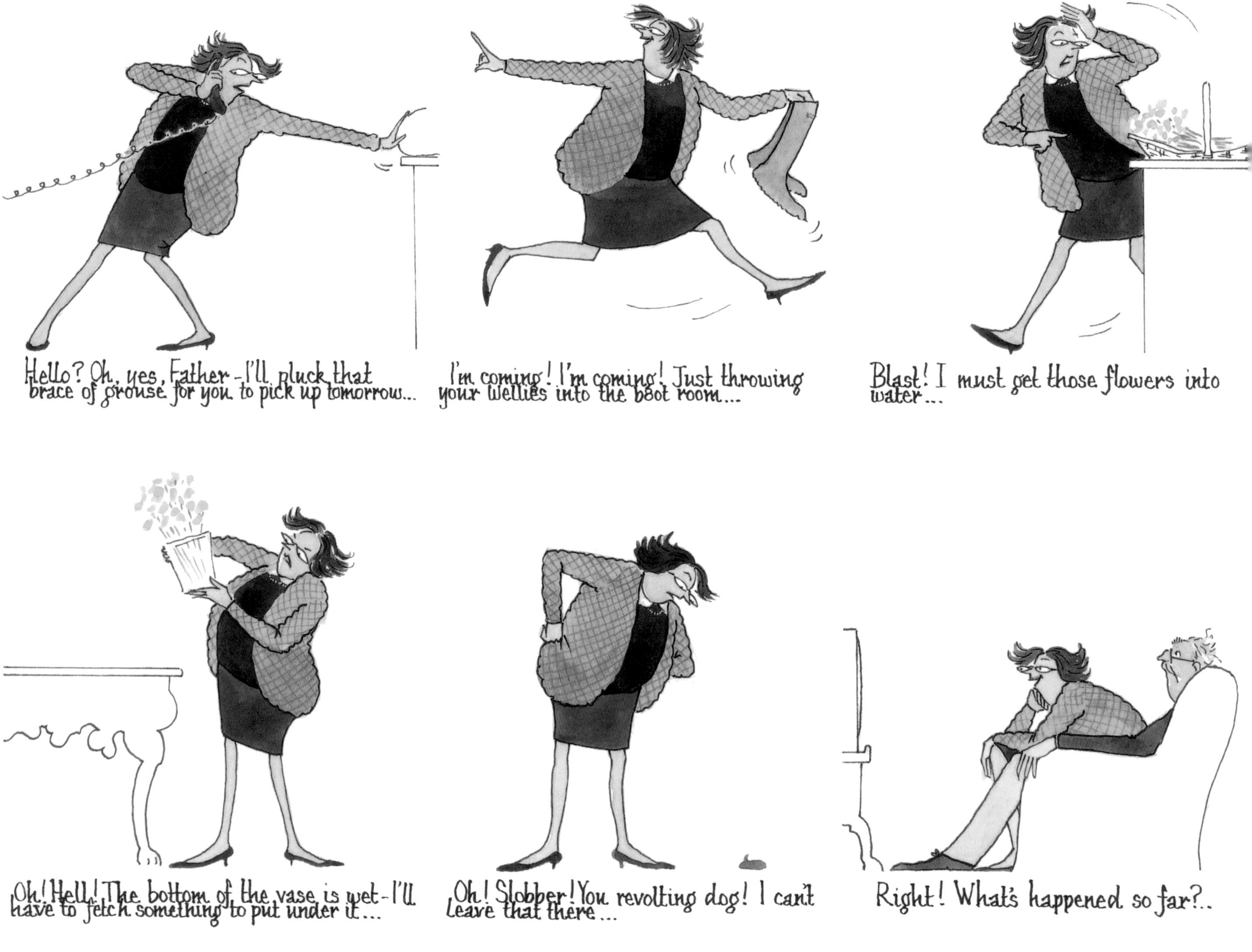
Hello? Oh, yes, Father - I'll pluck that brace of grouse for you to pick up tomorrow...
I'm coming! I'm coming! Just throwing your wellies into the boot room...
Blast! I must get those flowers into water...
Oh! Hell! The bottom of the vase is wet - I'll have to fetch something to put under it...
Oh! Slobber! You revolting dog! I can't leave that there...
Right! What's happened so far?..

I promise I'll settle down and watch the film with you in a moment...

...just give me two ticks to get a phone number from my handbag...

Damn! Where did I last have it?...I dropped Mrs Shagpile at Netto's...

Ah! Eureka! Your blazer button - better sew it on before it gets lost again...

Oh! Drat! I haven't taken anything out of the freezer for tomorrow's lunch...

Get that, would you, Dicky?...

October

1
_____

2
_____

3
_____

4
_____

5
_____

6
_____

7
_____

All them expensive hair gels are a con - marmalade is much cheaper
but you've got to be careful of wasps in the summer...

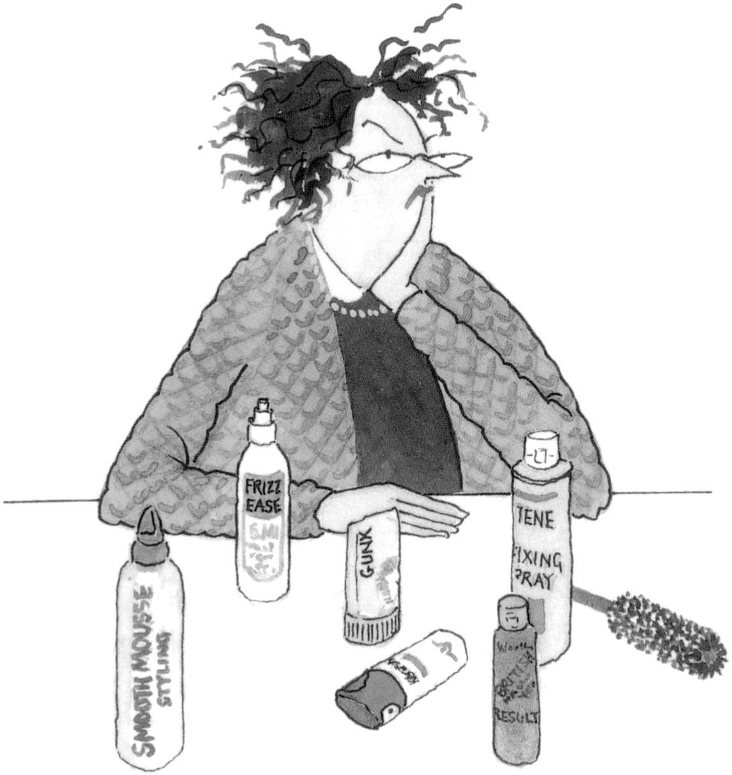
FRIZZ EASE
GUNK
TENE
FIXING
SMOOTH MOUSSE
STYLING
RESULT

BAD HAIR DAY

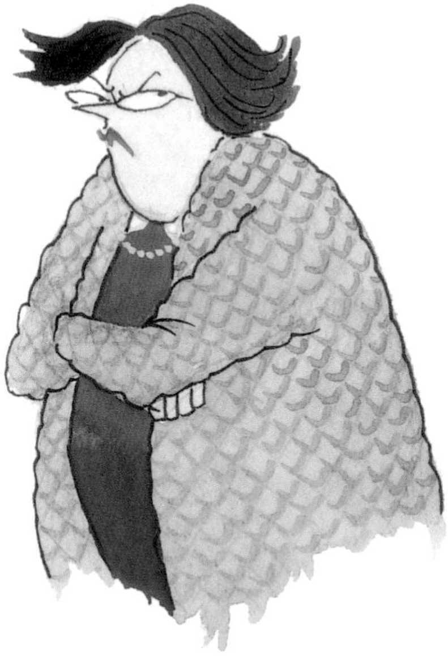

BAD MOOD DAY

The female angler fish weighs up to half a ton.. Her husband, however, is tiny and spends his entire life attached to his wife's nose...

OCTOBER

8
_____

9
_____

10
_____

11
_____

12
_____

13
_____

14
_____

Don Perignon was a blind Benedictine monk...

October

15

16

17

Our program, who art in memory,
Hello be thy name.
Thy operating system come,
Thy commands be done,
At the printer as they are on screen.

Give us this day our daily data,
And forgive us our input errors as we forgive those
Whose logic circuits are faulty.

Lead us not into frustration,
And deliver us from power surges.
For thyne is the algorithm,
The application
And the solution,
Looping for ever and ever.

AMEN.COM

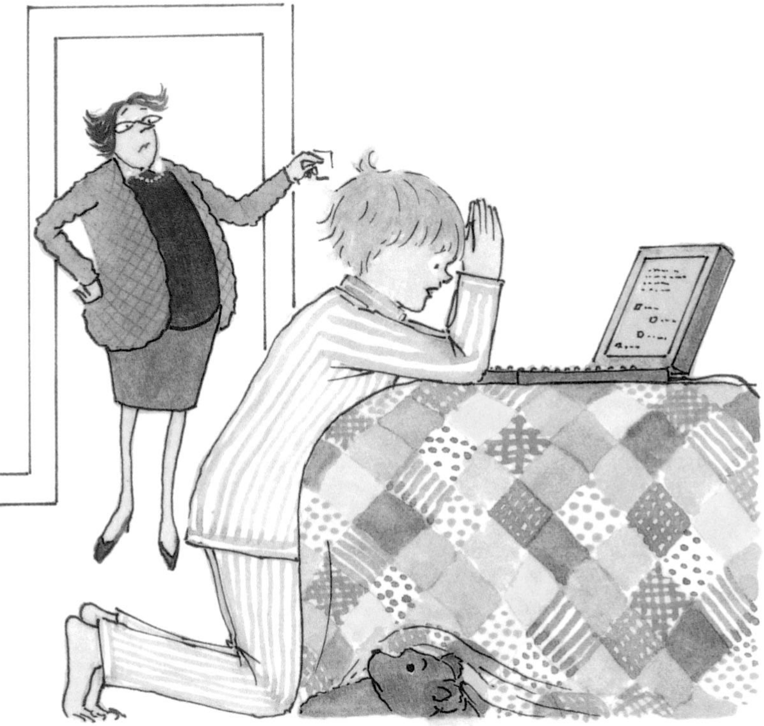

5 REASONS WHY COMPUTERS MUST BE MALE...

1. They're heavily dependent on external tools and equipment.
2. They periodically cut you off, just when you think you've established a connection.
3. They usually do what you ask them to do, but they won't do more than they have to and they won't think of it on their own.
4. They're typically obsolete within five years and need to be traded in for a new model. Some users, however, feel they've already invested so much in the machine that they struggle on with an underpowered system.
5. The only time you have their attention is when you turn them on.

5 REASONS WHY COMPUTERS MUST BE FEMALE...

1. No one but their creator understands their internal logic.
2. Even your smallest mistakes are immediately committed to memory for future reference.
3. The native language used to communicate with other computers is incomprehensible.
4. The message 'bad command or filename' is about as informative as 'if you don't know why I'm furious with you – I'm certainly not going to tell you!'
5. As soon as you make a commitment to one, you find yourself spending every spare penny on accessories for it.

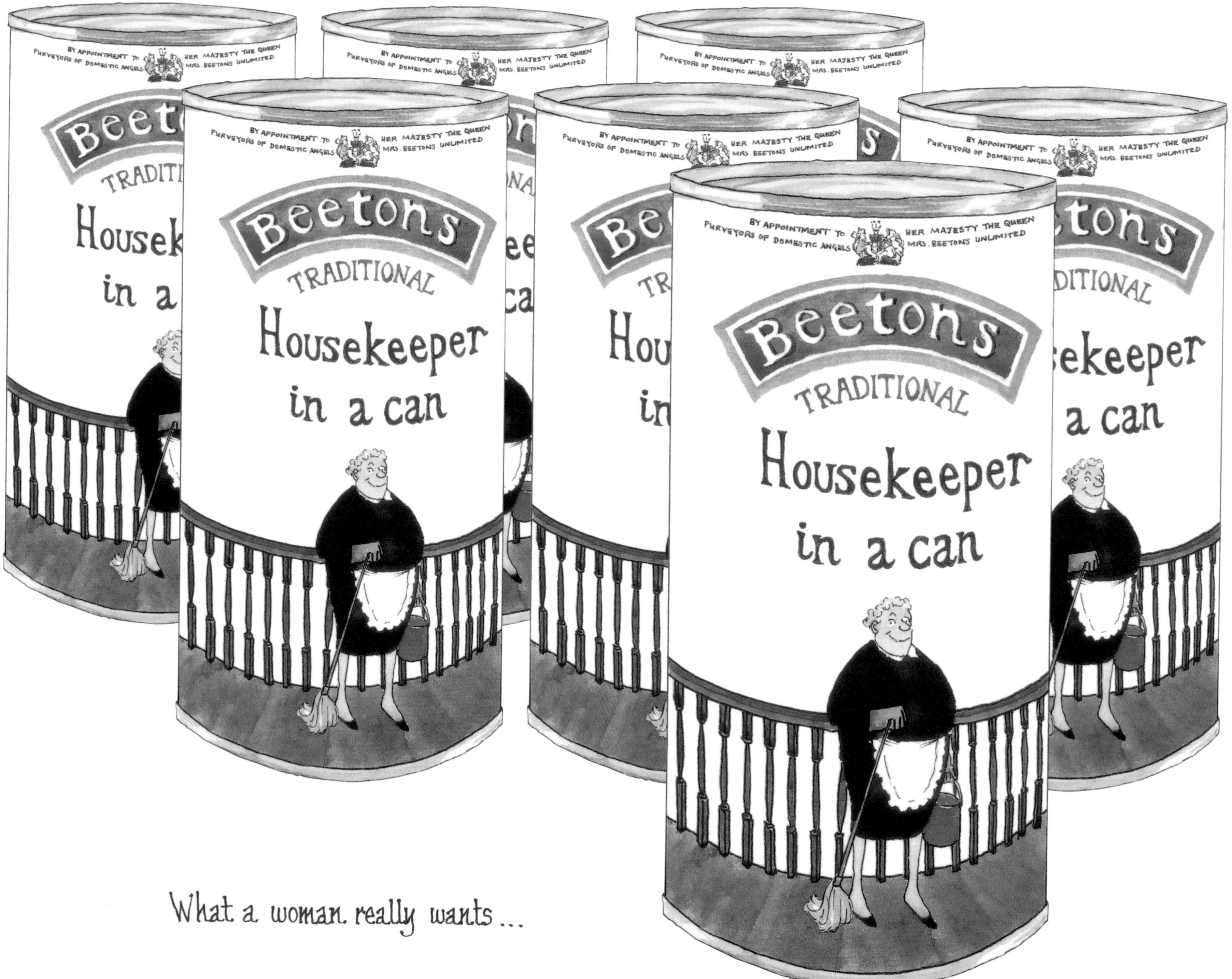
BY APPOINTMENT TO HER MAJESTY THE QUEEN
PURVEYORS OF DOMESTIC ANGELS MRS. BEETONS UNLIMITED
Beetons
TRADITIONAL
Housekeeper
in a can

What a woman really wants ...

Larder dreams...

OCTOBER

18

19

20

21

also available...

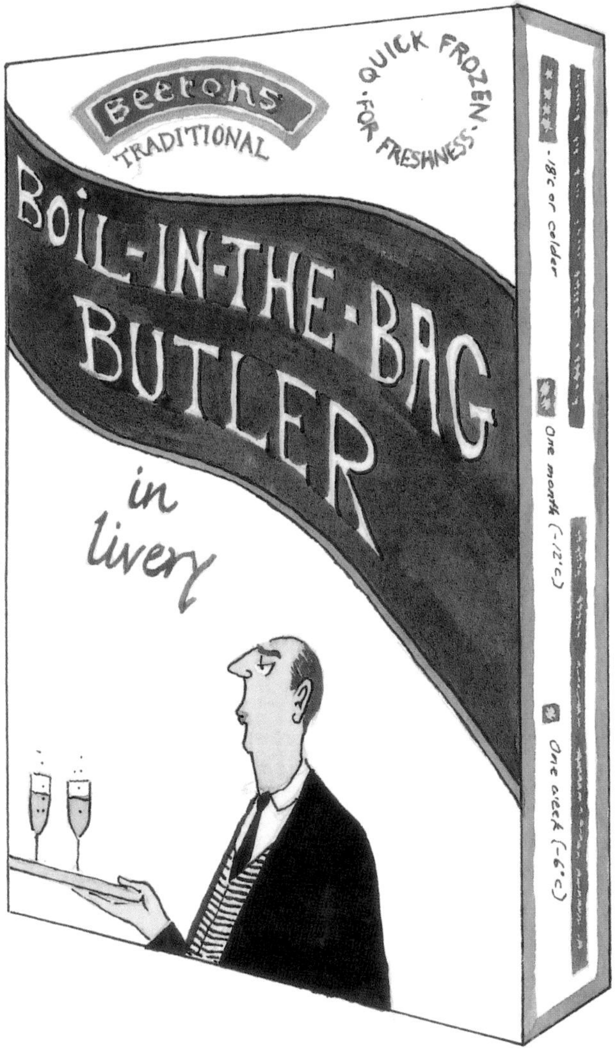

Beetons
TRADITIONAL
QUICK FROZEN FOR FRESHNESS
BOIL-IN-THE-BAG BUTLER
in livery
-18°c or colder
One month (-12°c)
One week (-6°c)

Tottering
tering Hall
ttingham,
nmshire

NB
Half
term-
Nit alert!

MUST GIVE
UP SMOKING
TODAY!

October

22

23

24 Bob

25

26

27

28 Clocks go back.

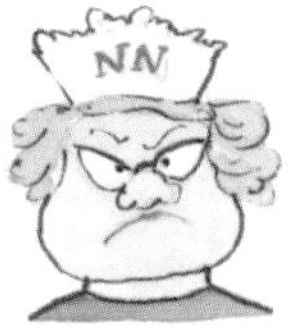
NN

The Nit Nurse's Advice

1. Don't ever allow your grand-children to come near you.

2. Alternatively, protect yourselves by wearing a cardboard box on your head at all times when they come to stay.

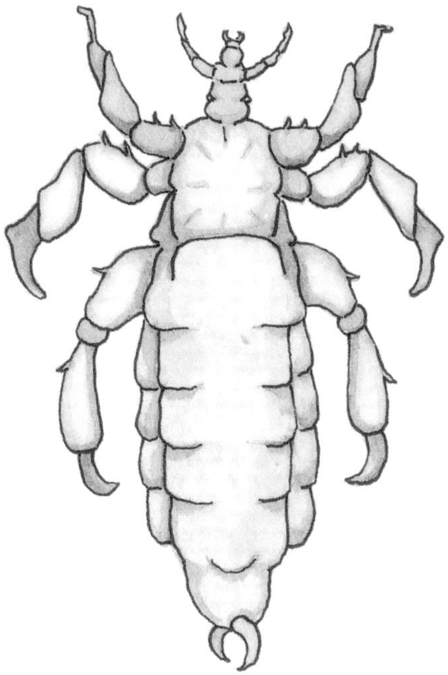

PEDICULUS CAPITIS
(a.k.a. 'Nasty Nit')

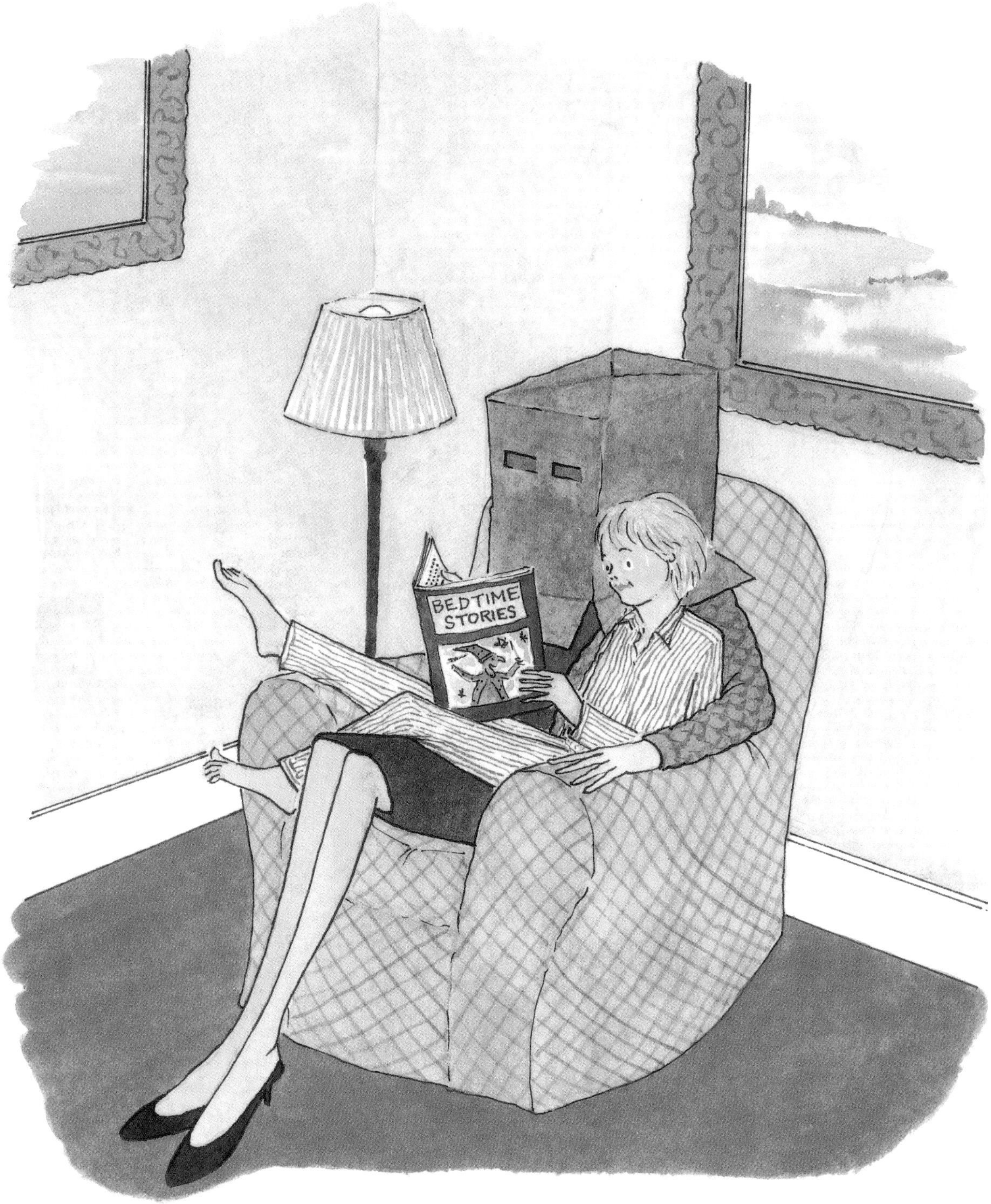
BEDTIME STORIES

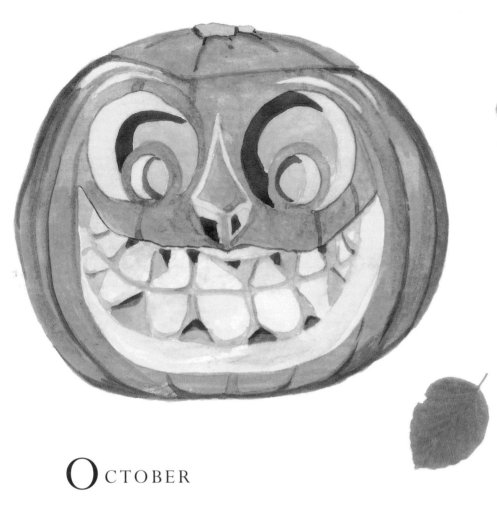

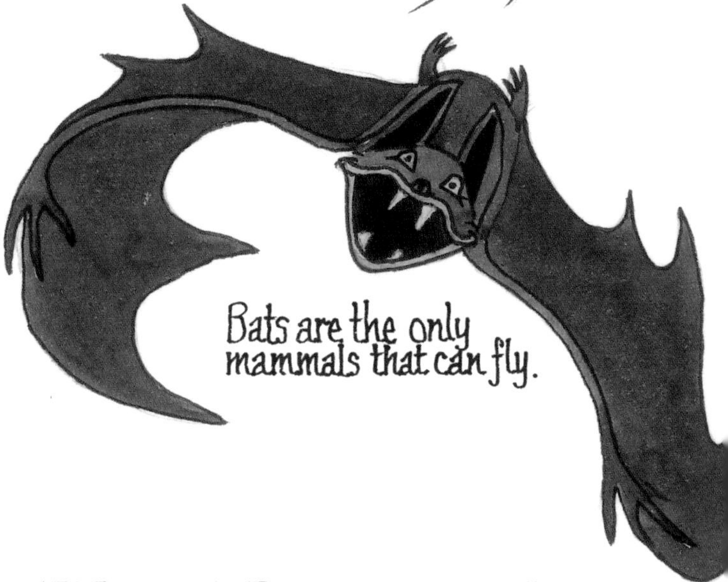

Bats are the only
mammals that can fly.

O CTOBER

29

30

31

DICKY'S OLD BAT →

TOTTERING TODDY

1 oz. Port wine (25g)
1 Pint fresh green tea (550ml)
4 oz. Sugar (110g)
Peel of 1 Lemon
1 glass of Brandy
1 bottle Scotch Whisky

Heat and serve piping hot!

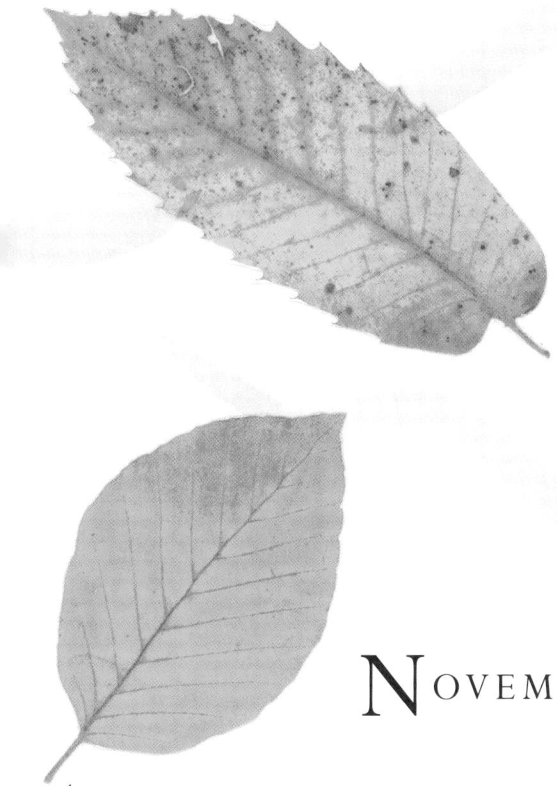

NOVEMBER

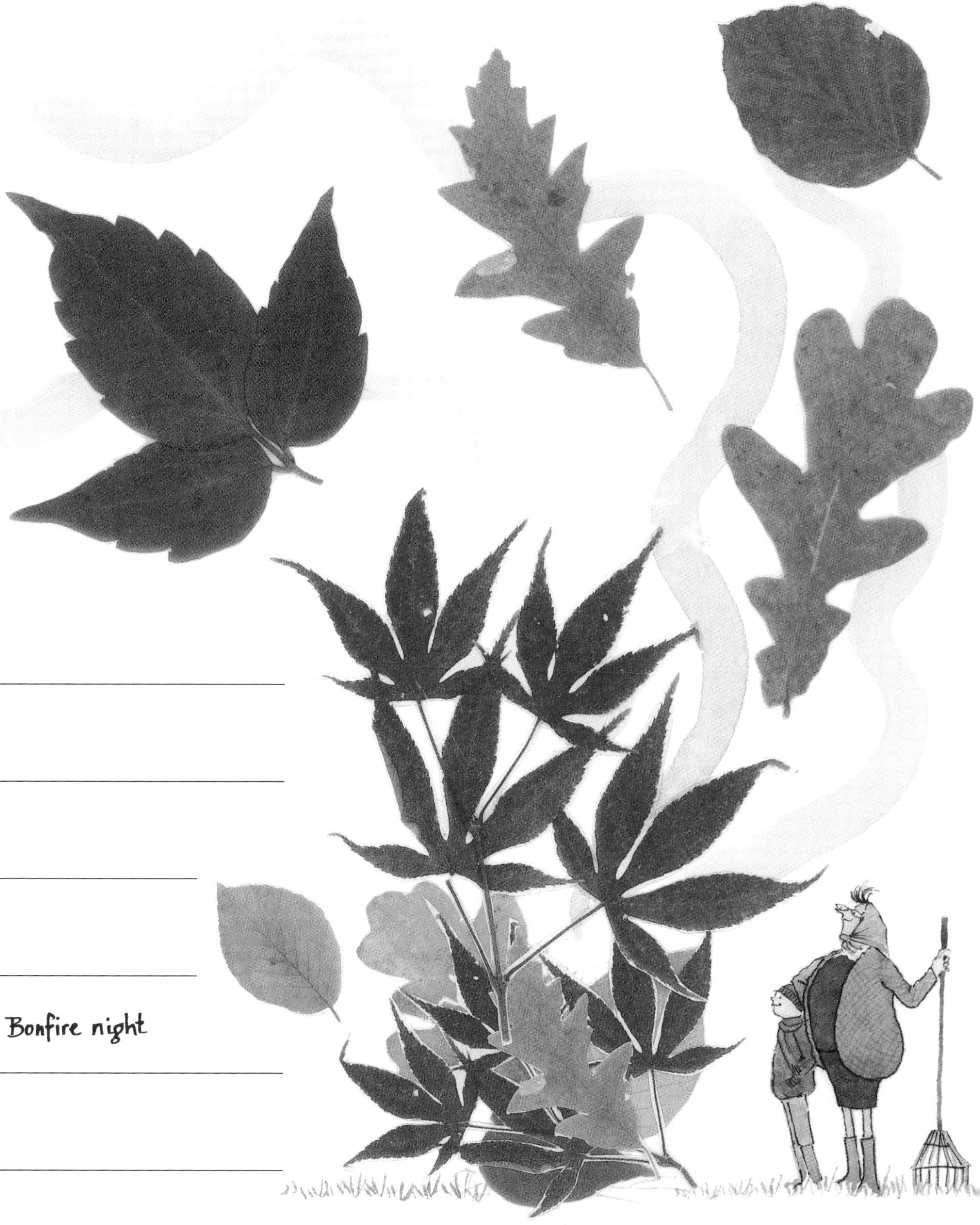

1

2

3 Ua Birthday

4

5 Bonfire night

6

A BRACE OF GAME BIRDS

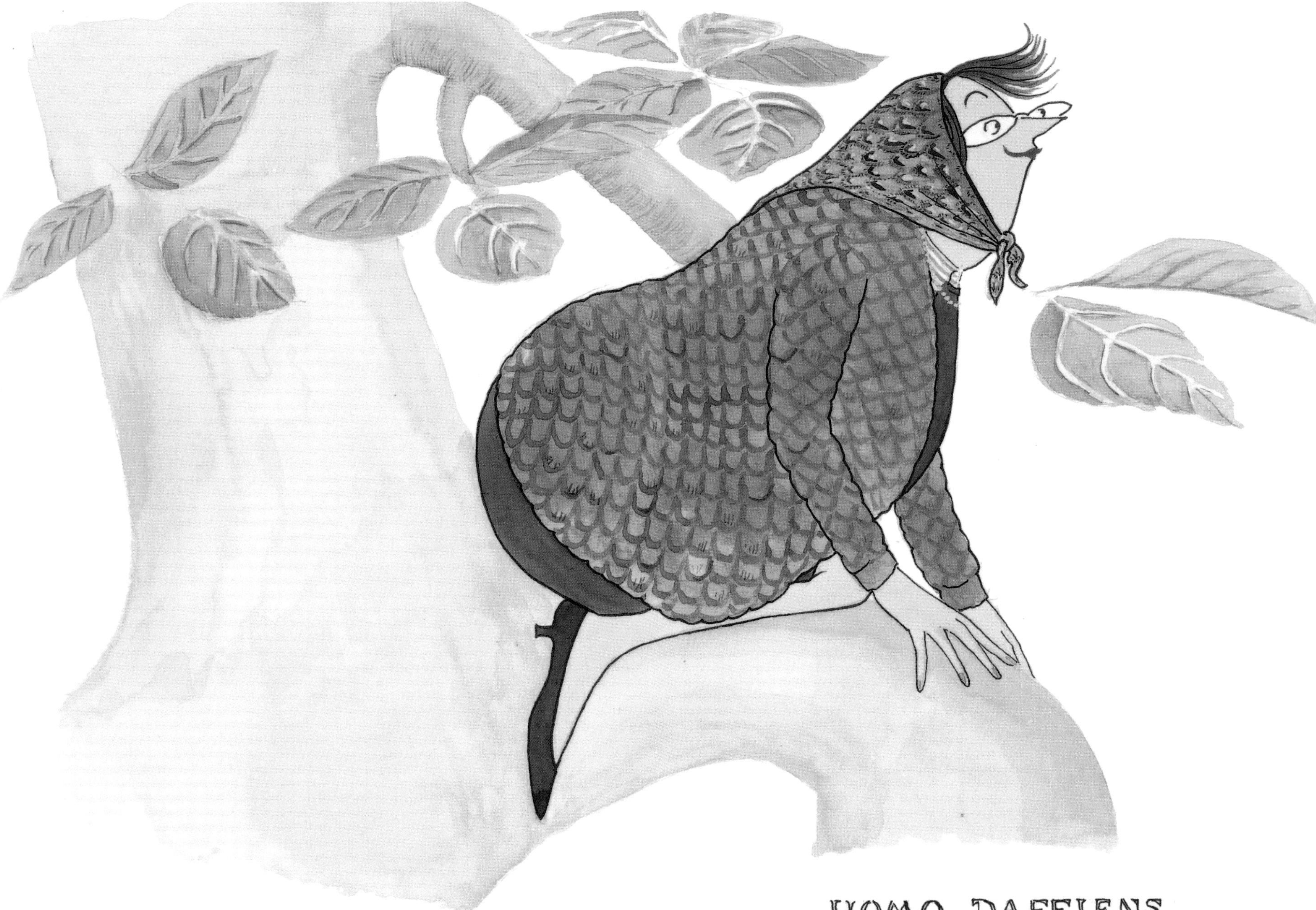

HOMO DAFFIENS

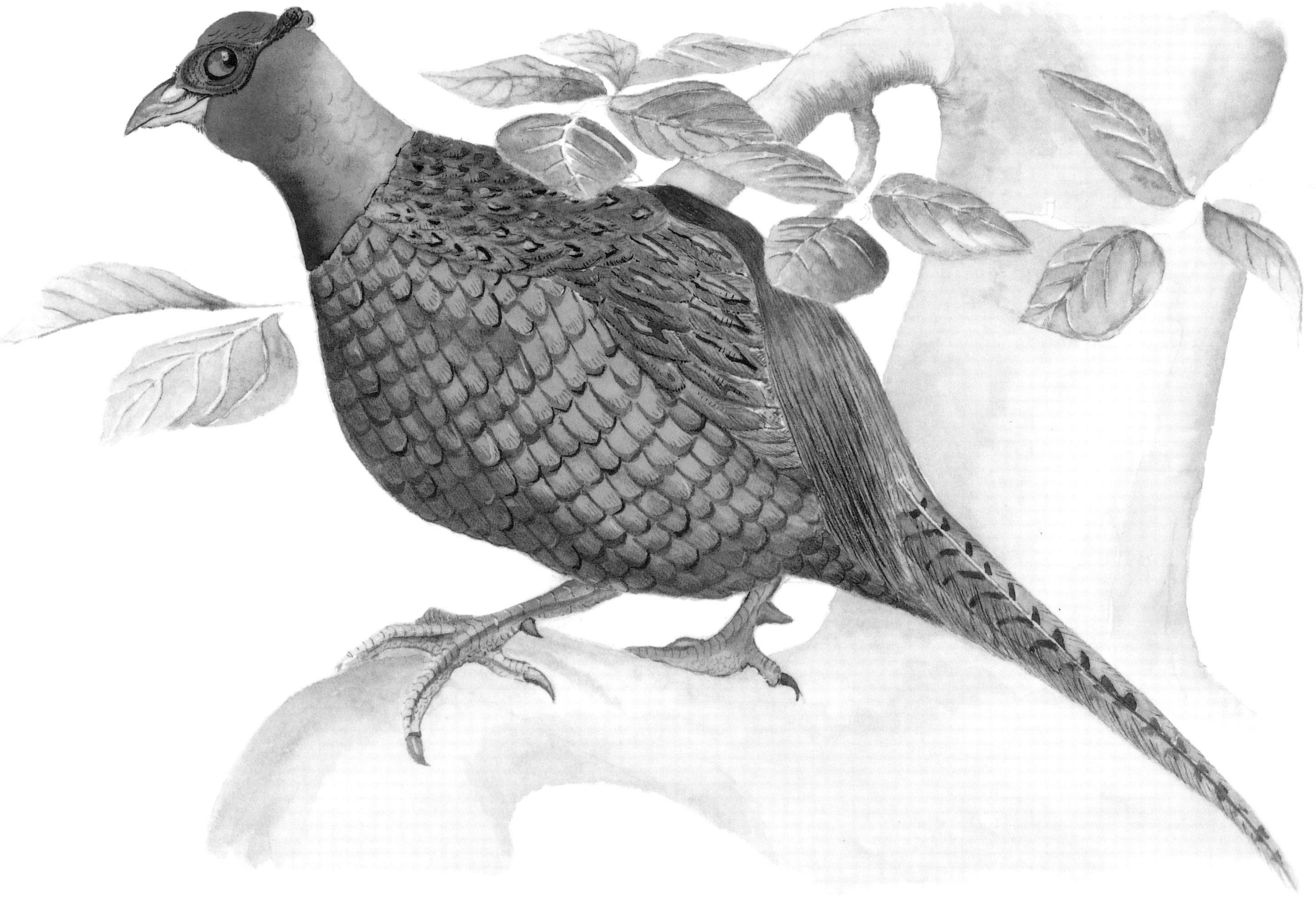

PHASIANUS HUSKYUS

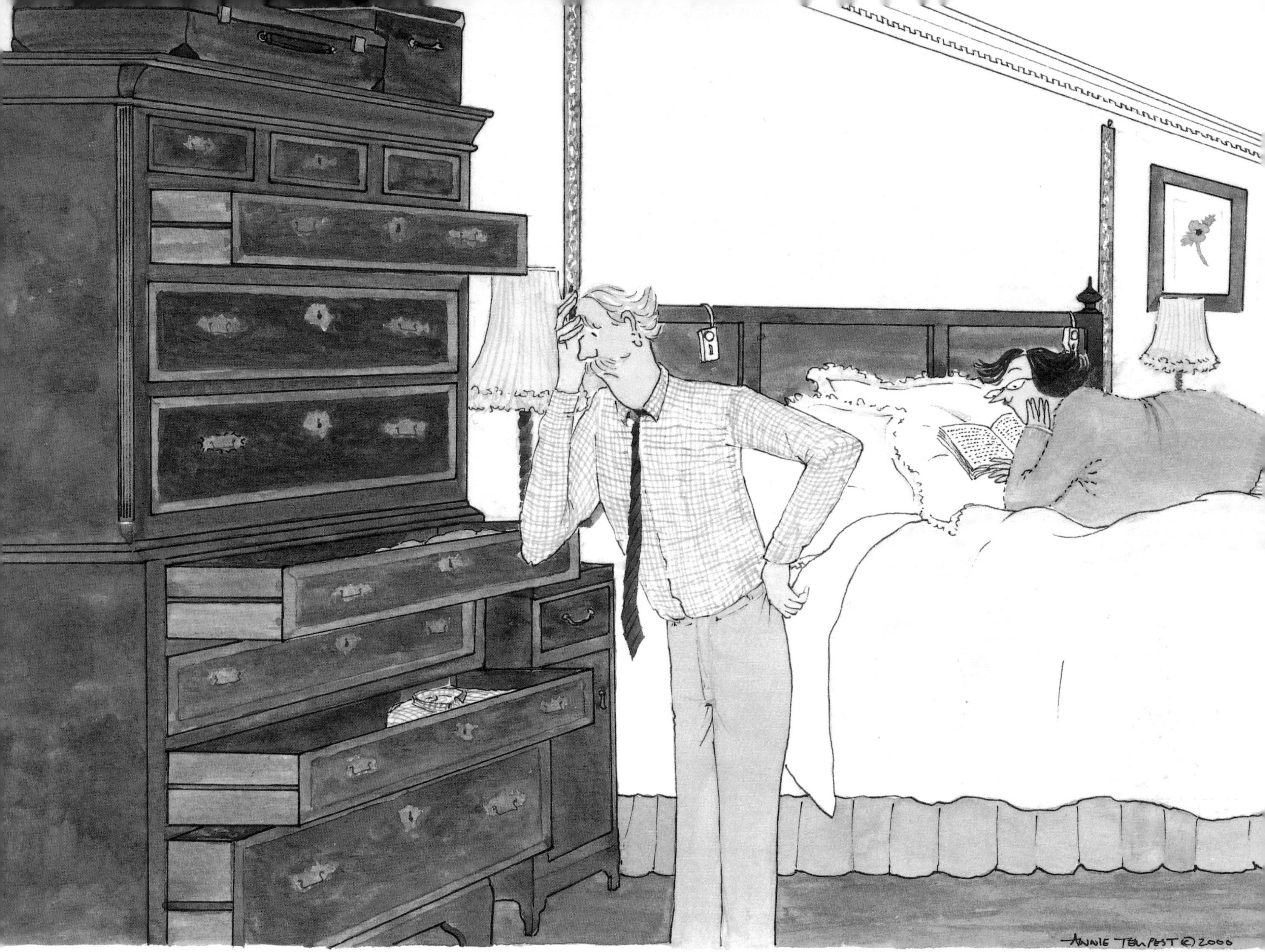
ANNIE TEMPEST © 2000

THE MALE CHARACTER: A tendency to mislay warm pyjamas and cashmere jumpers...

...and I shouldn't mind in the least if you borrowed my nightie...

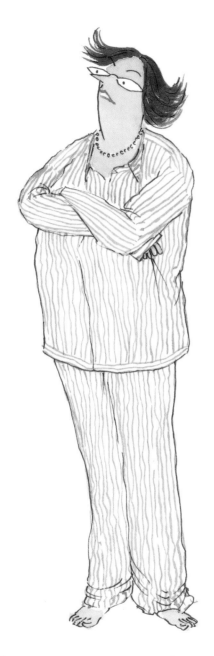

NOVEMBER

7 _____

8 _____

9 _____

10 _____

I could have sworn that when we got married we agreed that everything of yours was mine and vice versa...

Bloody women!

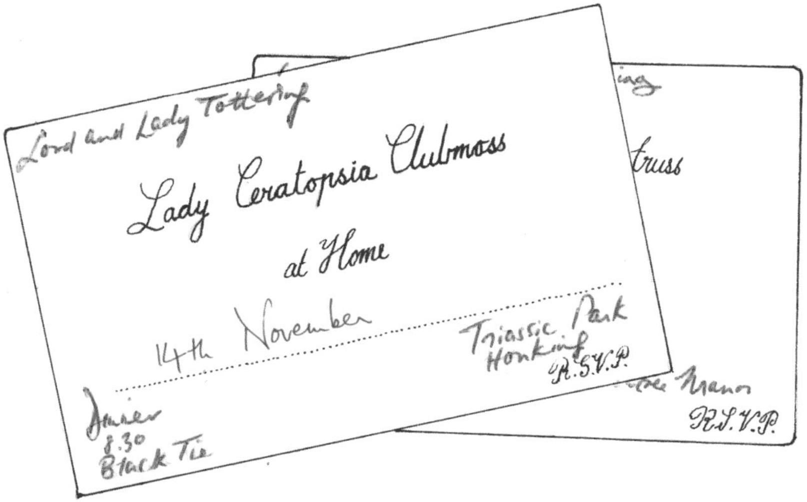
Lord and Lady Tottering
Lady Ceratopsia Clubmoss
at Home
14th November
Triassic Park
Honking
R.S.V.P.
Dinner
8.30
Black Tie
R.S.V.P.

NOVEMBER

11

12

13

14

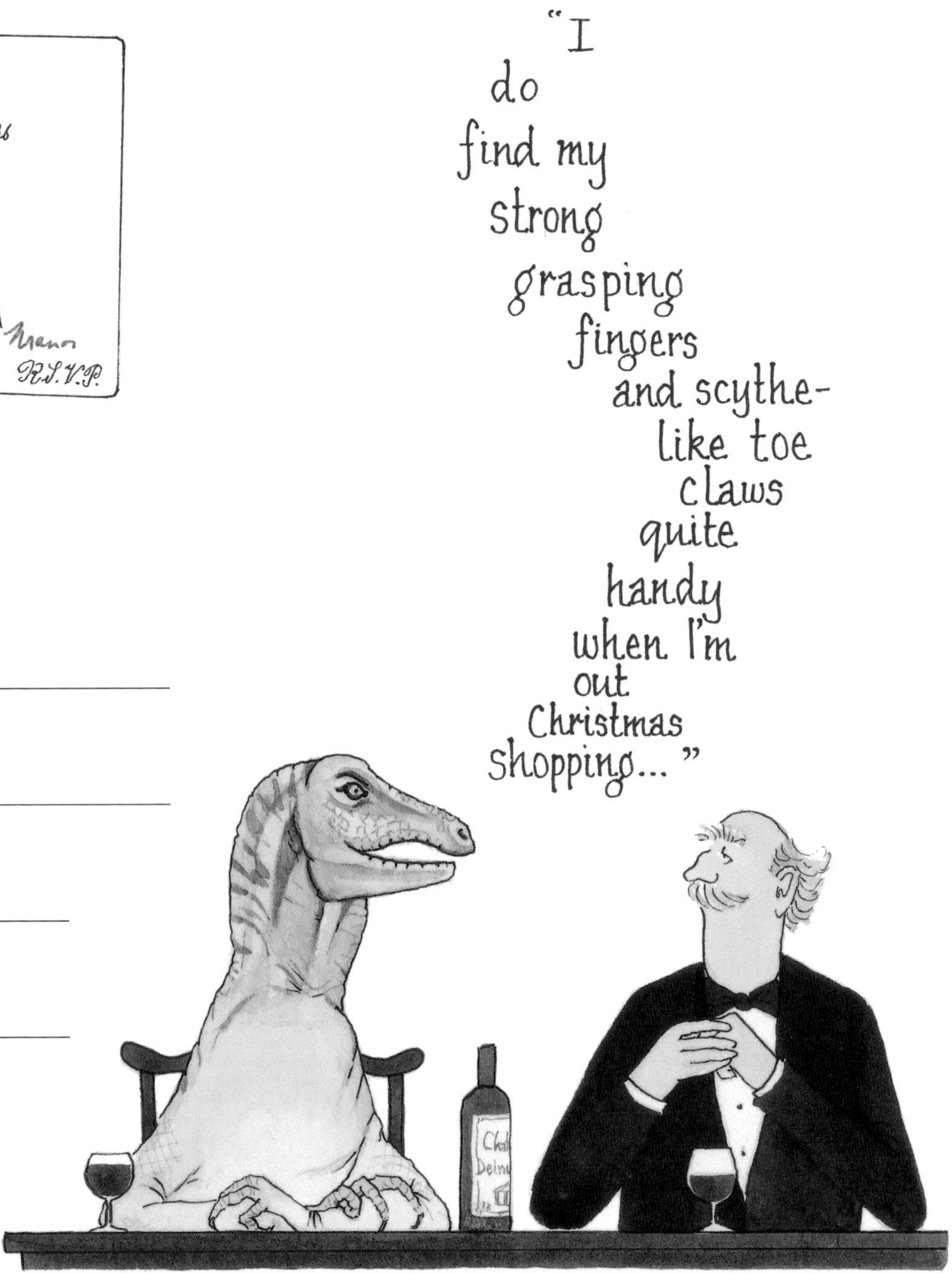
"I do find my strong grasping fingers and scythe-like toe claws quite handy when I'm out Christmas shopping..."

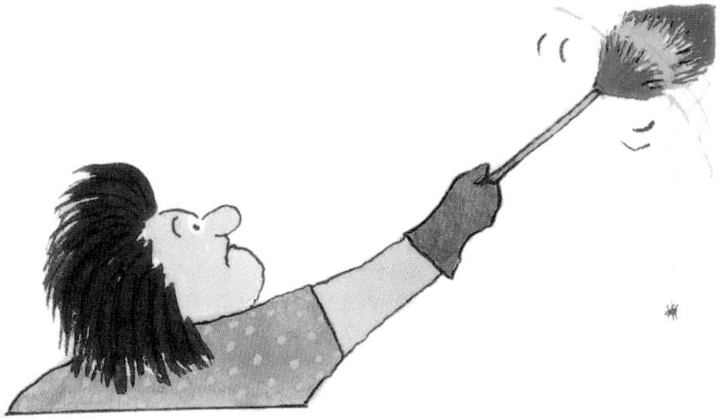

"I may be over 180 million years old but, thankfully, I've only had to survive 2000 Christmas shopping trips with my wife..."

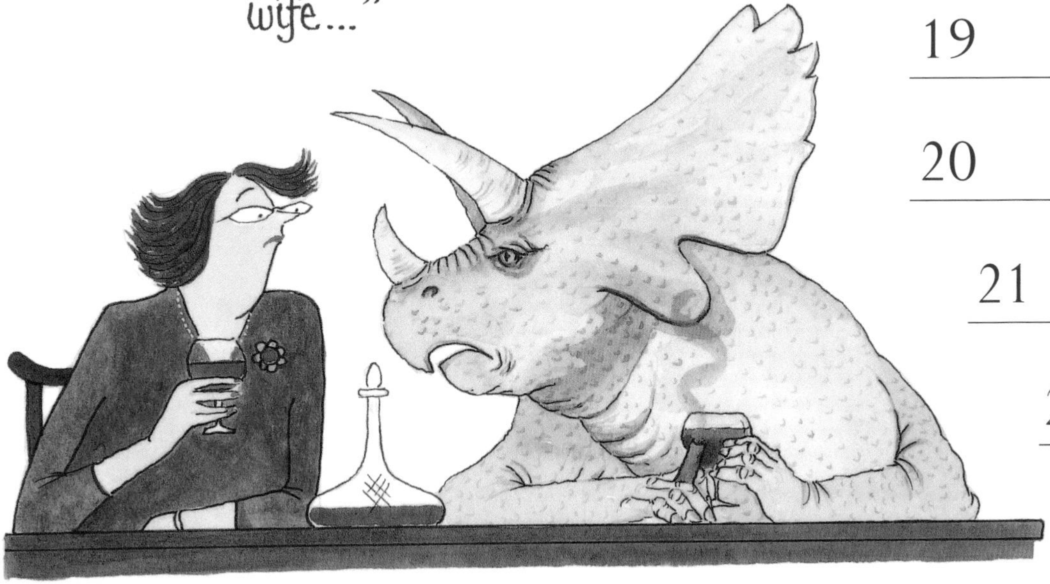

15

16

17

18

19

20

21

22

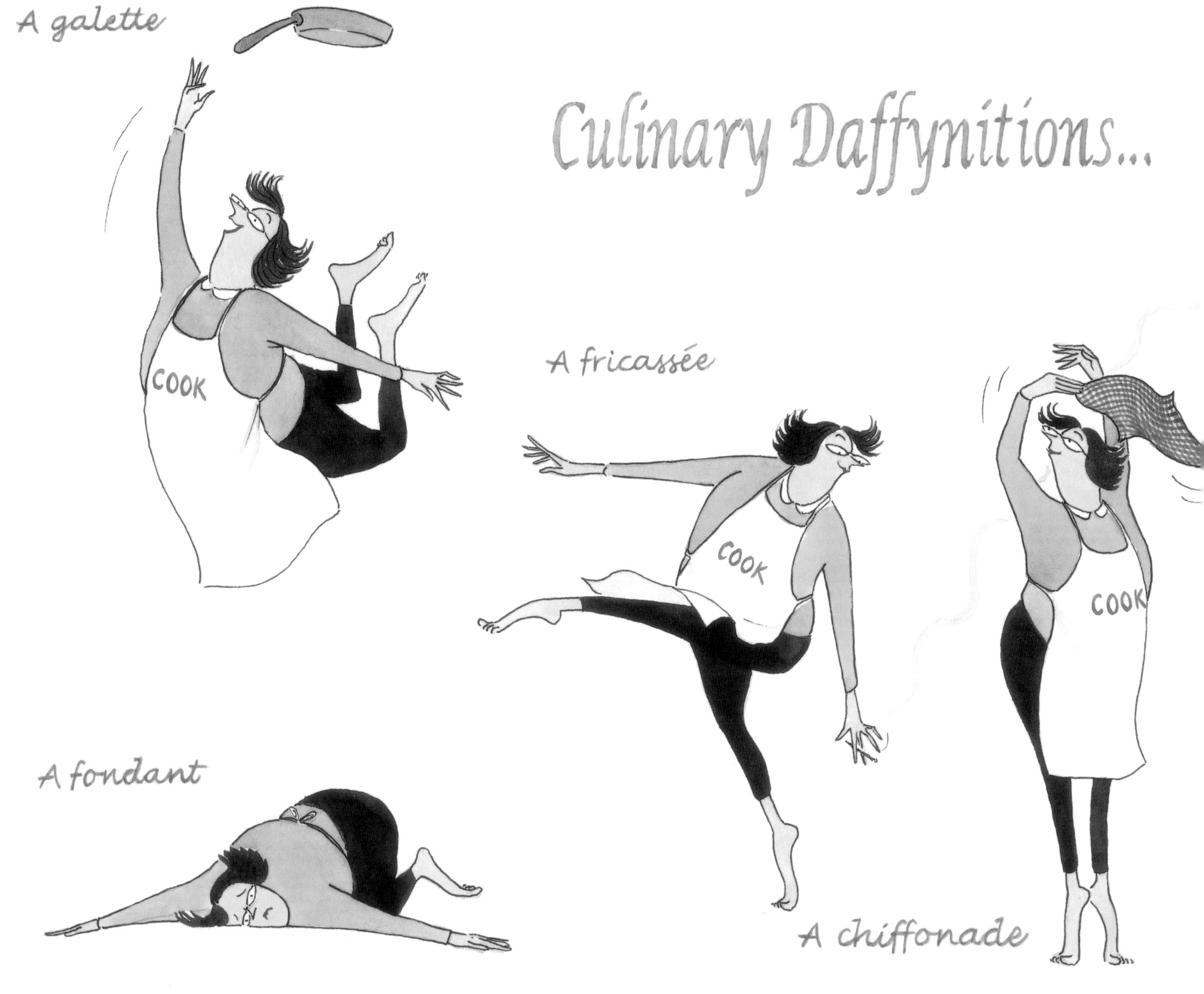
Culinary Daffynitions...
A galette
COOK
A fricassée
COOK
COOK
A fondant
A chiffonade

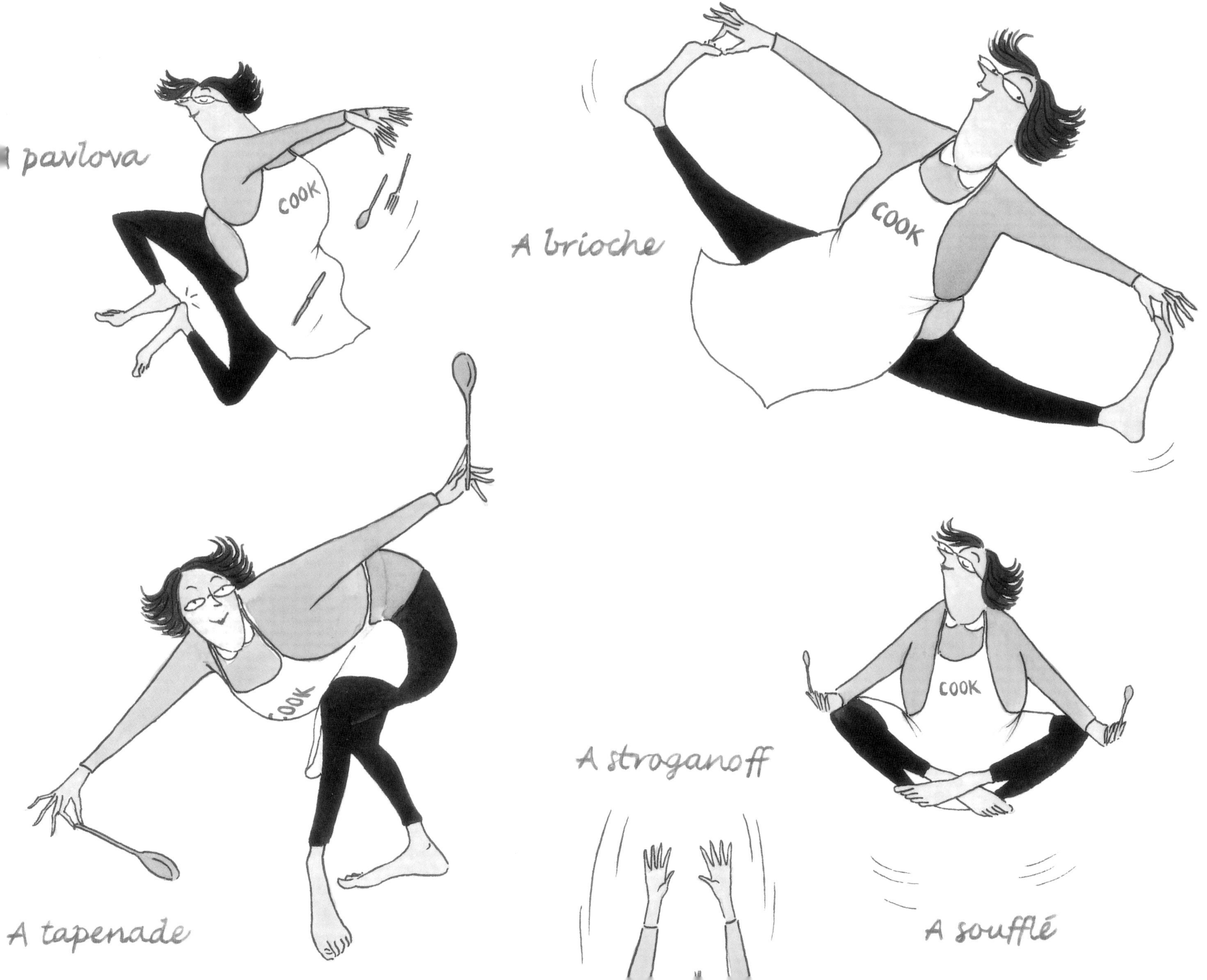
pavlova
COOK
A brioche
COOK
COOK
A tapenade
A stroganoff
COOK
A soufflé

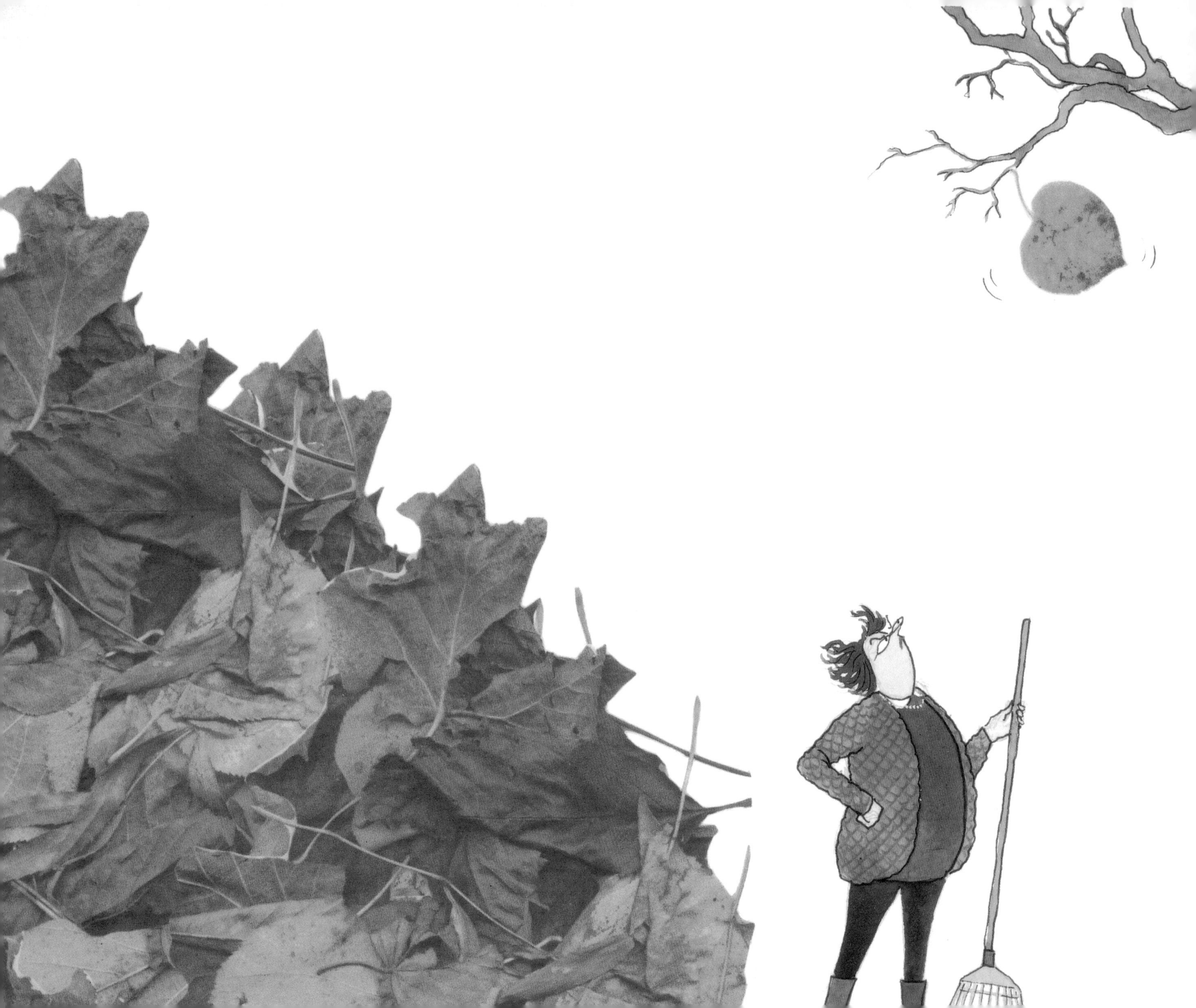

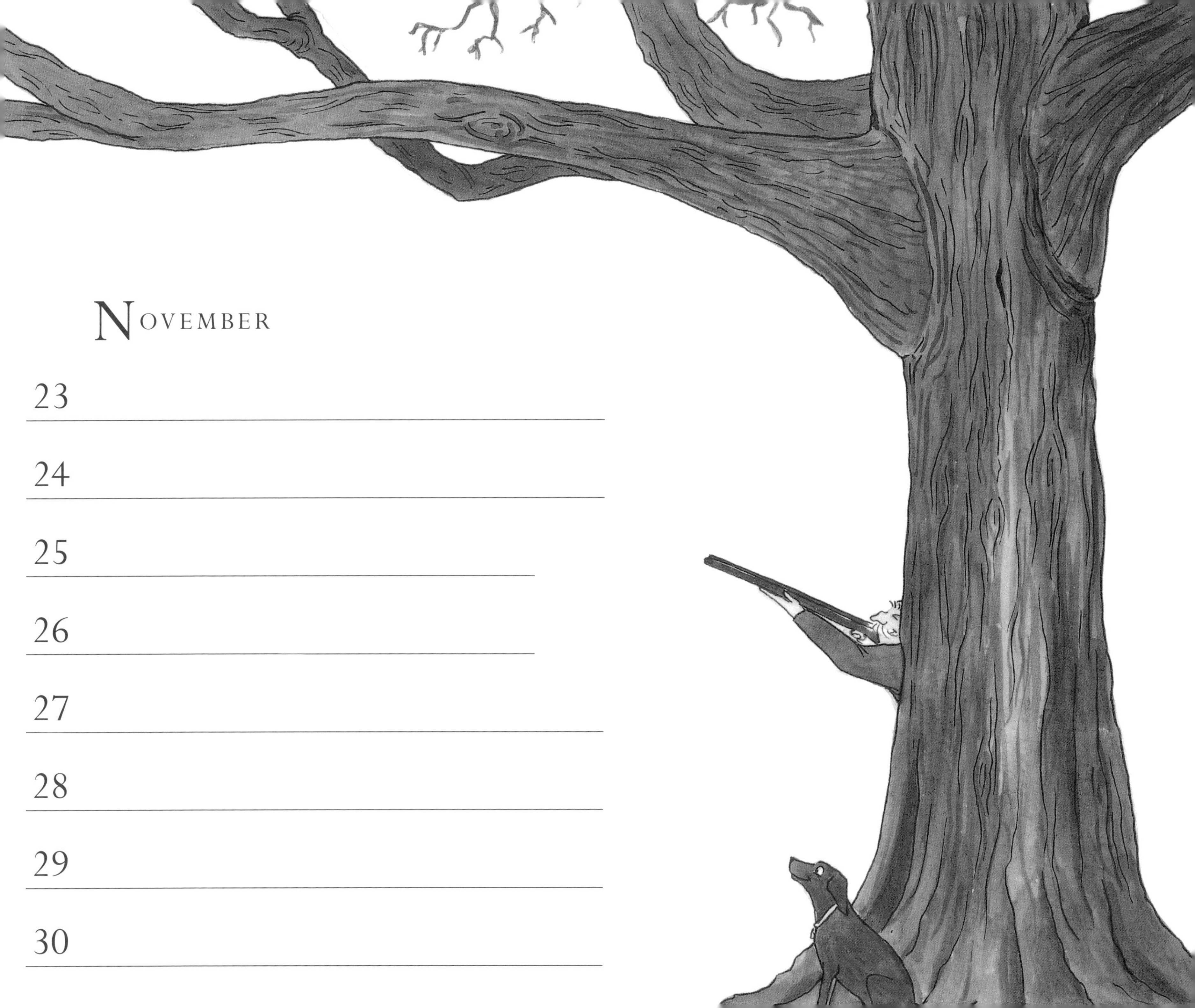

November

23

24

25

26

27

28

29

30

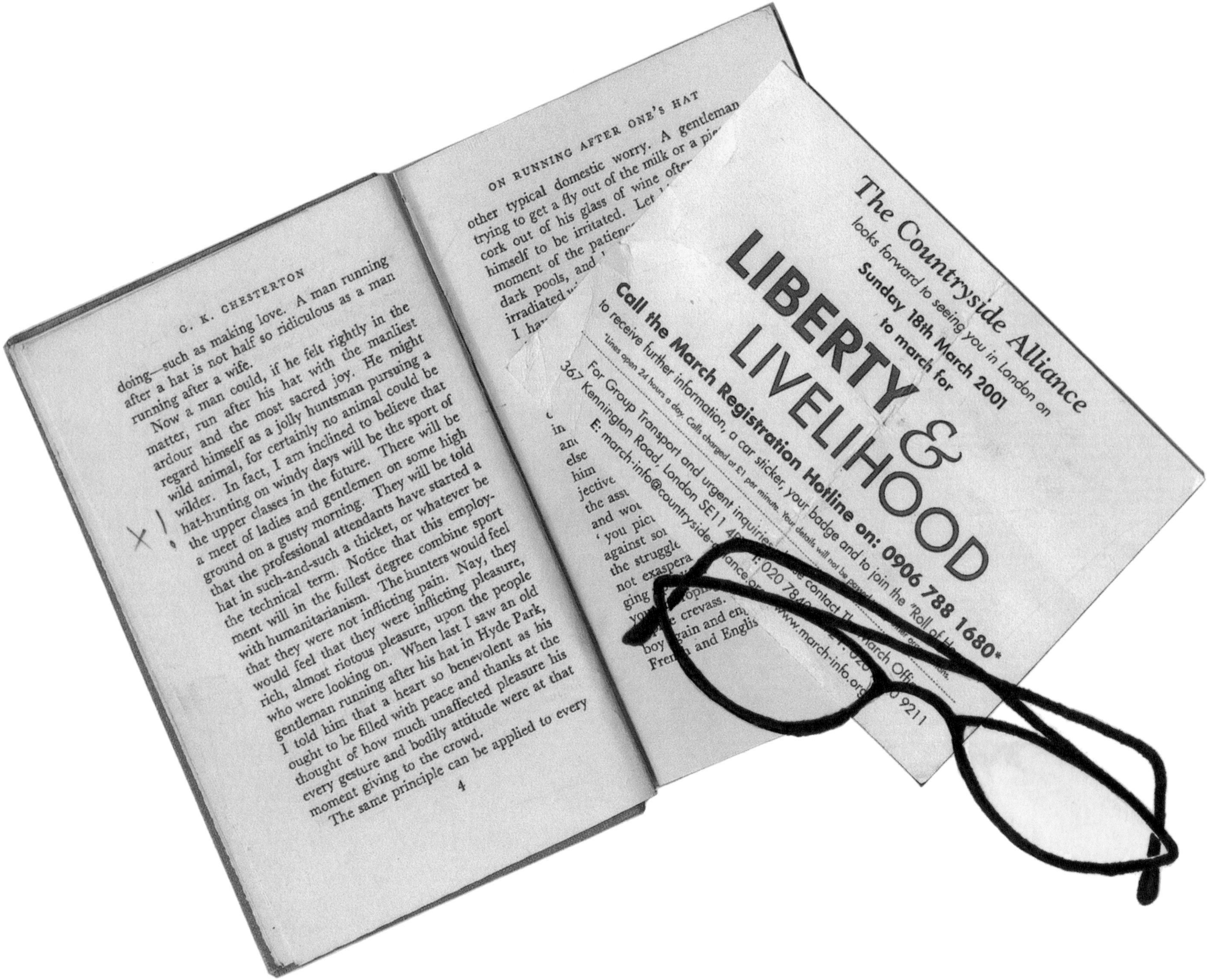
G. K. CHESTERTON
doing—such as making love. A man running after a hat is not half so ridiculous as a man running after a wife.
Now a man could, if he felt rightly in the matter, run after his hat with the manliest ardour and the most sacred joy. He might regard himself as a jolly huntsman pursuing a wild animal, for certainly no animal could be wilder. In fact, I am inclined to believe that hat-hunting on windy days will be the sport of the upper classes in the future. There will be a meet of ladies and gentlemen on some high ground on a gusty morning. They will be told that the professional attendants have started a hat in such-and-such a thicket, or whatever be the technical term. Notice that this employment will in the fullest degree combine sport with humanitarianism. The hunters would feel that they were not inflicting pain. Nay, they would feel that they were inflicting pleasure, rich, almost riotous pleasure, upon the people who were looking on. When last I saw an old gentleman running after his hat in Hyde Park, I told him that a heart so benevolent as his ought to be filled with peace and thanks at the thought of how much unaffected pleasure his every gesture and bodily attitude were at that moment giving to the crowd.
The same principle can be applied to every
4
ON RUNNING AFTER ONE'S HAT
other typical domestic worry. A gentleman
trying to get a fly out of the milk or a
cork out of his glass of wine
The Countryside Alliance
looks forward to seeing you in London on
Sunday 18th March 2001
to march for
LIBERTY & LIVELIHOOD
Call the March Registration Hotline on: 0906 788 1680*
to receive further information, a car sticker, your badge and to join the "Roll of
*Lines open 24 hours a day. Calls charged at £1 per minute.
For Group Transport and urgent inquiries
367 Kennington Road, London SE11
E: march-info@countryside-

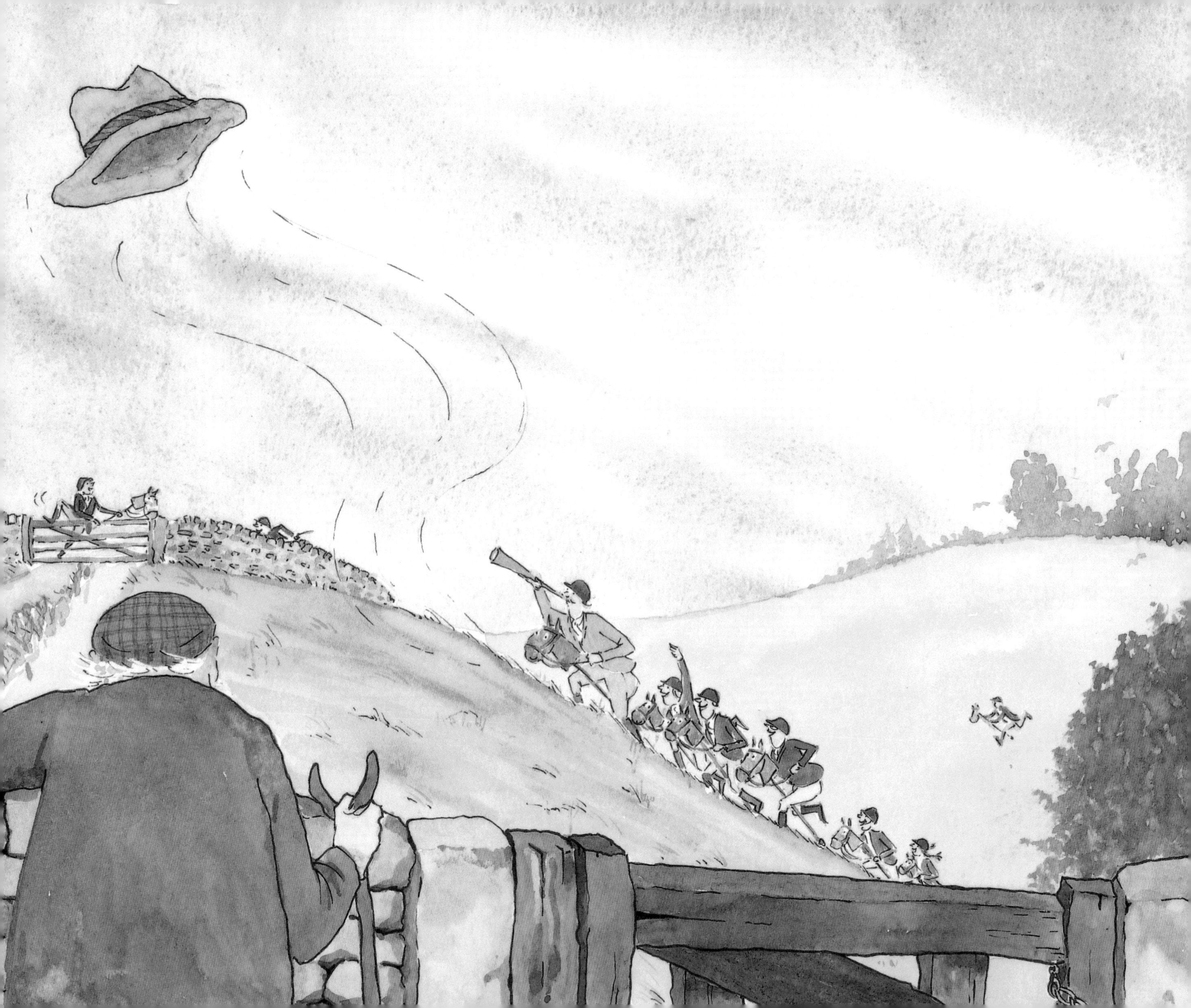

December

1

2

3

4

5

6

7

8

9

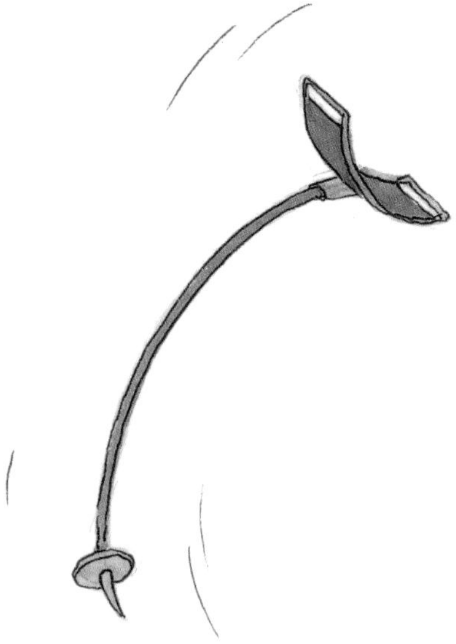

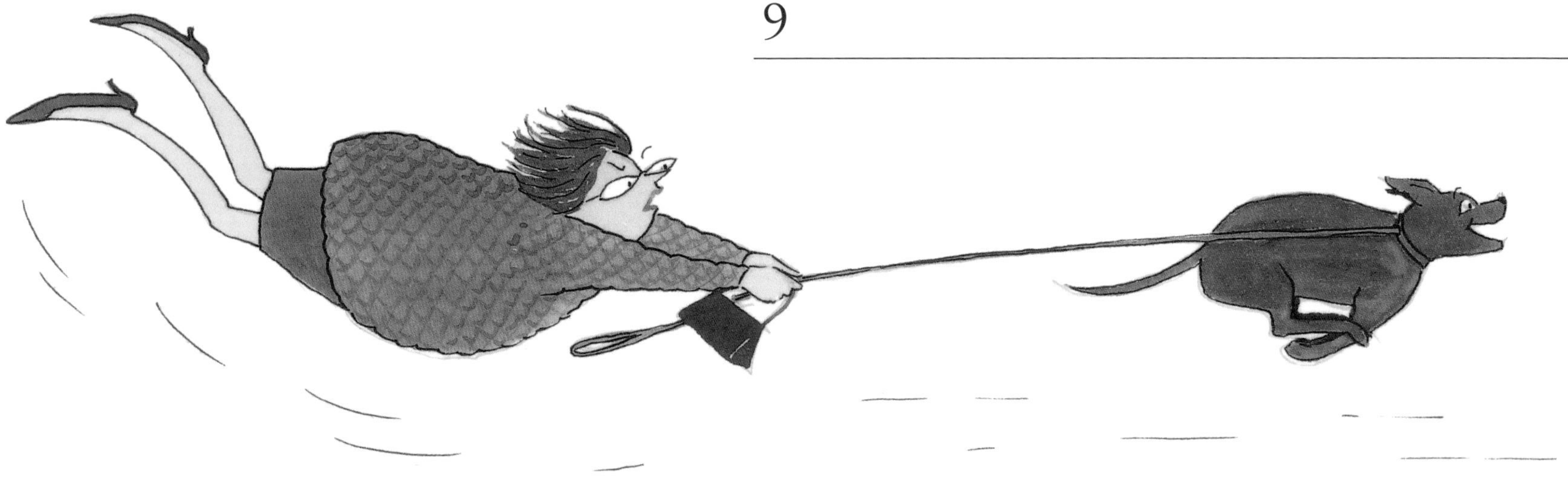

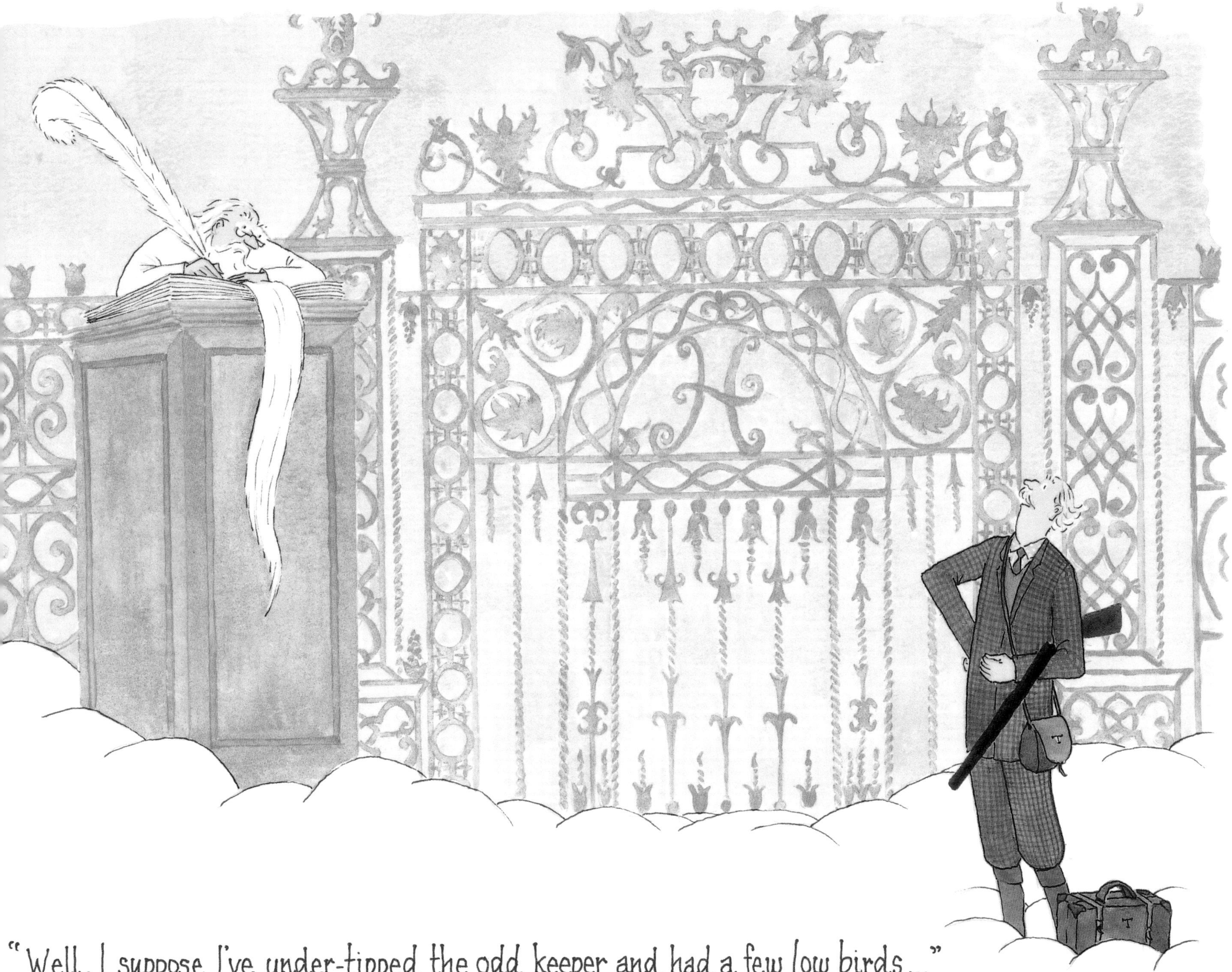

"Well, I suppose I've under-tipped the odd keeper and had a few low birds..."

I've got all those presents to wrap and
I've lost the sellotape...

Well, where did you have it last?

December

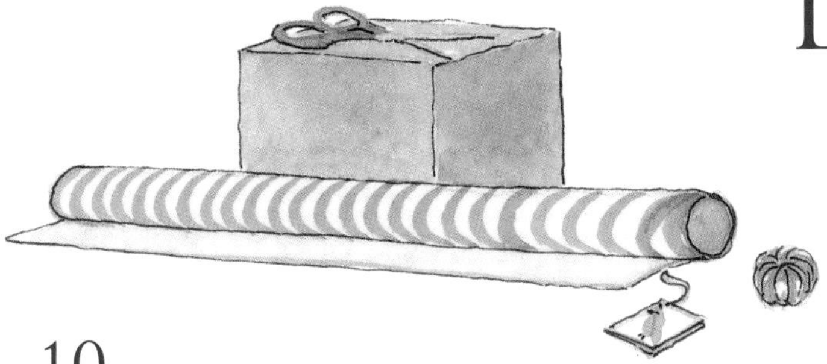

10

11

12

13

14

15 CALL RACHAEL MIDDLETON

16

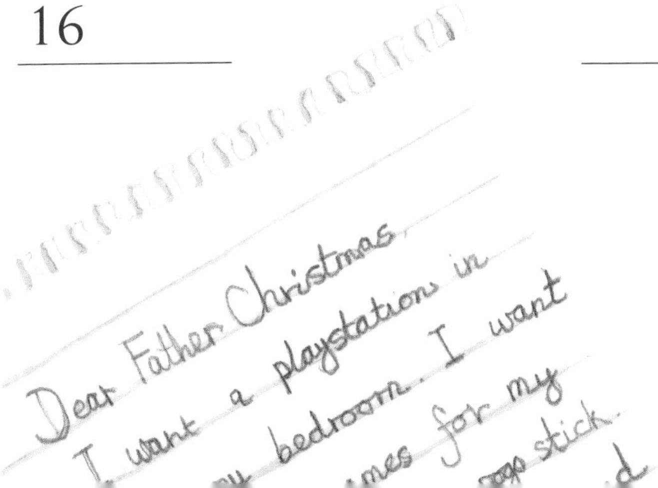
Dear Father Christmas,
I want a playstation in
bedroom. I want
for my
stick.

Why do husbands say that?...

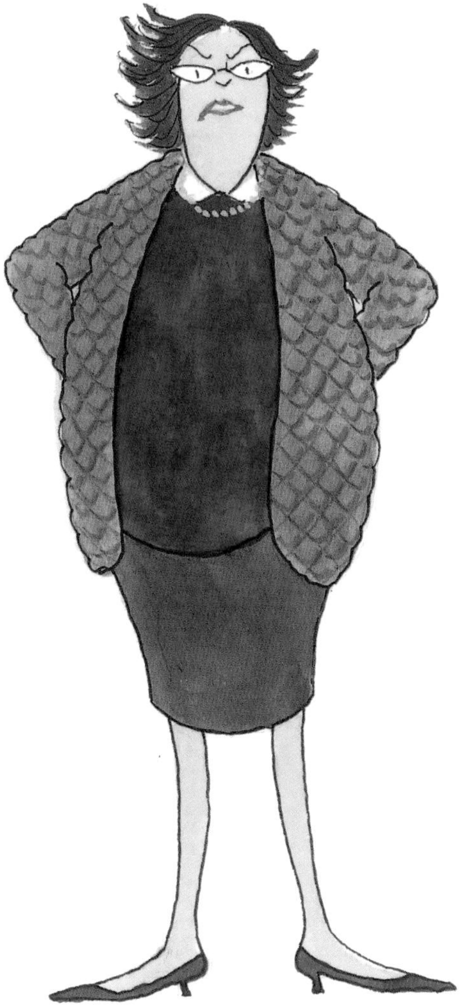

If you can master riding a unicycle with a stack of china cups on your head and juggle ten tennis balls while blind-folded, you should be able to please everyone at Christmas...

DECEMBER

17	*shopping*
18	*shopping*
19	*shopping*
20	*shopping*
21	*shopping*
22	*shopping*

Oh, what the hell!
It'll all be over in
a few
days...

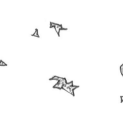

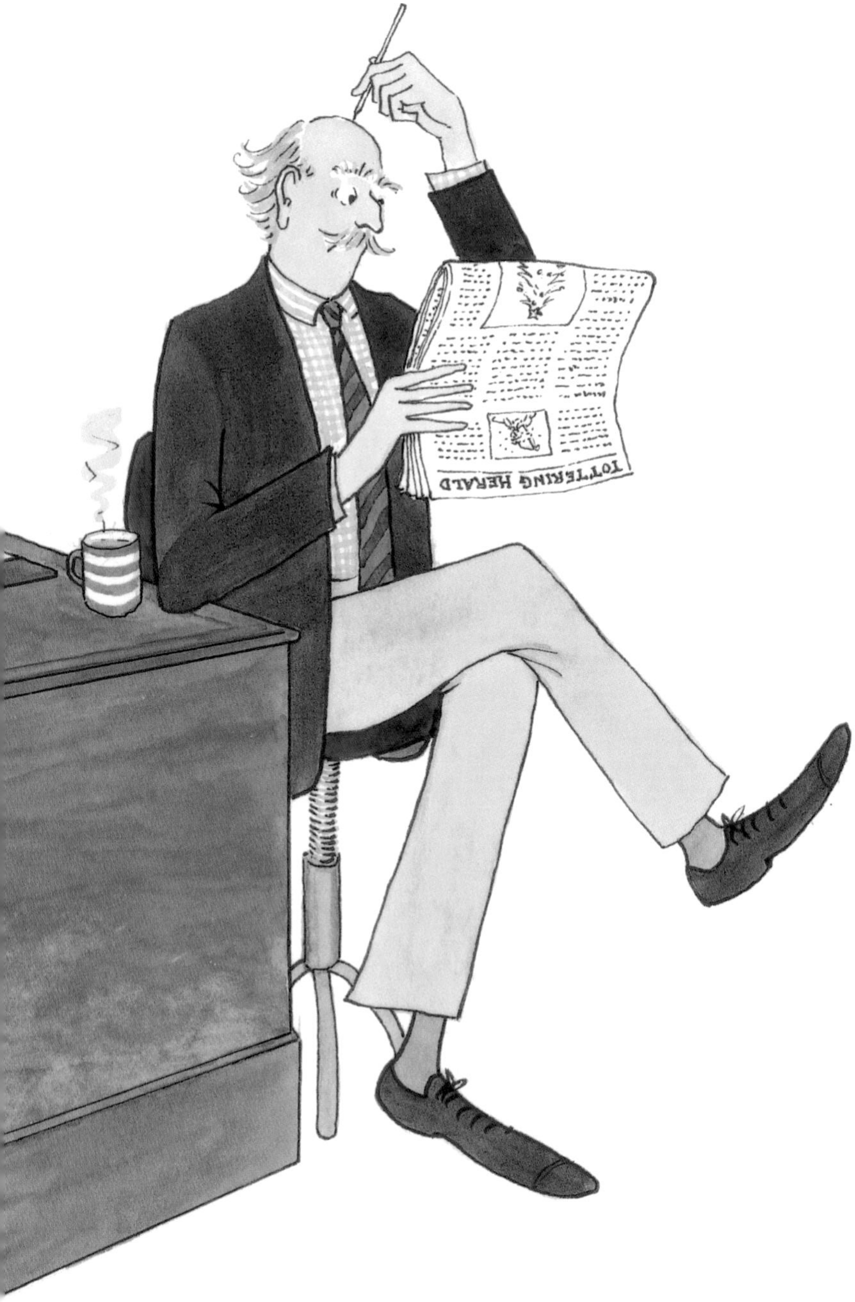
TOTTERING HERALD

TOTTERING CROSSWORD

ACROSS CLUES

1. Is Tottering putting up a false front? (5)
3. None of Daffy's (sober) fear Dicky. (9)
8. With 19, family home is staggering. (9)
10. Examine closely Daffy's breakfast offering. (5)
11. Little reward in remit for new building. (5)
12. Letting men go from poor housing Dicky's holding? (5)
14. In recess (for Freddy?) – mushy peas. (4)
15. Spurious alibi '<u>a cold</u>', – that's outrageous! (10)
18. Lose one's balance? Slips do heal in a disc. (2,8)
19. Ancient seat could be a bit of a drag, we hear (4)
21. Tottering Hall wants concession for exhibition (5)
23. 'Eden's Hybrid' are what's lacking (5)
25. Xanthine is the colour of what's in Dotty's dry martini (5)
26. Is duck one excuse for Daffy taking to gin? (9)
28. Such relics as Gladys? (9)
29. Pimmshire flower-girl? (5)

DOWN CLUES

1 & 24. Lady friend spotted with skin problem has a pet (5,5-4)
2. Operate boycott (3)
3. Decent hearing for Aunt Sally, perhaps? (4,5)
4. Appropriate party for the Totterings? (5)
5. Much disliked captain takes aboard unknown man for situation of 8 ac. (2-6)
6. Upper-class actors? I star in play (11)
7 & 2 Smooth short smoke for Daffy? (4,3)
9. The noble next to Dicky, almost ahead. (4)
11. Obedient servant, Mistress takes a nap twice. (3,8)
13. The long adherence Dicky has for Pratts? (3,7)
16. Tenners are curses without the Windsor possibly. (9)
17. Edging along the Hall roof, soldier takes step back (8)
20. Rank Honjon may live to see? (4)
22. Ivory one wrote about. (5)
24. Name of 1 d's solicitor. (4)
27. Gone away. (3)

Anne Bradford © 2002

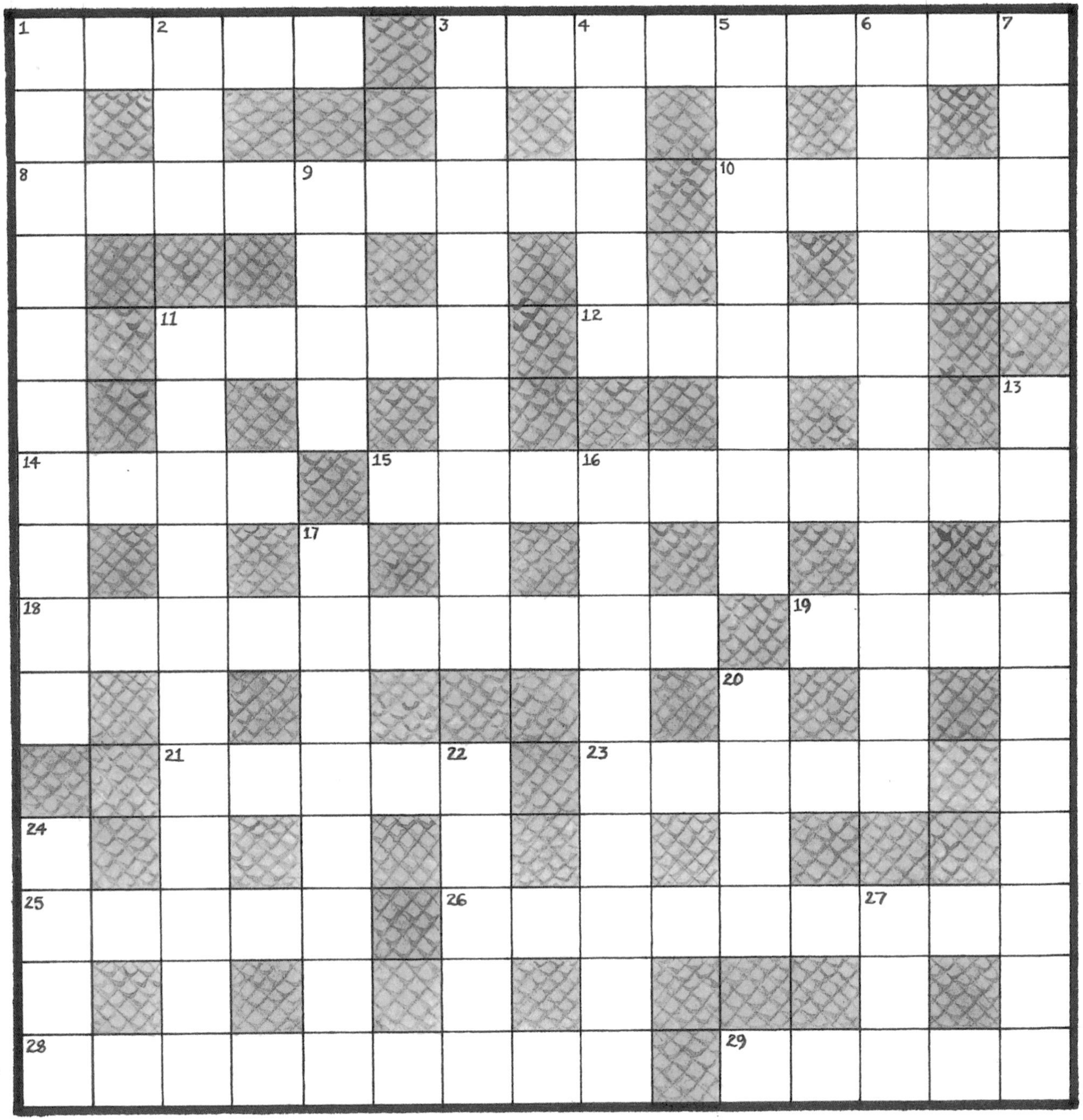

For solution visit our website at : www.tottering.com

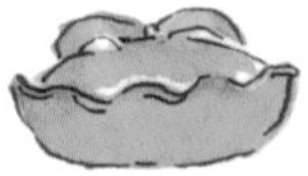

DECEMBER

23

24 *Midnight Mass*

25

26

27

28

29

30

31

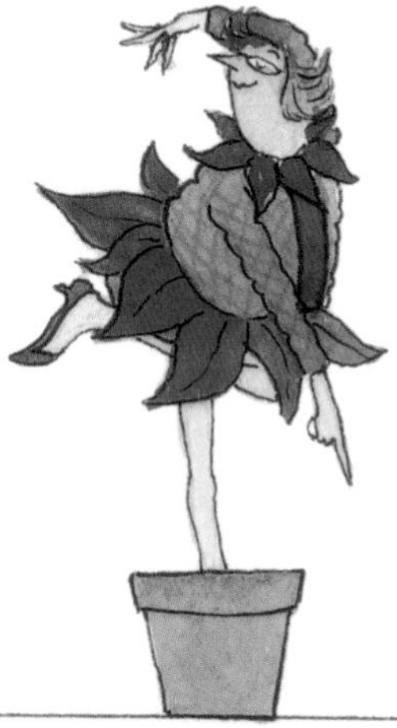

Poinsettia

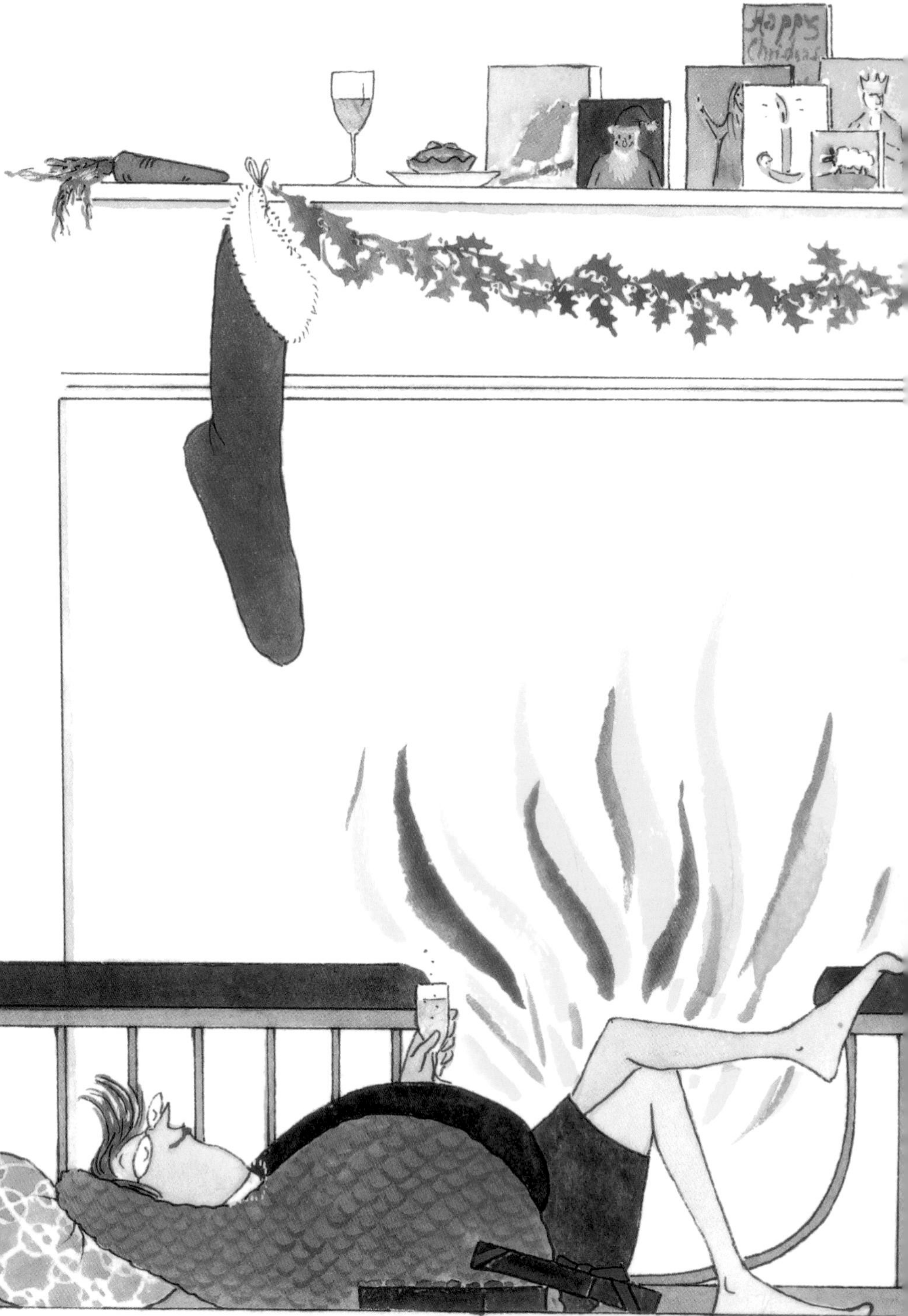
Happy

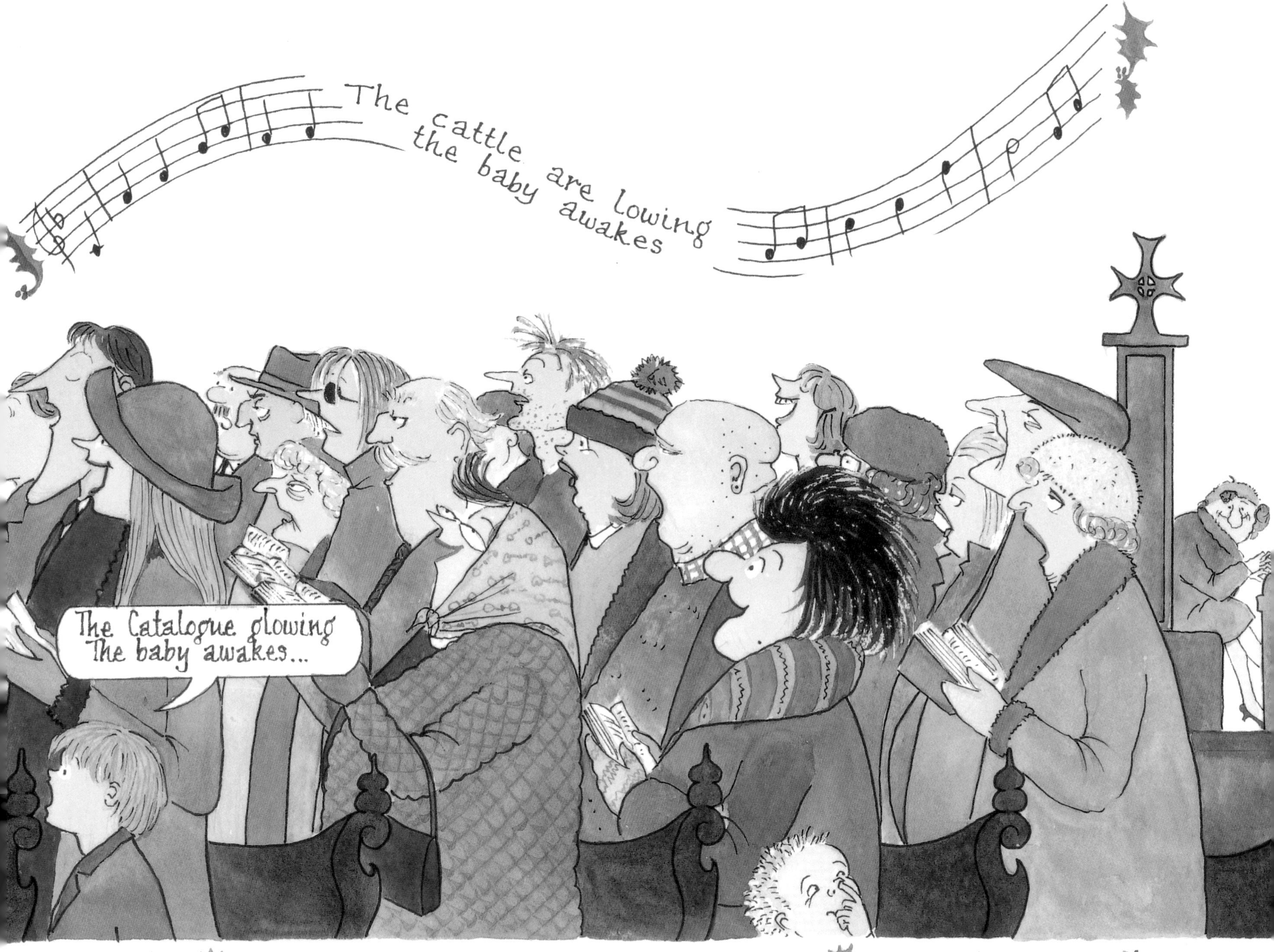
The cattle are lowing
the baby awakes
The Catalogue glowing
The baby awakes...

MIDNIGHT MASS

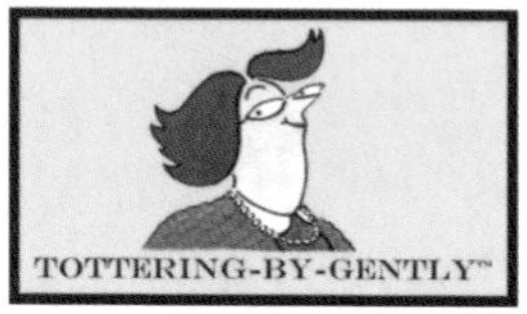
TOTTERING-BY-GENTLY™

ANNIE TEMPEST

Tottering-by-Gently™

Annie is one of Britain's best-loved cartoonists. She was recognised by her peers in the Cartoonist's Club of Great Britain as 'Strip Cartoonist of the Year' for her popular strip cartoon 'The Yuppies', which ran for seven years in the *Daily Mail.* In 1993 Annie embarked on her current internationally acclaimed cartoon strip, 'Tottering-by-Gently' for *Country Life* magazine. In 1995 The O'Shea Gallery, London, was appointed agent for Annie Tempest's originals and publisher of her books and prints. The gallery promotes and exhibits Annie's work worldwide.

Tottering-by-Gently is a village in the fictional town of North Pimmshire, in which Lord and Lady Tottering, affectionately known as Dicky and Daffy, inhabit the big house. Through them and their extended family, Annie Tempest casts her gimlet eye over everything, from inter-generational tensions and the differing perspectives of men and women, to field sports, diet, ageing, gardening, fashion, food, convention and much, much more. Her now large international following proves that she touches a note of universal truth in her beautifully executed and exquisitely detailed cartoons as she gently laughs with us at the stuff of life.

Annie has had nine collections of her cartoons published and has worked for most of our national newspapers and life-style magazines over the last sixteen years. As Sir Roy Strong observed: 'Annie Tempest has a great talent. She has the similar cult appeal of Osbert Lancaster and has created her characters from a certain set, but her observations are social as against political. They are gentler and beautifully observed. Annie Tempest is a bit of England – she articulates the things which set us apart and which form our identity.'

Tottering-by-Gently™
To receive information about Annie Tempest's original drawings, a catalogue of her signed numbered edition prints, and up-to-date listings of *Tottering-by-Gently*™ publications, products, and events, please contact: Raymond O'Shea, *Tottering-by-Gently*™, Twelve Acres, Valence, Westerham, Kent TN16 1QL. Tel: 01959 569301 Fax: 01959 569302 email: daffy@tottering.com website: http://www.tottering.com

First published in Great Britain in 2002 by
Orion in association with The O'Shea Gallery, London.
An imprint of Orion Books Ltd
Orion House, 5 Upper St Martin's Lane, London WC2H 9EA

Second impression 2004

A CIP catalogue record for this book is available from the British Library

ISBN 0 75284 108 4

Printed in Italy

ORION